ASHES
FEVER

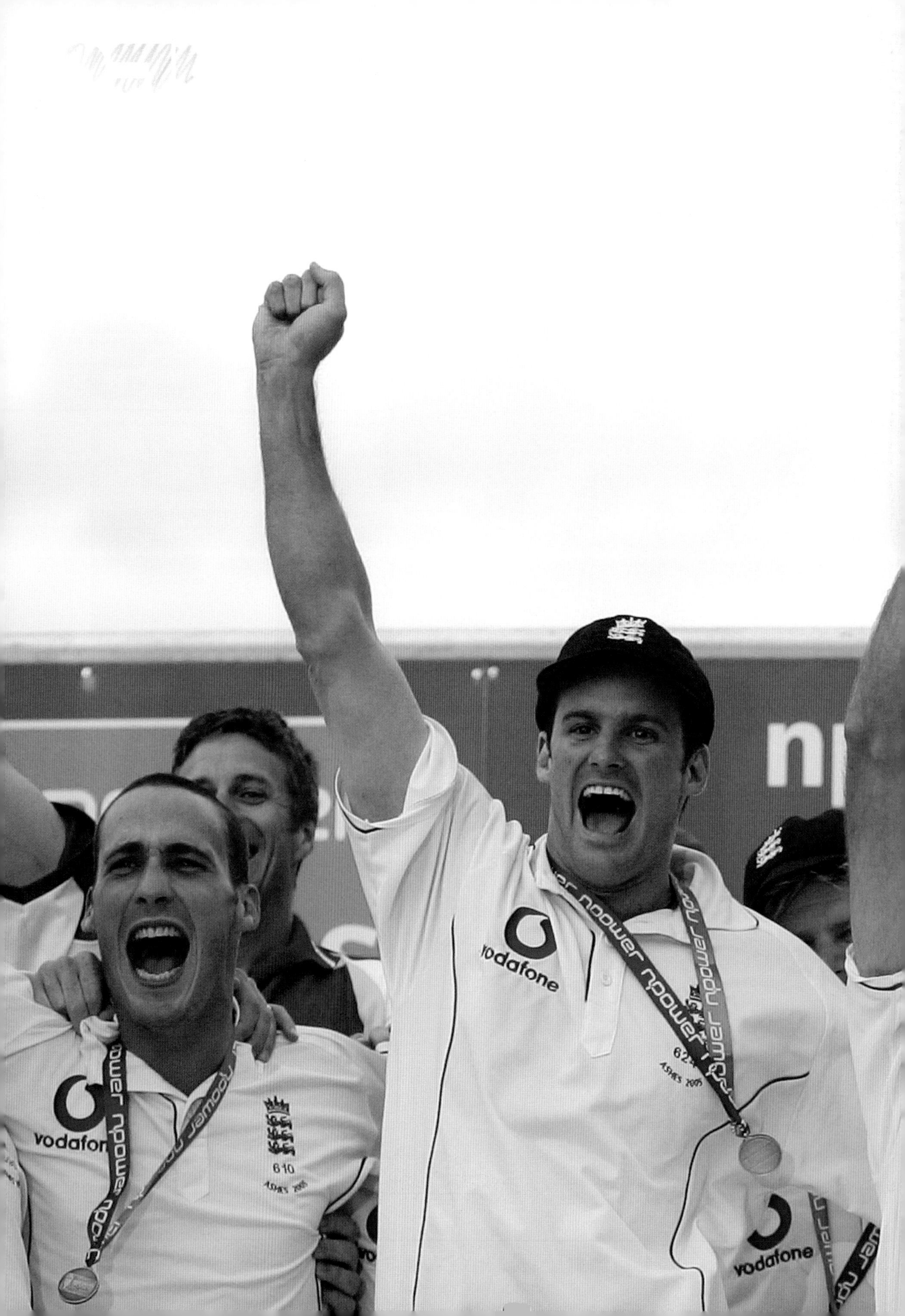
vodafone
vodafone
vodafone

Ian Stafford

PHOTOGRAPHS BY
Philip Brown

ASHES
FEVER

HOW ENGLAND WON THE GREATEST EVER TEST SERIES

MAINSTREAM
PUBLISHING

Copyright © Ian Stafford, 2005
All rights reserved
The moral right of the author has been asserted

Photographs © Philip Brown

First published in Great Britain in 2005 by
MAINSTREAM PUBLISHING COMPANY (EDI NBURGH) LTD
7 Albany Street
Edinburgh EH1 3UG

ISBN 1 84596 156 0

A catalogue record for this book
is available from the British Library

Production editor: Chris Marshall
Text and jacket design: Paul Cooper Design

The publishers would like to thank CricInfo.com for the information
contained in the scorecards and averages.

Typeset in Baskerville, Eurostile and Swiss
Printed and bound in Great Britain by
Butler & Tanner Ltd, Frome and London

CONTENTS

INTRODUCTION

English cricket has endured many a dark day over the years but none more so than 29 August 1882. It was on this day at London's famous Kennington Oval that an Australian fast bowler named Frederick Spofforth swept his country to their first victory on English soil with 14 wickets. That defeat inspired *The Sporting Times* to denounce the national team with a notice in their deaths column. 'In affectionate remembrance of English cricket which died at the Oval on 29th August, 1882,' it announced. 'Deeply lamented by a large circle of sorrowing friends and acquaintances. R.I.P.' Then, crucially, a footnote was added. 'N.B. The body will be cremated and the Ashes taken to Australia.'

The bails were subsequently burnt, with the ashes placed in a tiny, six-inch pottery urn. They never made their way down under to Australia, instead being kept inside a glass case at Lord's cricket ground in northwest London, the home of cricket. Over the ensuing years both England and Australia have won the little urn on

BELOW Glenn McGrath, metronomic pace bowler who needed just one wicket for 500 in Tests at the start of the first Ashes contest at Lord's.

many occasions, forging one of the great sporting rivalries in the process. Names such as Bradman and Hutton, Miller and Compton, Lillee and Boycott, and Border and Botham have stretched every sinew in their body to try and win the smallest, but one of the most important, trophies in world sport. In 1953 it was the Brylcreem Boy himself, Denis Compton, who struck the runs that won the Ashes. In 1981 it was the superhuman, all-round efforts of Ian 'Beefy' Botham that saw off Australia. But in recent times it has all been one-way traffic. And this has been deeply depressing for English cricket.

You had to go back to 1987 to recall the last time England had actually won the Ashes. Margaret Thatcher had just led the Conservative Party to their third general election victory, Pat Cash (an Australian) was the new Wimbledon champion, Jackie Wilson was Number One in the singles chart with a re-release of 'Reet Petite', and a pint of bitter cost just 83p. Mike Gatting's men went to Australia to pull off a stunning win with a team that included the likes of Botham, David Gower and Bob Willis. But it was all played out far, far away, on the other side of the world, and in the middle of the night for a UK audience. There was no satellite television in those days, and relatively little coverage. Within two years, when a wounded Australia came to England, the Ashes were gone again. Little did anyone know that the urn would be lost for 16 long years.

During this time England tried their hardest to wrestle the Ashes away from Australia. They enjoyed moderate success against other countries, but players such as Michael Atherton, Alec Stewart and Darren Gough could not find an answer against the Aussies. Ashes series came and went, and always England were beaten out of sight. The Australian team, from the moment they lost that 1987 Ashes series, became the most formidable Test team in world cricket. They reinvented the five-day game in the process, scoring their runs quicker than ever seen before and then hounding out the opposition with a fierce battery of fast bowlers, a penetratingly accurate bowler named Glenn McGrath, and a certain leg-spinner called Shane Warne. Throughout the 1990s and until midway through the first decade of the new Millennium, England had no answer to this pair of bowlers, nor to Australia's vast array of batting talent.

It would be this team that the 2005 England side would have to beat to win the Ashes.

A team that was brimming with sporting superstars. Aside from Warne, the highest Test wicket-taker of all

time, and McGrath, close to becoming the highest Test wicket-taker in history as a fast bowler, Australia boasted Brett Lee, the quickest bowler in the world, and fast bowler Jason Gillespie, so often the scourge of the English. They could field an opening partnership of Justin Langer and Matthew Hayden who between them had hit over 40 Test match centuries. Hayden was the former record-holder for the highest individual Test score, 380 against Zimbabwe. They had captain Ricky Ponting at number three, and Damien Martyn at four, two of the world's consistently best batsmen. And they had wicket-keeper Adam Gilchrist as well, a man with a Test batting average of over 50, and someone who could, and had, single-handedly won games for his country. They were, and indeed had been for 18 years, nigh on unbeatable. But they were also ageing. As happens to any great sporting team, an era was reaching closure. Most of their big-name stars were now in the twilight of their careers. This would be their last visit to England, their last Ashes series away from home. Could they muster one final, determined effort to beat the old enemy once again? Nobody doubted that they could. Nobody doubted that Australia would use everything at their disposal to do what they like best of all – to beat England and to retain, once again, the Ashes.

Yet for once England would enter an absorbing summer of cricket with hope – justifiable hope, too. Six years ago a new regime had begun under an understated Zimbabwean coach named Duncan Fletcher and the captaincy of Nasser Hussain. The omens were not good. They lost their first Test series against New Zealand at The Oval, and Hussain was roundly booed by a disgusted English crowd as he surveyed the scene from the England dressing-room balcony. The result had plummeted England to bottom in the world rankings. It was official. England had become the worst Test team in the world.

But then something very un-English happened. Nobody panicked. Nobody was dropped. No one became a scapegoat. Fletcher had seen enough, even in a harrowing defeat, to believe in the future. He believed, and soon that precious commodity – belief – came seeping through into the ranks of English cricket.

Defeats turned to draws. Draws then turned to victories. Young players became experienced players. A Yorkshireman called Michael Vaughan took over the captaincy from Hussain, seemingly passive and laid back on the exterior but with a determined fire raging inside. A big lump of a lad from Lancashire called Andrew 'Freddie' Flintoff decided one day to change his less-than-professional ways. Out went much of the booze, off flew the flab, and a young cricketer with bundles of talent but no sense of direction emerged like a butterfly from its cocoon to become a sporting champion. Another big

FACING PAGE The incomparable Shane Warne, leading wicket-taker in Test cricket history and believed by many to be the greatest leg-spinner who ever played the game.

man, Stephen Harmison, also went down the fitness trail to emerge as one of the most feared fast bowlers in world cricket. Matthew Hoggard perfected the art of swing bowling, Ashley Giles improved immeasurably as a spin bowler and, indeed, as a batsman. Marcus Trescothick began to flay opposition bowling attacks to all points of the boundary to become one of the most aggressive opening batsmen in the game.

Still England were not ready for a summit attempt. Down under, the boys were taught a lesson by the grown-ups. Vaughan became the best batsman in the world, and England were much more competitive than they had been for quite a while, but still they went down 3–1 to lose the Ashes once more.

Unperturbed, they returned to these shores, analysed the lessons learnt, and took the next, crucial steps. Into the side came a young opening batsman called Andrew Strauss who found Test cricket to his liking. He and Trescothick would soon forge one of the best opening partnerships in the world. In, too, came a wicket-keeper/batsman born in Papua New Guinea, but with Welsh parents, named Geraint Jones. And into the

ABOVE England coach Duncan Fletcher, who starred for Zimbabwe against Australia in the 1983 World Cup, with Marcus Trescothick, England vice-captain and one of the most aggressive opening batsmen in modern Test cricket. FACING PAGE Michael Vaughan of Yorkshire has topped the world rankings as a Test batsman and took over as England Test captain in 2003.

team as well came another Jones, Simon Jones, who would soon become one of the most respected fast bowlers in the sport with his reverse swing. In the summer of 2004 England put both the West Indies and New Zealand to the sword. In the winter they won a Test series in South Africa.

The final piece of the England jigsaw found its place on the eve of the 2005 Ashes series. A confident young man born in South Africa but discarded by his country's selectors qualified for England by virtue of his English-born mother. Kevin Pietersen was box-office material, and English cricket licked its collective lips at the prospect of him and Flintoff being let loose on Australia.

Now England were ready. If they were ever going to win back the Ashes, it was now. For the first time in 18

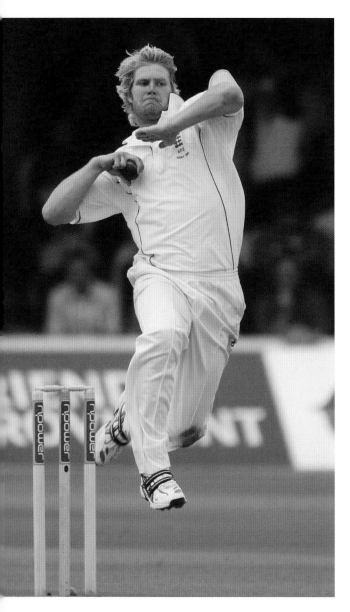

ABOVE Yorkshire and England swing bowler Matthew Hoggard.
FACING PAGE Kevin Pietersen – box-office material.

What followed was not only the greatest Ashes series of all time, and indeed the greatest Test series in the history of cricket, but one of the epic sporting clashes. This was cricket's version of Muhammad Ali versus Joe Frazier, Jack Nicklaus against Tom Watson, Pele and Bobby Moore. The sequence of events would, if scripted into a Hollywood film, have been ripped up and thrown away as too far-fetched for belief.

But everything that happened was for real. Australia hammered England in the First Test at Lord's and looked certain to back up their own prediction of a comfortable series victory. A freak injury and an absurd captaincy decision swung the series back in England's favour in the Second Test at Edgbaston, where Freddie Flintoff came of age in a game considered one of the finest, and closest, of all time. The Third Test was equally close, and as dramatic. It may have ended as a draw, but England were now on top and Australia were beginning to hang in there. By the end of the Fourth Test, a match England won narrowly and dramatically thanks in no small part to Flintoff again, Ashes fever had gripped the nation. Cricket was the new football. The England players had become household names. And phrases such as 'slider', 'Warney', 'KP' and, of course, 'Freddie', were being uttered by formerly non-cricket followers around the land.

By the time the Fifth Test at The Oval came around, England's quest to regain the Ashes had become the biggest news item in the country. England were 2–1 ahead and needed only a draw to achieve their goal. Two years previously the England rugby team won the World Cup, beating Australia in Sydney in the final. The win was met with national celebration, but even this was being dwarfed by what was now being undertaken by 22 men in whites. The Fifth Test became the biggest sporting occasion played out in this country since the England football team won the World Cup at Wembley Stadium in 1966.

In keeping with the rest of this amazing series, the Fifth Test did not disappoint. Just after lunch on the final day it looked like Australia were on course to win the match, draw the series and retain the Ashes. Up stepped Kevin Pietersen to play one of the greatest Test match innings you are ever likely to see. The crowd remained tense throughout. It was only after 5.00 pm that they began to believe that the Ashes were coming home.

And so, on the final day of the final Test, the destiny of the Ashes had come right down to the wire. England had prevailed, captain Michael Vaughan received the famous old urn and celebrations like never before engulfed English cricket.

The very next day the England team were treated to an open-top bus parade around the packed streets of London, a journey that ended at Trafalgar Square, where

years there was a belief that an Ashes series would, at the very least, be close. But these Australians were still so very good. Some called it a narrow win for Australia. A few brave souls predicted a series draw. That would have been some result for England, but a draw would still have been enough for Australia, as holders, to retain the Ashes. There must be someone out there, somewhere, who predicted before the first ball was bowled that England would win the Ashes. Certainly I neither heard nor read such a prediction from anyone.

the players gazed down on a sea of jubilant English cricket supporters.

Against the odds, and against all predictions, England had prevailed. The summer of 2005 would never be forgotten, either by the players, or by the rest of us who found ourselves immersed in the most compelling, dramatic and nerve-wracking two months of our cricketing lives.

This, then, is the story of how England won back the Ashes.

PROLOGUE
PHONEY WAR

FACING PAGE Man of the Match Kevin Pietersen celebrates taking a catch during the Twenty20 international against Australia at his home ground of the Rose Bowl. RIGHT Brett Lee completes a swing and a miss against Darren Gough in the NatWest Challenge match at Headingley.

Quite when the countdown to the Ashes began is open to conjecture. Certainly in the summer of 2004, as England were building an impressive run of wins against New Zealand and the West Indies, Australia were taking note. When England then beat their oldest and fiercest rivals in the semi-final of the Champions Trophy in the September of that year, a minor marker had been laid down.

Over the ensuing winter England continued to impress the watching world of cricket. Captain Michael Vaughan's increasingly merry men left South Africa with a 2–1 series win under their belts, no mean achievement, especially when it was accomplished following a South African comeback that saw the Test score levelled at one apiece. All through that tour the spectre of the Ashes series was raised, and all through the tour England insisted they were concentrating entirely on beating the South Africans.

Deep down, though, they knew, the Australians knew, and we all knew that the summer of 2005 might, just might, produce the kind of Ashes series for which the cricket world, let alone England, had been crying out for many years.

Brett Lee, Australia's demon fast bowler and all-round nice guy – at least off the pitch – admitted with still six months to go that he was expecting a tight tussle for once between the two teams. 'The way the next Ashes series is shaping up it could be the best ever,' he said, unwittingly making a prediction so precise that a future as a soothsayer awaits him. 'Both teams have fantastic squads, have been winning games and playing great cricket. It's very rare that two very strong teams come together and world-class teams do not usually meet in the same arena.'

His captain, Ricky Ponting, soon restored our faith in the now well-versed, hard-nosed Aussie psyche when it

comes to playing the Poms. 'Sides can lose form and individual players can go downhill so the Ashes is still some way off,' he said. 'England's performances have been good but we've not been up all night worrying.' Little did Ponting know at Christmas that his comments about players losing form would prove to be correct, although it would be his own seeming untouchables he would be inadvertently speaking about.

By April our pulses quickened just a little with the announcement of the Australian squad to tour England for the triangular NatWest Series One-Day International competition against England and Bangladesh, the NatWest Challenge three-match ODI contest against England and, most important of all, the Npower Ashes Test Series.

Australia had just hammered New Zealand in both a one-day and Test series and boasted a team that was bursting with not only experience but players who knew how to win the Ashes, over and over again. Moreover, only four of the squad – Adam Gilchrist, Brett Lee, Jason Gillespie and Brad Haddin, the reserve wicket-keeper – had never played county cricket. The other 12 members of the Test squad were well accustomed to English summer conditions.

FACING PAGE The Australians arrive. Adam Gilchrist and Brett Lee at Heathrow Airport. ABOVE Matthew Hayden, half of Australia's highly successful Test opening partnership, gets a nasty one against the PCA Masters XI.

Wherever you looked the Australians were bursting with match-winners. Gilchrist, the most destructive batsman in the world, had destroyed New Zealand only a few weeks before. The partnership of Matthew Hayden and Justin Langer formed arguably the most formidable opening pair in the world. Ponting and Damien Martyn both sported averages in the high 40s, while Lee was officially the fastest bowler in the world. And then there was Glenn McGrath and Shane Warne, without argument the two best bowlers in world cricket. Warne would be hoping to snare his 600th Test victim some time during the Ashes series, thus extending his own world record, while McGrath was on the verge of claiming his 500th. These two alone could win the series before it had barely started.

The only sliver of hope for England, besides their own good form and confidence, was the collective age of the Australian squad. Only two players in their assumed 1st XI arrived in England under 30, Michael Clarke and Simon Katich, and the latter would pass the milestone in between the Third and Fourth Tests. With Warne and McGrath both 35, Langer 34, Martyn, Gilchrist, Hayden and fast bowler Michael Kasprowicz all 33, the Australians had an ageing look about them. With the five-Test Ashes series packed into seven weeks later in the summer, could their bodies withstand the pressure?

It was a straw for English cricket to clutch at in the face of the facts. And the facts were that England last won the Ashes in 1987, Australia would come to these shores looking for a record ninth winning Ashes series, and that while England had undoubtedly become a potent force in becoming the second best international team in cricket, they had not played the all-conquering, seemingly unbeatable Australians.

Indeed, in readiness for Australia, England would play Bangladesh in a two-Test series in May. This was an immediate concern, for, although Bangladesh need such challenges for them to gain credibility in the world of international cricket, this series appeared hardly the appropriate preparation for the challenge ahead. In football parlance, it was like England playing Andorra in readiness for a World Cup final against Brazil.

Still, they had a job to do, and the squad announced for the two Tests against Bangladesh saw Warwickshire's Ian Bell, who impressed with his 70 against the West Indies on his Test debut the previous summer, claim the fourth batting spot ahead of Kevin Pietersen, who had announced his arrival on the international scene by smacking three centuries in South Africa during the losing one-day series in the winter. Robert Key, who held the number three spot for the last three Tests of the previous summer, also missed out, as Graham Thorpe, subject to his back spasms clearing up, was marked down in his customary spot at five in the batting order.

In late May England duly went about their routine business. At Lord's they beat the hapless Bangladeshis by just about as big a margin as is possible, in a Test that threatened to end in just two days. The hosts having bowled Bangladesh out for a paltry 104, with Matthew Hoggard taking 4–42, England's batsmen then gorged themselves in a run feast. The tried and trusted opening pair of Marcus Trescothick and Andrew Strauss put on a destructive 148 for the first wicket, before Strauss fell on 69. Vaughan would be the next out, but by this time he and Trescothick had rocketed the score on to 403, with the captain having accounted for 120. Trescothick finally went for 194, which left Bell and Thorpe to hurry the scoreboard along to a final total of 528–3 declared.

If Vaughan had declared 100 runs earlier, then this match, for sure, would have become just the fifth post-war Test to end inside 48 hours, but he felt, rightly, that Bell needed time at the crease. Besides, it hardly mattered. Bangladesh finished the second day on 90–5, and were put out of their misery before lunch on day three, bowled out for 159. England had won by an innings and 261 runs.

It did not get much better in the second Test, either, played for the first time at the Riverside Stadium at

Chester-le-Street, the home of Durham CCC and a certain Steve Harmison. After propelling himself to number one in the world's bowling rankings the previous summer, when he terrorised Kiwi and West Indian batsmen, a subdued and homesick Harmison was below par in the winning series in South Africa. Back in England, though, and appearing on his home pitch, he

RIGHT England's preparation for the expected Australian onslaught was two Tests against Bangladesh, both of which they won by an innings. Here Matthew Hoggard dismisses Aftab Ahmed lbw in Bangladesh's second innings at Lord's.

bounced back with five wickets as Bangladesh were bowled out in their first innings for 104. By then England had already posted an impregnable 447–3 declared, with Trescothick hitting an imperious 151, Bell an innings of 162 not out which further enhanced his credentials in Test cricket, and Thorpe a typical unbeaten 66. Bangladesh fared much better when asked to follow on – they scored 316 all out, with Hoggard taking a five-wicket haul, and Andrew Flintoff easing his way back into cricket following an ankle operation with three wickets. England's winning margin was by an innings and 27 runs.

England's performances when the quality of the opposition was considered would hardly have had the

ABOVE Graham Thorpe with Duncan Fletcher during the First Test v Bangladesh at Lord's. By the time selection for the Ashes came round, Thorpe's Test place was under threat from Kevin Pietersen, who eventually got the nod ahead of the Surrey stalwart. FACING PAGE Ricky Ponting enjoys a laugh at Arundel before the serious business of the tour got under way.

Australians quaking in their cricket boots, even if many plusses had emerged, notably the return of Harmison, the rise of Bell, a century for the out-of-sorts Vaughan and the sparkling form of Trescothick. It was pretty obvious, though, that in taking on Australia England's challenge would be very different.

The word games and the psychological war that would provide such a fascinating sub-plot to the summer's events began from the moment Australia touched down at London's Heathrow Airport on the same day that England wrapped up proceedings against Bangladesh in Durham.

Ricky Ponting was well aware that his squad had been out of action for seven weeks. He had also observed the tour schedule laid out before him and he liked what he saw. 'We have a one-day series to play first and that is our main focus at the moment,' he announced, blinking as a multitude of cameras flashed away at the greatest collection of cricketers currently in the game. 'I think it will work pretty well for us that we've got a lot of cricket under our belts before the Tests come around. Hopefully all the guys will be fully fit and raring to go by then, with plenty of match practice behind us. It is an advantage for us the way the summer has panned out. We've had a long break before we've come here, then to have ten one-dayers before the first Test and having England at the end of a long summer of cricket for them is good news. It's a good time for us to be playing a Test series against them. I'm certainly not looking at it as me potentially being the first captain in years to lose the Ashes. It's more like I will be the latest captain to retain them. Pretty much every series we've played in the last ten years we've been expected to win. This is no different.'

With that, he and his squad, struggling with jet lag, prepared for a trip the next day, courtesy of Eurostar, to the war memorials of Northern France dedicated to their countrymen and other First World War Allied soldiers. It was an idea first thought up by previous captain Steve Waugh who, four years earlier, stopped off en route to the UK at Gallipoli in a trip that certainly brought inspiration and determination to his fellow cricketers. Ponting this time chose the Western Front.

It appeared to work instantly. With Australia's very first ball of their tour to England they grabbed a wicket, Brett Lee bowling the New Zealand captain, Stephen Fleming, for a golden duck in the one-day game against the PCA Masters at Arundel. After the Masters scored just 167, Australia knocked off the runs for the loss of only two wickets, with Matthew Hayden scoring 79.

Two days later they made similarly short work of Leicestershire in another one-day game, scoring 321 runs in their allotted 50 overs. Hayden this time helped himself to 107, the dangerous one-day player Andrew Symonds made an unbeaten 92, while Damien Martyn added 85. Leicestershire could only muster 226 in reply, losing the game by 95 runs.

England, meanwhile, warmed up for their looming first clash against Australia with a useful practice match against Hampshire. Batting first they acquired 238 runs, with Andrew Strauss scoring 85 and that man Pietersen, back in the fray now that England were playing overs matches, 77. His county side replied with 85 all out, Simon Jones and Darren Gough grabbing three wickets each, the latter with a hat-trick.

The stage was set, then, for the opening encounter between England and Australia. Unprecedently, this would take the form of a Twenty20 match at Hampshire's Rose Bowl ground just outside Southampton. To make any comparisons between this match and Test cricket would, of course, be ridiculous. After all, we are talking about a three-hour game and 240 balls as opposed to a five-day game and 450 overs. Whatever the result, it would not make a difference.

Not entirely true. England scored 179–8 off their allocation of 20 overs, a respectable total. They then bowled out Australia, the one-day world champions as well as the best Test team in the world, for just 79 from 14.3 overs in front of a capacity crowd who could not quite believe what they were watching.

In Twenty20 cricket a 100-run defeat is huge. Indeed, Australia's 79 was the second lowest ever score witnessed in England in this type of cricket. And it could have been even worse. At one stage Australia were 31–7 after just six overs. Those seven wickets fell for eight runs in a mad period of 20 balls, with Pietersen taking three catches. Earlier Trescothick had bludgeoned 34 from just 16 balls, despite facing Lee's third ball of the innings measured at 93 mph, and Paul Collingwood a crucial 46.

Captain Vaughan had asked his team to hit the ground running against Australia, and to face them head-on from the very first minute of summer action. It may have been only a Twenty20 game, but it was an encouraging start, to say the least. 'I wouldn't read too much into it, but it's always good to beat the best team in the world,' he said afterwards. His counterpart, Ponting,

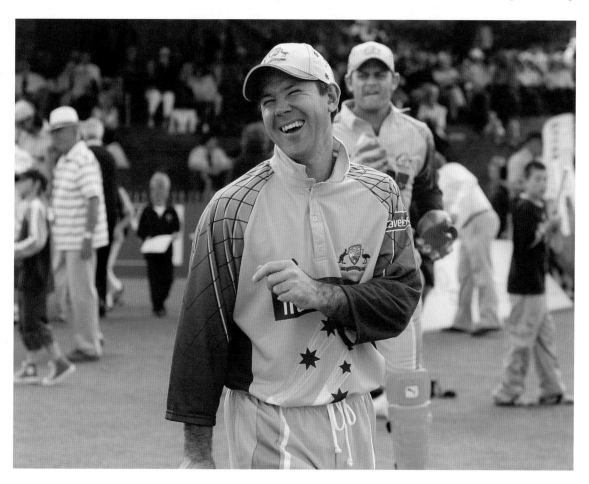

seemed unperturbed. 'I don't think the result will do them much good or us much harm,' he insisted. 'If anything, it will make us more determined.'

It was the beginning of a quite remarkable week for Australia – remarkable for the wrong reasons. In what should have been an easy canter against Somerset in another one-day warm-up match, they somehow contrived to lose. Ponting admitted that there were 'angry words' in his dressing room after seeing his men fail to protect a massive total of 342 in 50 overs. Instead Somerset, an understrength second division county side, won by four wickets with 18 balls to spare. To be fair, the West Countrymen sported South African captain Graeme Smith and former Sri Lankan captain Sanath Jayasuriya as their opening pair, and both hit centuries, but it was still a sorry display from Australia.

'We are going to sit down and take a long hard look at things,' Ponting added. 'We have to get things out in the open and see where we can improve. I don't know if it was the execution or the thought process that was wrong, but something was.'

England, by contrast, started the triangular tournament with Australia and Bangladesh by battering the latter by ten wickets. Bangladesh were bowled out for 190 in 45.2 overs, with Harmison capturing four wickets and Gloucestershire swing bowler Jon Lewis, three. In reply Trescothick scored exactly 100 not out, ably assisted by Strauss, who ended the day unbeaten on 82.

The next day's game in Cardiff against an obviously weak Bangladeshi side appeared to provide Australia with the chance to get a foothold on their summer tour in England. Instead one of the greatest upsets in sport

ABOVE Bangladesh celebrate after their earth-shattering victory over Australia at Cardiff. FACING PAGE Ricky Ponting congratulates Mohammad Ashraful on his hundred.

took place. After Australia posted a respectable 249 in their 50 overs, Martyn top-scoring with 77, Bangladesh knocked off the runs with four balls to spare for the loss of five wickets, with their number four batsman, Mohammad Ashraful, proving to be the hero by scoring exactly 100 runs. The world champions had been beaten by, statistically, the worst international team in the world. 'It's about as bad as it could get,' a stunned Ponting would confess afterwards. 'It's one of the biggest upsets in the history of the game.'

One day later they would lose their fourth one-day game in a week, and this time it was against England once more. The bare facts are that Australia scored 252 runs for nine wickets in 50 overs at Bristol. England, in reply, won with three wickets and 15 balls to spare.

The truth is that Kevin Pietersen stole the show once again. The South African-born batsman had taken on his former countrymen almost single-handedly in the losing one-day series the previous winter, and now he was at it again. In the 38th over England were well behind the run rate and had slumped to 160–6. Less than ten overs later they were home and dry after Pietersen had completed a 65-ball, unbeaten 91, a knock that included four sixes hammered into the 15,000-strong crowd. By the end Australia had run out of clues when it came to controlling the man. Pietersen's thrilling knock not only added another hammer blow to the aura that had previously surrounded Australia but also made his

dismiss Matthew Hayden after the opener had cut the ball for what looked a sure-fire boundary.

'Kevin was a genius out there,' was Vaughan's response after seeing his new boy destroy Australia. 'He got us over the line and his innings was very special. He has played some great knocks in the short time he has been in the team, but with the pressure on against Australia and having to bat at the end with the bowlers, I haven't seen many better than that.'

Harmison, who had bagged 5–33, including Gilchrist, Ponting and Martyn in one over, was equally impressed. 'We couldn't believe it,' he reported of his colleagues sitting on the Bristol dressing room balcony. 'I was sitting there with Darren Gough with our pads on waiting to go in wondering what on earth he was going to do next. It was just a fantastic knock. It's probably the best innings I've seen chasing a target.' As for that over he bowled to dismiss three of the world's top batsmen? 'That was about as good as it gets,' he replied.

The mood of the country was already high after this. 'Jerusalem' was belting out of the tannoy system at Bristol and Australia seemed to be lurching into an early tour crisis. What with four defeats – including the Twenty20 hammering, the embarrassment of Somerset, and the utter humiliation by Bangladesh – coupled with off-field problems such as a disciplinary rumpus surrounding Andrew Symonds, who was suspended by his own management after some late-night drinking, nothing seemed to be going right for the tourists.

inclusion in the forthcoming Test series beyond debate. There was one other major highlight at Bristol. Paul Collingwood pulled off one of the finest catches ever witnessed when he produced a flying leap at point to

England dismissed Bangladesh once more at Trent Bridge, with pace bowler Chris Tremlett picking up 4–32

on his international debut. The star of the show, however, was Paul Collingwood, who followed up an unbeaten 112 with bowling figures of 6–31. England's mammoth 391–4 also saw Strauss hit 152. Bangladesh answered with 223 all out. England then journeyed north to Collingwood's native Durham to face Australia again two days later. They would be without captain Vaughan, out with an injured groin, and would be skippered by Trescothick. The big news from the northeast prior to the start of play was how the Australians were convinced that their accommodation, Lumley Castle, was haunted. Members of the management team plus all-rounder Shane Watson had all revealed that strange and spooky goings-on had been witnessed during the night. To add to Australia's misery, England's Darren Gough made a point of imitating a ghost when Watson came out to bat.

Ironically, it would be Australia who were laughing at the end of a game in which, by beating England by 57 runs, they had finally returned to some kind of form. This was not Australia at their best, but after suffering four back-to-back one-day defeats, any kind of win was most welcome, even if England gave them a helping hand by first electing to bowl and then handing their

Let the good times roll. FACING PAGE TOP Hit man Kevin Pietersen is all smiles after bringing England home at Bristol with a brilliant 91 not out. RIGHT Andrew 'Brocket' Strauss hits out during his 152 against Bangladesh at Trent Bridge. BELOW Fans construct a lengthy 'beer snake' out of plastic pint pots as Australia take on Bangladesh at Headingley in the NatWest Series.

rivals some cheap wickets. Australia's 266–5 was made thanks largely to a 73 from Symonds and an unbeaten 68 from Martyn. In reply England slumped to 6–3 before producing a first glimpse of Flintoff and Pietersen together out in the middle. The partnership whose potential had English fans salivating with the Ashes ahead, lasted just 14 balls. In the end it took a last-wicket partnership of 50 between Gough and Harmison to add a little credibility to England's disappointing display.

Normal service was resumed for both chief combatants as they saw off Bangladesh in respective games at Old Trafford and Headingley. England won the latter comfortably after Flintoff's four wickets kept Bangladesh down to 208–7 off their ration of 50 overs. In reply a 98 from the in-form Strauss helped England home by five wickets. With the final of the NatWest Series set for Lord's and both finalists already known, England's third and last group game against Australia at Edgbaston appeared to be nothing more than a dead rubber. It would, however, throw up the first heated flashpoint in a summer that would be riddled with controversy.

The game's facts were not the major talking point. In a match that was abandoned after rain poured out of the Birmingham night-time skies, Australia batted first and posted a par total of 261–9, with Symonds proving his one-day worth once again with a useful 74. Darren Gough was the pick of the English bowlers with three wickets. In response England began well enough, notching up 37–1 off their first six overs before a thunderstorm deposited its load over Edgbaston, complete with spectacular, forked lightning. One positive that came from England's interrupted batting display was how Strauss took five boundaries off Glenn McGrath in quick succession, providing proof that the great, and usually miserly, medium-quick bowler could be attacked.

However, the aftermath of the game concentrated on one major incident that appeared to light the fuse for the rest of the summer. Australia's barrel-chested opener, Matthew Hayden, confronted Simon Jones angrily out in the middle after the pace bowler, in an attempt to run Hayden out, instead hurled the ball from his own bowling so wildly that it hit the Australian full on the chest. Hayden slammed his bat down on to the pitch after Jones's throw bounced back off the ground and hit him. Although the bowler's hand shot up immediately in apology Hayden lost no time in telling Jones exactly what he thought of the incident.

In what was an interesting sub-plot – and a telling one, too, as England made it clear that this summer, unlike others, they would not be giving ground nor standing in awe of the world champions – both Collingwood and Strauss swooped on Hayden to back up Jones and to show the opening batsman that they would not allow him to abuse their team-mate after what had been an unfortunate accident. Collingwood is known to

LEFT Ne'er a backward step. Kevin Pietersen and Andrew Symonds have a heated exchange after the latter's run-out at Edgbaston in a game also marked by a confrontation between England's Simon Jones and Australia's Matthew Hayden. FACING PAGE Ricky Ponting can only watch as Man of the Match Geraint Jones takes a diving catch down the leg side to dismiss him off Steve Harmison in the NatWest Series final at Lord's.

have some fire in his belly. But for Strauss to become involved – he is nicknamed 'Lord Brocket' in the England changing room because of his supposedly posh voice – provided more evidence that this England team would not be taking a backward step against Australia under any circumstances. The temperature continued to rise when England came out to bat and Australia saw Strauss emerge. McGrath, a former Middlesex colleague of Strauss's, launched a sledging assault on the England opener. Then spinner Brad Hogg barged into Strauss as he ran past him between overs before the skies became as electric as the atmosphere out on the pitch.

Despite Jones's apology Hayden, who has a reputation for having much to say to opposing batsmen in the middle, refused to let the matter drop afterwards. 'I am in my crease and away from my stumps and he fires the ball at me as hard as he can,' explained Hayden, sporting bruised ribs. 'You tell me whether that's fair or not. You can't get out of the way. It was like a baseball throw from ten yards. He missed his target by about four feet and I have no right of reply. There's no doubt it should be discouraged. To me it's not acceptable.'

In what appeared to be a provocative challenge for the rest of the summer Hayden added, 'What you've got

ABOVE Excitement on the England balcony as Giles and Harmison scamper two runs off the final ball of the NatWest Series final to bring about a tie. FACING PAGE A disappointed Brett Lee awaits the presentations after the final, a match that Australia seemed to have in the bag after reducing England to 33–5.

to understand is our culture, in which there's gamesmanship from five years old upwards. That's the way we play. If England decide that's the way they want to play, then it's just "play on" as far as I'm concerned.'

A bemused Vaughan attempted to cool the atmosphere later, but he not only admitted he expected more similar incidents before the summer's end but also expressed how delighted he was to see the degree of support from his England colleagues. 'I wouldn't think it will be the last time England and Australia have a few words in the middle,' he said. 'I'm sure it will happen throughout the summer. The incident probably shouldn't have taken place and you don't really want to see it on a cricket field. It was a bad throw. But it's good to see the England team were all together. You have to stick together when there's a little bit of confrontation. That's exactly what other sides do and we didn't step over the line.'

Jones appeared pretty unrepentant, happier to focus on the message portrayed by his team-mates' reaction to Hayden. 'We are a team, aren't we?' insisted the Welshman. 'We are all together and we want to work

hard for each other. It's not about backing down or not. It's just that we are pretty confident at the moment.'

One way or another, Australia were not a happy bunch. In an attempt to stir up a little patriotism, the England and Wales Cricket Board had arranged a tunnel of St George's flags, carried by children, that both teams needed to negotiate in order to enter the field at the start of each innings. The children were bunched together to ensure that it was nigh on impossible for the Australian players to avoid the flags, something they saw as an irritating distraction to their well-set routines. Hayden was forced to strenuously deny a leaked and unverified story that he had verbally abused one of the flag-bearing youngsters at Edgbaston, following on from his altercation with Jones, Collingwood and Strauss. Add to this the tourists' displeasure at the limited dressing room facilities and shared player viewing area at an Edgbaston pavilion that needs upgrading, and it was clear that quite a bit had got up Australian noses.

It was in this light, after Australia had beaten Bangladesh in the last round-robin game, that the two sides met in the NatWest Series final at Lord's. Already it had been quite a summer, and we had only just crept into July. Although Australia had shown flashes of their best, England had more than held their own, both on and off the pitch. Now would come the first real epic of the tour. It would not, of course, be the last, but right now the Ashes Test series still seemed some way off.

Just before 7.00 pm England's last pair of Ashley Giles and Steve Harmison somehow scrambled two runs off the last ball of the match, bowled by McGrath, to bring the scores level and thus produce England's fourth tie in their one-day history. It was their second against Australia, the other having been at Nottingham back in 1989. The episode not only ended a compelling game but provided yet more evidence that England really were a match for their illustrious opponents. True, it was only a tie, not a win, but in achieving it England staged one of the great comebacks in the one-day game and ensured that the first piece of silverware on offer during this incredible summer of cricket would be shared between the two combatants.

When Australia managed only a modest 196 all out with seven balls remaining of their 50 overs, nothing suggested what was to come. England had won the toss and invited Australia to bat. Gilchrist and Hayden launched into Gough and Jones to race away to 50 in just the seventh over. But when Harmison and Flintoff took over to exploit the variable pace, movement and bounce in a lively Lord's strip, Australia were reduced to first 93–5, and then 196 all out. Only Michael Hussey offered

any kind of real resistance, his unbeaten 62 proving invaluable. Flintoff and Harmison grabbed three wickets apiece and bowled economically to boot.

When England came out to bat, a home win looked the likely outcome. At 33–5 in the tenth over, though, an England defeat appeared to be odds-on. The Australian opening bowling pair of McGrath and Lee did the damage, with figures of 3–9 and 2–20 respectively at that point. Trescothick, Strauss, Vaughan, Pietersen, registering his first real failure in English colours, and Flintoff were all back in the pavilion, and all England's last hopes appeared to rest with their final two recognised batsmen – Collingwood at six and wicket-keeper Geraint Jones at seven.

The latter had been selected before this one-day series to open the innings with Trescothick, a move designed to emulate the success Australia had enjoyed with their wicket-keeper, Adam Gilchrist, who had long destroyed opposition opening bowlers in one-day cricket before reverting to type and the number seven batting position in Test cricket. Jones had proved to be a moderate pinch-hitter, no more, and for the NatWest Series it was decided by England coach Duncan Fletcher

LEFT Michael Vaughan was full of praise for his side's performance in the NatWest Series, yet in no time at all he and his side were practising at Headingley ahead of another competition against Australia – the NatWest Challenge. FACING PAGE Marcus Trescothick crashes Brad Hogg for six during his 104 not out in England's nine-wicket win at Headingley.

to go back to their tried and tested batting order. Strauss went up the card to partner Trescothick, and Jones returned to number seven.

He and Collingwood put on a partnership of 116 from 205 balls, a partnership that began slowly and painstakingly. Initially the order was to simply rebuild. If England were to lose this final, then at least Collingwood and Jones could add some respectability to the margin of defeat. The more these two batted, the higher the ambition became, from avoiding humiliation, to damage limitation, to respectability and, finally, to the chance of an unlikely win. Jones reached his half-century first, from 86 balls and with two sixes. By the time Collingwood reached the mark after 108 balls, the pair could have been forgiven for believing the win was on. But after Collingwood was run out for 53 and Jones followed shortly afterwards, leg before to Hogg for 73, the game appeared to be up.

Giles and Gough had other ideas, though. The two had brought England to within sight of a win when Gough was run out off the penultimate ball of the innings. Out strode Harmison, no doubt relieved to see

that Giles and Gough had crossed during the run out and that it would be Giles to face the final ball. Needing two to tie, Giles thrust out his bat and pad to McGrath's final delivery. There was a huge shout for lbw, but Giles had somehow got a small nick on the ball and as it trickled its way down to third man the England pair scrambled the couple of runs required in front of a Lord's crowd of 28,000 who sat rooted to their seats as the drama unfolded in front of them.

Afterwards Jones, who also claimed five catches behind the wicket, and Collingwood received the praise they deserved from a grateful Vaughan for their match-turning sixth-wicket stand. 'They set up an enthralling finish with both batting beautifully,' said the England captain. 'At one point we looked down and out but some low-scoring games can sometimes be the most exciting. We did fantastically well to restrict Australia to 196 but at 33–5 in reply we were struggling and I thought the game was gone.' His counterpart, Ponting, was clearly disappointed once more. 'It was a game we should have won,' he stated.

Harmison's return to world-class form did not go unnoticed, either. 'Harmison was outstanding in this series,' Vaughan pointed out. 'Just because he had a couple of bad games in the winter doesn't make him a bad bowler.' He also received encouragement from McGrath, of all people. The Australian is usually explaining how his side will beat England whenever asked, but even he had to acknowledge his bowling counterpart's role in the series. 'To have a bowler bowling at that pace, with bounce and movement, Harmison's current form must be giving the England team tremendous confidence,' he admitted.

Both England and Australia had precisely five days to recover from the nerve-jangling events of Lord's and the NatWest Series final. Then it was off again, like two boxers rising from their respective corners to slug it out once more. The NatWest Challenge, a three-game tournament between the two sides, would soon begin at Headingley, but not before Australia's coach, John Buchanan, had delivered some choice views on England.

His assessment of England's batsmen after the NatWest Series final was withering, to say the least. 'What I saw on Saturday at Lord's was very, very encouraging from our point of view in terms of the way a lot of English players were dismissed, especially their top order,' Buchanan announced, before homing in on

ABOVE Andrew Flintoff opens his shoulders against the bowling of Andrew Symonds during his innings of 87 in the second NatWest Challenge match, at Lord's.

England's top three. Speaking about Trescothick, he added, 'We see him very much as still the same batsman who is vulnerable to bowling angles across him.' On Strauss, 'It's not so much the quick bowling, rather the line you bowl at him. He's been troubled by McGrath as much as by Lee.' And on Vaughan, 'I'd like to hear England coach Duncan Fletcher's views on how Michael has got out against us so far this summer.' Then he turned on England's fielding. 'I think they've only got three good fielders. Paul Collingwood is obviously a very good fielder, so too is Vikram Solanki, and Kevin Pietersen is quick to the ball. But others are quite lumbering in the field.'

These were words that would hit the Australian coach full in the face come the first tie of the three-game NatWest Challenge at Headingley. England not only won

the game. They handed out a severe and emphatic beating. Australia, put in to bat, could only muster a below par 219–7 in their 50 overs, with Collingwood's awkward medium pace resulting in figures of 4–34. Gilchrist, Martyn and Hussey all contributed with useful knocks, but no Australian went on to make the big score the side required. Simon Jones had the dubious honour of being the first player substituted in international cricket after he had completed his ten overs, the pace bowler being replaced by 'super-sub' Vikram Solanki, in accordance with regulations decreed by the game's rulers. It was not the accolade Jones would have wanted, but better things would lie ahead for the Welshman. In reply England knocked off the runs with four overs still to spare for the loss of just one wicket, Strauss, who made 41. Trescothick continued his golden summer run spree with an unbeaten 104, while Vaughan chipped in with 59 not out.

With the countdown to the start of the Ashes having now reached 13 days, both teams were looking for psychological pointers. For Australia it would be how well their opening attack of McGrath and Lee would fare against England's opening batting pair of Trescothick and Strauss. On this evidence the latter, having put on 101 for the first wicket, had their noses in front.

Trescothick, in particular, would have been pleased with his 134-ball stay at the crease, an innings that included one six and eight fours. Talk of him being easy meat for McGrath on previous evidence was put to bed after this, while coach Buchanan's earlier comments looked decidedly ill-advised. While Vaughan had an excellent record against the world champions, and Strauss had no record against them at all, Trescothick's previous experiences against Australia had been modest. In Tests he averaged only 29, and in one-day cricket only 28 in 15 outings. Before this game his best score in any form of cricket against Australia was 82. He had been criticised for his lack of foot movement, yet his innings was faultless save for his being caught on the third man boundary off a Lee no-ball when on five, an incident that would repeat itself in various forms on numerous occasions as the summer's continuing drama unfolded. After an early summer of bullying Bangladesh, this ton would have meant a great deal more to the Somerset player. He even produced a statement of intent against Lee, who had almost decapitated him with a beamer in the NatWest Series final at Lord's the previous Saturday. This time Trescothick, on 85 and with the game all but won, went down the wicket to face a Lee ball.

Clearly the new regime in the Trescothick household was doing wonders for his cricket. At the start of the season he had played poorly, amassing just 96 runs in four Championship appearances for his county. This, in part, he put down to being a doting father since the birth of Ellie Louise Trescothick in April. After repeated attempts to fit his sleep patterns around his newborn baby daughter, Trescothick had finally caved in to the continual 3.00 am wake-up calls and opted for the spare room. 'A couple of weeks ago it got so bad that I found myself yawning as the ball was coming down,' Trescothick admitted. 'Fatherhood has been fantastic, but waking up at 3.00 am and feeding the baby hasn't helped my cricket. I told my wife I needed more sleep so I've popped off to the top floor of my three-storey house to get away from it all.' It seemed to have done the trick in good time for Australia.

There was no doubt that it was a vital toss to win at the home of Yorkshire cricket. The morning was overcast, making the ball hard work for the batsmen in Headingley's notorious conditions. Perhaps Darren Lehmann might have profited, the Australian batsman having played a number of seasons for Yorkshire, but he had not been selected for this tour and was instead sitting up in the commentary box. Then, when England came in to bat, the clouds dispersed and the sun came out to shine on English cricket as they rattled up a nine-wicket win. This was their largest ever margin of victory against Australia in one-day cricket.

Three days later at Lord's, this compelling pendulum of a one-day series would swing again, and this time in Australia's favour. A win for England would have wrapped up the best-of-three series even before a ball had been bowled in the third and final encounter at The Oval 48 hours later. Instead, the two sides would reconvene in south London all square on one apiece after Australia this time saw off England at Lord's with their most emphatic win of the summer to date.

Moreover, this proved to be a good day for the beleaguered Australian captain, Ricky Ponting. He had enjoyed a few beforehand in his role as skipper but not as an individual cricketer on this tour. At Lord's a Ponting century revealed not only why he is regarded as one of the finest batsmen in world cricket but also, and worryingly from an England perspective, that he had returned to form. He pulled off a stunning catch as well, to dismiss Giles off Lee's bowling.

The only real positive for England was that in their disappointing 225–8 in their 50 overs, having been asked to bat first, Andrew Flintoff hit 87, his first score of significance against Australia. England, Australia, in fact everyone knew that if England were to compete against Australia in the forthcoming Test series, let alone win the Ashes, then Flintoff needed to be in form with both ball and bat. Flintoff bludgeoned two sixes and ten fours in his 87, but not even he could produce a complete batting recovery after England's first three fell for just 28 between them. From 45–4 Flintoff and the increasingly dependable Collingwood, who chipped in with 34, did well to revive England, but their total appeared 30 to 40 runs short of a testing target for Australia to chase. Lee was in fiery form as he picked up four wickets, while Michael Kasprowicz compensated for the continuing loss of form by Jason Gillespie, who was hit once again to all four corners of the boundary, as indeed he had been since arriving on English shores.

England's one-day new ball opening partnership of Gough and Jones lasted only four overs before they had were removed from the fray and replaced by the more heavyweight first change bowling pairing of Flintoff and Harmison. Gilchrist and new opening partner Simon

Katich made light of the absence of Hayden, out with a shoulder problem, but it was Ponting who stole the show. In scoring his seventeenth one-day century the captain put himself just one ton behind Mark Waugh's Australian record of 18 limited overs international centuries. His exuberant joy as he reached three figures was an indication of the pressure he had undoubtedly been under since Australia's horrible start to their summer tour. He fell eventually for 111, leaving Martyn and Symonds to notch up the few remaining runs required for victory.

As the sun went down over the home of cricket, Ponting reflected that his innings, and the manner of Australia's win, could prove to be a watershed for the remainder of the tour. 'In the context of the tour this was a big game for us,' he admitted. 'We had built this game up among ourselves and it could be a turning point. It has been a long, hard road on this tour but this time we were really able to prepare properly. It shows what we are capable of when we perform close to our best.'

Not a particularly good day for the England cricket team, then, but a good day for cricket and for sport, as Lord's was full to capacity in a veritable show of public defiance three days after London had been stunned by

terrorist bomb attacks on the Underground and bus network that led to over 50 deaths. In fact, just about the biggest cheer of the day came when an old Second World War Lancaster bomber flew over Headquarters.

And so the decider of this three-match series would unfold at The Oval two days later. The seven one-day matches between England and Australia, including the Twenty20 encounter a month before, had been full of twists and turns, high drama, and plenty of action – and England could argue that, largely, they had enjoyed the best of it.

But there were signs, worrying signs, that Australia were finally discovering their form. Certainly their comfortable win at Lord's seemed to have made a marked transformation in the general mood inside the Aussie camp. For a start those arriving at The Oval early

The Australian response. FACING PAGE Ricky Ponting jumps for joy after completing his hundred in the Lord's NatWest Challenge match. BELOW A shrinking Jason Gillespie gets a laugh out of Glenn McGrath during an official team photo. Gillespie struggled for form at the start of the tour but came good in the NatWest Challenge game at The Oval, in which he took three key wickets for 44 runs.

ABOVE Adam Gilchrist on his way to a 101-ball 121 not out at The Oval. FACING PAGE Captain Ricky Ponting and his team celebrate winning the NatWest Challenge.

would have seen the Australian players working through a newly extended series of pre-match preparations. More vigorous training the day before had seen an optional but fully attended net session. Moreover, there appeared to be a sense of renewal about these Australians.

Maybe the team who had smashed New Zealand 5–0 in their previous set of ODIs prior to arriving in England had sound reasons for their stuttering start. Their schedule, after all, had been hectic bordering on insane, but it was both interesting and worrying that for the first

time all summer Australia had managed to have six travel-free days in the same London hotel in preparation for the two remaining NatWest Challenge internationals.

One month of cricket in pyjamas came to a shuddering end at The Oval. What had begun with an emphatic win for England in the Twenty20 version of the game down at the Rose Bowl in Hampshire, a result that created instant grounds for optimism for the summer ahead, was completed with a heavy dose of reality in south London. Australia may have started a month of limited overs cricket out of sorts, but they ended it looking precisely what they were supposed to be – one-day world champions, and the best team in Test cricket in the world, by some distance.

It was not just the fact that Australia won the series decider to take the NatWest Challenge Trophy. It was not even the manner of victory, as one-sided as it proved to be – having asked England to bat first, Australia restricted the home side to 228–7 in 50 overs before reaching their target for the loss of just two wickets with an enormous 15.1 overs to spare.

It was more the fact that, at last, Australia were revealing their true colours. With the First Test of the Ashes series just nine days away at Lord's, this was precisely the wrong moment, from an English point of view, for Australia to gain the upper playing and psychological hand.

England's innings, not for the first time, relied heavily on Kevin Pietersen. Without his 74, plus super-sub Solanki's unbeaten 53 and 25 not out from Giles at the end, England would have amassed no total at all. Apart from Strauss, who scored 36, England's other recognised batsmen failed collectively, with Messrs Trescothick, Vaughan, Flintoff, Collingwood and Geraint Jones scoring 30 runs between them. Trescothick slashed

Lee to third man for a duck, Vaughan ran himself out attempting a suicidal run, while Flintoff wafted at Kasprowicz to be caught behind. Pietersen revealed excellent timing to produce, by his thrilling standards, a more measured innings with Test match selection to be decided the following day. While batsmen around him fell on their swords, Pietersen showed that he is able to reconstruct an innings as well as simply smash the ball to the boundary. Indeed, his first 30 runs were gathered almost in a conservative fashion. After that, as he and Solanki enjoyed a 93-run stand, he reverted to type, smashing two sixes before being bowled by Gillespie.

The Australian fast bowler, with his shaggy, long hair, beard and headband, had endured a horrendous tour to date. Formerly one of the most feared strike bowlers in Test cricket, this amiable, almost Bohemian character off the pitch suddenly rediscovered his line and length to claim three wickets. It was an especially admirable performance considering that he had been subjected to ridicule from a largely partisan Oval crowd for first letting through what should have been no more than two

runs to the boundary after some poor ground fielding, and then dropping what seemed to be a straightforward skied chance from Vaughan.

Gilchrist, too, had been guilty of an equally embarrassing dropped catch when he fumbled a high, looping chance off the edge of Strauss's bat. None of these errors made a jot of difference to the eventual outcome of the game, and those in the crowd who hooted their derision at Gilchrist may have thought about their response later that day as the wicket-keeper/batsman finally found his form with a vengeance.

If the return to form of Gillespie was a concern to England, the way in which Gilchrist announced himself should have created sleepless nights beyond the Trescothick household. Up until this point Gilchrist, by his own high standards, had been missing from action.

One of the most destructive batsmen in the game, and one of the major aces in the Australian Test pack, he had not got going yet in the batting department, and had been less than his usual tidy self behind the stumps.

At The Oval Gilchrist announced that his demise had been exaggerated. By scoring an unbeaten 121 off just 101 balls, he turned what could have been an interesting if not especially taxing run chase into a procession. With Hayden and Ponting enjoying the action from the other end of the wicket, and adding useful contributions themselves, it was left to Gilchrist and Martyn to see Australia home. If Ponting's celebrations on passing a hundred at Lord's two days earlier had been ecstatic, then Gilchrist's own way of showing his pleasure in passing the mark bordered on orgasmic. In truth it was the lifting of a heavy burden off the affable player's shoulders.

England's bowlers had no answer to this slaughter. Only Flintoff produced satisfactory bowling figures. Of the Test bowlers used, Harmison went for 81 runs off 9.5 overs, and Giles 64 in ten overs. It was a hammering delivered at the best time for the visitors, and the worst for England, a fact pointed out by a euphoric and clearly relieved Ricky Ponting afterwards.

The Australian captain revealed how his team had vowed to put things right after their humiliating nine-wicket defeat to England at Headingley in the first of the three NatWest Challenge matches. 'There was a lot of soul-searching about where we were going wrong, and today was as close to perfect as one-day cricket gets for us. The way we've turned it around since Leeds has been very pleasing.'

Gilchrist admitted later that he and his team-mates had been stung into action by the extent of the hurt felt within the Australian camp. 'We've been copping it both on and off the field,' he said. 'People have laughed about us and made things up about us and we showed great character today to play that way and put things right.'

The next day England's selectors would be meeting to name their Test XI to start at Lord's. Pietersen's latest knock meant that three batsmen appeared to be vying for the number four and five spots in the England middle order. Would England go for the young and

their hitherto fragile confidence restored. To all intents and purposes it was the nightmare scenario many had feared when the schedule for the summer was first announced, and Ponting's opening comments on arrival at Heathrow seemed to be ringing true. How English cricket fans wished England had taken on Australia in a First Test played in mid-June, when Australia were still so rusty and underprepared. By July England could have been two Tests up. Instead Australia had been allowed to find their feet, with devastating results. Even the most optimistic pundits could not see England getting any closer than a 3–1 Ashes defeat after what had happened at Lord's and now at The Oval. Australia at their best appeared to be better than England at theirs.

Vaughan, quite rightly, tried to downplay the messages from the last two One-Day Internationals of the series. 'At Leeds we were told the Ashes momentum was with us and now people are saying it's with Australia,' he commented. 'We are not reading too much into either argument. History tells you that one-day cricket has little impact on the five-day game.'

Maybe, but the sight of Australia's Test match men not used in the one-day series arriving in England would hardly have eased England's sudden woes. Shane Warne and Brad Hodge had already been warming up courtesy of their English counties, Hampshire and Lancashire, while reserve spinner Stuart MacGill and reserve pace bowler Shaun Tait arrived in time to watch Australia batter England at The Oval. Opener Justin Langer, meanwhile, had been in the country a few days more, having been working out previously at home with the trainers of Australian boxer Danny Green.

Warne made a point of informing English cricket that his widely publicised marriage break-up in June would not distract him from trying his best to beat England. 'Over the years one of my strengths as a cricketer has been my mental capacity to focus on the job in hand,' he insisted. 'As with many people who have to face up to their job each day, no matter what is going on in their private lives, I have been able to focus on my job. This will not be any different.'

One of his best friends in English cricket is Hampshire colleague Pietersen, who received the happy and not totally unexpected news the day after The Oval that he would be making his Test match debut the following week at the expense of Thorpe. The fact that the 25-year-old's first Test would be the opening encounter against Australia in the most eagerly awaited

promising Bell, who had started his Test career with such aplomb, the experienced and proven Graham Thorpe, or Pietersen, who had kicked down the selectors' door with his virtuoso performances? 'Pietersen has given the selectors a headache,' admitted Vaughan. 'That's all you can ask of a player.'

For a day this was not England's biggest concern. As they packed away their blue and red pyjamas and took out their cricketing whites in readiness for the first Test, just nine days away, they would have realised that Australia had suddenly claimed the psychological edge for the first time all summer.

A look back over the past month of one-day cricket made reasonable reading for England, considering that at the start of the summer Australia were hot favourites to win everything. Three wins, a tie, a no-result and three defeats was hardly a disgrace against the best team in the world. But in the past three days England had lost much if not all of the pre-Ashes momentum initially gained.

Australia had suddenly discovered the feel-good factor, their routine seemed to be back on track, and

Ashes series for a long, long time would have suited Pietersen just fine. As far as he was concerned, the bigger the challenge the better. 'I'm the happiest boy in the UK,' Pietersen declared when told of his selection. 'Since coming into international cricket there's been a lot of pressure on me and I've come out all right. I'm going to enjoy the moment now.'

The selection provided yet more evidence that England were looking to the future, and forging a more aggressive approach to their cricket. The choice had been difficult. The 35-year-old Thorpe had just racked up his hundredth Test appearance in the Second Test against Bangladesh, won by England, and had scored runs in both Tests, admittedly against sub-standard opposition. He had earned the respect of previous Australians for his gutsy displays against them, notably former captain Steve Waugh, who said of Thorpe, 'He was someone who was mentally strong, who always stood up to you and fought.'

It must have been very tempting to stay with the tried and the tested. Thorpe averaged 44 in Test cricket. Amazingly, against Australia his average improved to 45, and against Shane Warne it stood at 46.

Yet chairman of selectors David Graveney pointed out how Pietersen had clearly revealed an ability and character beyond slogging the ball during the one-day series that had swung the verdict his way. 'If you look at the times he has been coming in to bat they have already been difficult situations,' he explained. 'Under Michael Vaughan there has been a fantastic atmosphere in the dressing room and Kevin has contributed to that.' What also worked against Thorpe was his pre-summer statement that he would retire from international cricket after the Ashes series. 'We would be lying if we pretended that we weren't aware of that fact,' Graveney added.

Thorpe was diplomatic in his response to the news that his Test match credentials had been discarded, most probably for the final time. 'I'm disappointed not to be selected but I respect and understand the selectors' decision,' he stated. 'I wish Michael Vaughan and the England players all the best.' Before the Ashes series was concluded Thorpe would also announce his retirement from first-class cricket.

The other Test debutant in an otherwise expected 12-man squad was the 6ft 7in Hampshire pace bowler Chris Tremlett. In picking the 23-year-old, England showed yet again that youth would be their policy. Only Giles was over 30 in the England team, while only Katich and Clarke were under 30 in the Australian Test starting XI. Tremlett was odds-on to be 12th man, but it was still a significant step forward for a man who, with five Ashes Tests crammed into barely seven weeks, stood every chance of making his Test debut some time during the remainder of the summer.

Out after the one-day series went the likes of the unlucky Collingwood, Solanki and Gough, and in came Ian Bell, with a Test average after three innings of 297.00, and the Yorkshire seamer Matthew Hoggard, who had already played a substantial part in England's success story over the past couple of years, and had enjoyed rich pickings during the successful winter Test tour of South Africa.

Hoggard lost no time in throwing himself right into the very epicentre of the last-minute Ashes build-up. Choosing words that threatened to haunt him in later weeks, he suggested that Australia were both running scared and over the hill. 'They are scared and trying to put us down by talking like bullies,' Hoggard said. 'They say we are good, but we aren't as good as them. Well, we will see about that. They are putting themselves in the

BELOW AND FACING PAGE Opinion had long said that England needed Harmison and Flintoff to be fit and in form to stand a chance of beating Australia. The one-day series suggested they were. Could they transfer their success to the Ashes arena?

spotlight and bigging themselves up. But we are second in the world and capable of beating them and we intend to show this.'

The man with the floppy, blonde hair, who loves nothing better than to walk his dogs on the Yorkshire moors, then homed in on the collective ages of the Australian bowling attack. 'Age will be a factor,' he insisted. 'The wickets will be flat and their bowlers will have to bowl a lot of overs. It will be tough for Glenn McGrath and it will be interesting to see if he is still the world-class performer he was and if Jason Gillespie can find some form. It will also be interesting to see if Shane Warne can produce his best because he is getting on a bit as well and he isn't the force he was. He comes around the wicket a lot now and that's a defensive measure.'

Meanwhile, Pietersen urged the Lord's crowd to leave their usually conservative behaviour at home and instead give Australia a hard time. 'I don't think Australia like it,' he explained. 'It would be good for the crowd to really get behind the England team and absolutely nail the Aussies from ball one. They didn't like

the stick they got at the start of the tour and it would be fantastic if the crowd could give it to them.'

It had been six long weeks since the Australians had first arrived on British shores. The one-day competitions had been a fascinating duel, of that there was no doubt. England had fared much better than anyone had dared to expect. We had seen batsmen such as Trescothick, Strauss, Flintoff and Pietersen hit Australia's much-vaunted bowling attack all over the place, and witnessed the likes of Harmison and Flintoff, in particular, strike fear into the hearts of Australian batsmen.

But the prevailing feeling throughout was that all this, as watchable and exciting as it had been, was no more than a prelude, an hors d'oeuvre, to the main event. At last, after seemingly an interminably long time, the pyjama cricket was done with and the serious business of the summer was about to get under way.

There was no escaping the fact that Australia had started the summer as clear favourites to retain the Ashes. It was also clear that England were capable of giving them a run for their money this time. But on the evidence of the past week it was also clear that Australia were sitting in the box seat.

Australia for the Ashes? If there were those who still doubted this assumption, the next four days would appear to remove any lingering English hopes.

LORD'S
1ST TEST
21 JULY–24 JULY

FACING PAGE Glenn McGrath takes his 500th wicket in Tests – Marcus Trescothick caught by Justin Langer for four. RIGHT Australian fans play cricket outside Lord's as they wait for bought-back tickets for the First Test to go on sale.

E ven had you discarded the events of the previous week, cricket historians would have feared the worst on the first morning of the Ashes series. If the First Test had been at Headingley, then England, with a magnificent record against Australia at Leeds, would have been filled with optimism.

But Lord's? The facts made sorry reading. England had not beaten Australia at Headquarters for 71 years. Indeed, Bill Brown, the Australian opening batsman, is the only participant alive today from that match in 1934. Since then Australia have won eight times and drawn nine in seventeen tests. Undoubtedly they were saved by

rain on a couple of occasions, but largely Australia have had it all their own way.

Nobody, it seems, enjoys the ground, with its notorious slope, more than Glenn McGrath. Maybe it is because he had a spell with Middlesex. Or maybe it is simply because his tight, fast-medium pace that strangles the opposition is ideally suited to the place. Whatever the reason, his first innings figures of 8–38 in 1997 are the best recorded by an Australian in the 32 Tests between the teams on the famous old ground. He and Jason Gillespie both have their names up on the honours boards that hang on the walls of the dressing rooms. The

qualifications for such an honour are a century scored, five wickets in an innings or ten in a match. Only Australia's Keith Miller's name is up on all three boards.

Strangely, Shane Warne's name is absent from the boards. The world's leading wicket-taker has three times collected four wickets in an innings at Lord's, but never five. He has his portrait hanging on the wall of the Long Room, but it was a place on the honours boards that he really wanted. With this being his last Test appearance at Lord's, Warne knew it would be now or never.

Perhaps a glance up at the boards would encourage the English players. Trescothick, Strauss, Flintoff and Vaughan were all up there, the last-mentioned five times, while Giles also appeared for his one five-for.

Yet England went into the Ashes with a lot of unanswered questions. They brought to the First Test a captain short of runs, numbers four and five with three Tests' experience between them, and a six in Flintoff making his Ashes debut. Youth equalled fearlessness was the positive argument. With such inexperience there would be no baggage from previous Ashes beatings. But

BELOW Steve Harmison bowls the first ball of one of the most keenly anticipated Test series for years.

pace, bounce and aggression, claiming five Australian scalps. The England team left the field to a heroes' welcome from an old pavilion almost buckling under the weight of MCC members, resplendent in their egg and bacon striped ties. Half a day had gone out of a possible 25, and suddenly the unlikely dream of the Ashes coming home seemed to be entering people's thoughts.

could such inexperience seriously handle the worldliness of McGrath, Warne and company when the heat was on?

For all the foreboding prior to the start of the First Test, it began well enough for England. Michael Vaughan, using a special coin to commemorate the 125th anniversary of Test cricket in England, lost the toss and knew that his counterpart, Ricky Ponting, would elect to bat. By mid-afternoon Australia had been bowled out for just 190 in only 40.2 overs, with Harmison, all

By the end of the first day's play, however, that dream had been shattered. England concluded the evening session staggering on 92–7 after being obliterated by the incomparable McGrath. After all the build-up, and all the hype, the Ashes series had begun with the fall of 17 wickets on the very first day. It was some start, and it provided the yardstick for the days to come in the series.

First came the positive. England's bowlers had clearly done their homework on the Australian batsmen and, like the great West Indies side of the 1970s and

FACING PAGE **Ricky Ponting is patched up by Errol Alcott after being struck by a Harmison special.** BELOW **Not long afterwards, Harmy had his man, caught by Strauss for nine.**

1980s and Australia themselves ever since, hunted in a pack of four. Australia began as if batting in a One-Day International, but from the moment Hoggard, the least impressive of England's four-pronged pace attack, bowled Hayden, the visitors were under siege.

The chief protagonist was Harmison, who laid into the Australian batting line-up like a man possessed with a major grievance. A thoroughly laid-back, family man off the pitch, Harmison, when the mood takes him, is transformed into a veritable monster with ball in hand. At one stage his hostility led to the Australian physiotherapist, Errol Alcott, acting more like a cuts man in the corner of a boxing match as he patched up the bloodied face of Ponting, struck on the visor by a lifter from the England fast bowler. Not surprisingly, shortly afterwards Harmison got his man. It was his rough-house treatment of the top three Australian batsmen that paved the way for his colleagues to exploit.

Simon Jones had not enjoyed the best form or luck during the one-day series, but his fortunes took an abrupt U-turn for the better when he took a wicket with his first ball in an Ashes Test since suffering a horrific knee injury in Brisbane in 2002 that so nearly ended his career. Damien Martyn could only waft at Jones's delivery, the batsman's fourth, which moved off the pitch, giving Geraint Jones behind the stumps a simple catch. Then Jones the bowler claimed Michael Clarke, too, with an inswinging ball that caught him plumb leg before wicket. With Flintoff adding the vital wicket of Gilchrist, edging to wicket-keeper Jones, to the earlier wicket of Justin Langer, caught by man of the moment Harmison, it was left to the big, hulking Geordie to finish off the Australian tail with a ferocious onslaught of top-class pace bowling. In a 14-ball spell his figures read 4–7. With the wickets of Katich, Warne, Lee and Gillespie, plus that of Ponting, Harmison ended with first innings figures of 5–43, and a place on the Lord's honours board. This was already the sixth time Harmison had bagged a five-for in his still relatively short Test career.

For Harmison, this was a welcome return to world-class form after a disappointing time in South Africa the previous winter. Twelve months before that he spent the winter training with his beloved Newcastle United football team to improve his fitness. After a winter tour to the West Indies, and two summer series against the Windies again and New Zealand, Harmison had become the number one ranked fast bowler in the world and the top wicket-taker in world cricket for the calendar year, but his form deserted him in South Africa and he longed to be back home with his wife and two young daughters. Homesickness has always hit Harmison harder than it

has any other member of the England team. He used to run away from school, and he also ran away from his first England cricket tour, with the Under 19s in Pakistan. He did not exactly run away in South Africa, but he was barely half the player he had been for the previous 12 months. 'It will always be there, even when I'm 30,' Harmison admitted. 'I miss home like others are scared of the dark.' It speaks volumes for his team-mates that they could still pull off a series win in South Africa without Harmison getting even close to top form. But that was then, and even during his unhappy time in South Africa the Ashes were never far from the 26-year-old's thoughts.

'I would be lying if I didn't admit that I was thinking about the summer even when playing in South Africa. On my own at night I'd often think about the Australians. I couldn't wait for the Ashes series to start. I knew everything about the Australian thing growing up. It's always been the be-all and end-all and we'll be judged by how we fare in this series against them much more than how we've done against the other teams in the world. The Australian factor has to be knocked out. We have to stop playing against Australia, and start playing against 11 other blokes. That said, it doesn't get any better than going out in front of a full house on the first morning of the Ashes Test knowing that Langer and Hayden were gunning for me. It's the ultimate challenge in cricket.'

Australia would have had every right to be disappointed. Their intention, having been sent out to bat, would have been to take an immediate stranglehold on the game. This has always been their style. Take early command, and then squeeze the life out of the opposition. Langer, Katich and Gilchrist had all played themselves in and were all looking likely to score a half-century when they got out, their wickets falling at inconvenient intervals. Langer and Katich, in particular, were dismissed after senseless hook shots, while Gilchrist's edge to the England 'keeper followed a loose shot. Warne, too, with a 28, suggested he was on for a useful score, even though his previous batting average made him an all-rounder only in the loosest sense. In truth he had always been the world's finest spin bowler who could bat a bit as well. His first innings score, modest as it may appear, was a precursor of greater things to come.

All in all England should have been pretty pleased with their half-day's work. Their achievement could have been even greater had Pietersen not marked his Ashes debut by dropping two catches, the first a difficult chance off Australian skipper Ponting, but the second a relative sitter when Brett Lee edged at a comfortable height to the debutant, who first fumbled and then failed to hold on to the rebound.

FACING PAGE Australian wickets continue to tumble – Michael Clarke is lbw to Simon Jones for 11.

When Ponting led Australia out to field in the afternoon he sported stitches in his cheek and another grievance to add to his many so far on this tour. By the end of the first day, however, his scowl had been replaced by a grin after seeing McGrath, branded too old by Matthew Hoggard the week before, destroy the top half of England's batting line-up.

A year earlier the bowler, suffering from an injured ankle, was beginning to look like a spent force. Those who witnessed his opening spell for Australia at Lord's that afternoon would vouch that McGrath was anything but spent. Having survived the minor, pre-tea session from McGrath and Lee, England's batsmen then folded like a pack of cards. While Australia's batsmen succumbed to Harmison's provocative bowling, England fell victim to a bowler with the precision of a surgeon, who used the slope's assistance to move the ball in

towards the right-handers, and away from left-handers such as Marcus Trescothick.

First to fall was Trescothick, nicking the first ball after the resumption of play in the final session to Langer in the slips. If it was any consolation at all, Trescothick could always view himself as McGrath's 500th wicket in Test cricket. It was almost an honour. McGrath had always predicted that Strauss would be his 500th victim, but there were no complaints from the New South Welshman when it turned out to be Trescothick. There was always the danger that McGrath's reaching such a magnificent landmark would lift both the bowler and his

team-mates, and so it proved. Ten for one shortly became 11–2 when Strauss edged McGrath to Warne behind. Vaughan, Bell and Flintoff were all clean bowled by McGrath, who utilised the unique conditions at Lord's to perfection by bowling down the slope and swinging the ball late into the batsmen's stumps. Both Vaughan and Flintoff could argue that the ball appeared to keep low, while Bell played on to his stumps after looking reasonably solid, but their footwork looked suspiciously wanting in the process.

In his initial burst after tea McGrath took five wickets for two runs in thirty-one deliveries, producing one of the most devastating spells of bowling of his whole, illustrious career, and his twenty-seventh Test match five-wicket haul. It left England stumbling around on 21–5 like a drunkard in the dark, their lunchtime euphoria rapidly erased by the most masterful display of seam bowling you could wish to see. The standing ovation they received after dismissing Australia earlier in the day was in danger of becoming the high point of their summer.

By the end of the first day's play England's position had marginally improved, thanks partly to a resolute 30 from Geraint Jones and 11 from Ashley Giles, both batsmen falling to the red-hot pace of Brett Lee. The fact that England would start the second day still batting, however, was largely down to that man Pietersen, who put up two hours' worth of resistance and ended the day having scored an uncharacteristic 28 not out.

He had been given the nod ahead of Graham Thorpe because the selectors decided he would be a more exciting bet for England in this Ashes series. The irony of the first day, however, was that Pietersen produced the kind of innings that Thorpe would have been proud of. While wickets fell around him, and in the face of open hostility that saw Ponting earlier sledge Vaughan as the England captain came to the crease, Pietersen stood firm. With his bottom-handed batting style, and his preference for hitting as much as he can to the leg side, there were many who had questioned whether Pietersen, for all the fireworks he had displayed in the one-day game, really possessed the technique to succeed in Test cricket. His first-class average of 52 should have answered that question, but if there were any lingering doubts, his gutsy display on that first day buried the argument for good.

The fact that Pietersen was still in was the only positive to end the day on. True, England had bowled Australia out, but they ended proceedings 98 runs behind, and in familiar territory. Australia had them on the rack, and already only a miracle could save England.

That night McGrath spoke of a day that would remain forever in his memory. 'When we won the toss and were batting first I was hoping I'd be waiting until the end of day two to take my 500th wicket,' he admitted. 'I thought I'd put my feet up, enjoy the day and worry about it again tomorrow. To have 500 in the bag, plus four others, at the end of day one is strange. My spell was one of my best ever. I felt I could take a wicket with every ball and that doesn't happen often.

'I had watched England bowl on that wicket and I thought it was more suited to hit-the-deck type of bowling. Harmison and Flintoff got more out of it than Hoggard and Jones. But they bowled too short. They unsettled our batsmen but I thought you'd get more pressure on the batsman if you pitched it up. I learnt from England. Maybe there was an extra spur for me as

well, having seen three Australian batsmen hit by Harmison. I certainly felt that I had a point to prove to those who feel I might be past my prime.

'I've always loved playing at Lord's. It is unique. The crowd is so quiet and the slope really suits my style of bowling. You see the names of the guys that have taken five wickets in an innings, ten in a match and scored a hundred. My wife, Jane, and our two children, James, 5, and Holly, 4, were watching from the Mound Stand while, elsewhere in the ground, were my mother, Beverly, and my father, Kevin, who I shared a beer with after the end of play. This was the first time Dad had ever left Australian soil after a lifetime of farming sheep and wheat in Dubbo, in New South Wales.' McGrath, incidentally, had ended the Australian innings earlier in the day on ten not out, sending a message that he, for so long one of the true rabbits of Test cricket, had worked on his batting as well.

Nothing he had seen that day had convinced him of changing a view he held before the Lord's Test. 'I could

FACING PAGE AND BELOW After the carnage, England staged a fightback through Kevin Pietersen and Geraint Jones, here surviving a spirited appeal for lbw from Jason Gillespie.

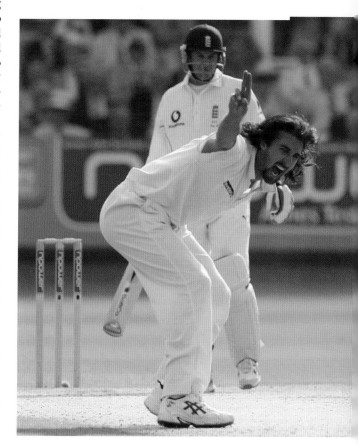

see England's recent record in Tests, and the fact that with their new players they didn't carry any baggage of previous Ashes defeats, but I also knew that playing against Australia would be like nothing they'd experienced before. The plan is to exert immense pressure on them. In this series we're going to make sure it's bearing down on them ball after ball. It'll be interesting to see how they cope.'

LEFT Brett Lee strikes, dismissing Geraint Jones for 30 as England stagger towards the close of the first day.

conclusive. 'I never believe we're going to lose a match,' he said. 'We go out to win every game we play. I wouldn't be true to myself nor my team-mates if I didn't now say we're going to win 5–0. That's exactly how I see it.'

Brought up on a 1400-acre farm 200 miles from Sydney, McGrath first learnt to play his cricket on a matting wicket situated between the grain silo and the shearing shed. So isolated was he from the rest of Australia that the name of the local cricket club he played for as a kid was 'Backwater'. At 19 he went to Sydney to see if he could crack it in the sport he loved, choosing to live in a caravan on Bondi Beach to make his stay cheaper. 'My philosophy hasn't changed in the 17 years since,' he said. 'I like to keep things simple. Less can go wrong that way.'

In fact, the only thing that had gone wrong for him in recent times was having to confront the cancer that his wife contracted before they were married. Jane underwent chemotherapy, beat the disease, and is now the mother of McGrath's son and daughter. 'We're very happy and Jane's thriving,' he reported. 'And I couldn't have thought of a better place to have taken my 500th wicket than at Lord's in front of my whole family.'

The situation England found themselves in as they woke on the Friday morning was not good, but neither was it a lost cause. They still had Kevin Pietersen at the crease and, once again, much of the day's key moments centred around the 6ft 5in 25-year-old.

From the moment it became clear that he was eligible to play for England, Pietersen had been the chief subject of cricketing debate. Even though he had met all qualification rules, there were some who questioned whether a man born in Durban who had lived all his childhood in South Africa and who bore a strong accent from his native country should be allowed to play for England. Then Pietersen decimated his former countrymen in a series of violent batting onslaughts in the One-Day Internationals in South Africa in the face of much resentment from the crowds and the opposing players, a feat he had followed up to an extent against Australia the previous month. Then there was the Graham Thorpe debate. And now English hopes appeared to rest with a man making his Test debut.

At first he did not disappoint. With only Hoggard, Harmison and Simon Jones as batting partners, Pietersen reverted in style from the previous day's cautious to his more natural, all-out attack. Never mind the fact that England were in such a precarious position. And never mind that he was playing at the home of cricket in one of the most eagerly anticipated Test matches of all time. Pietersen went to work on two of the

At the start of the tour McGrath had said that Australia might win the Ashes by only 3–0. 'That's because the weather might play up,' he had explained. Now he believed the result would be even more

greatest bowlers in the history of cricket, Warne and McGrath, both of whom found themselves staring into the stands after being hit for six. In Warne's case the ball ended up in the hospitality boxes. The two Hampshire colleagues and friends exchanged knowing grins. In the case of McGrath the ball was deposited high and straight back over the bowler's head and into the pavilion, and this with McGrath operating from the Pavilion End, from which he had dealt so much damage to the English cause the day before. Indeed, Pietersen brought up his half-century by hitting McGrath for a four, a six and then a

cover drive to the boundary in three successive balls, leaving the great bowler to walk back to his mark shaking his head in bemusement. In three deliveries Pietersen had taken twice as many runs off him as McGrath had conceded in taking five wickets the previous day.

Pietersen's one-man show of defiance came to an abrupt halt courtesy of one of the finest catches you are ever likely to see in the deep. When the England number five cross-batted a Warne delivery high over mid-wicket, it was initially just a question of whether the shot would earn him four or six runs. Damien Martyn had other ideas, though. Sprinting at speed, he made 20 metres, dived and caught the ball a couple of inches from the grass at full stretch just a foot inside the ropes and in front of a packed and stunned Grand Stand. Pietersen had gone for 57, marking his debut innings in Test cricket with a half-century.

| BELOW Day one ends as another Lee express accounts for Ashley Giles, who edges to wicket-keeper Gilchrist and steps on his stumps for good measure. FACING PAGE Eight down. Matthew Hayden catches Matthew Hoggard at slip off Shane Warne early on the second morning.

England were bowled out eventually for 155, which was not exactly how they had seen their much-vaunted batting line-up responding to Australia's poor total. It could have been a lot worse had it not been for Pietersen's belligerence and a last-wicket stand of 33 between Harmison, who fell finally to a Martyn catch off Lee, and Simon Jones, who remained 20 not out and batted with style for a Test number 11. Nonetheless, England were still 35 runs behind. In claiming Harmison's wicket Lee finished with a three-for, while Warne grabbed two late wickets with the fall of Hoggard and Pietersen.

There was the best part of an hour before lunch for Australia to bat again, and for Pietersen's golden morning to continue. Justin Langer had made just six runs when he tried to pinch a single to cover in the sixth over but was run out after Pietersen's athletic swoop, pick-up, transfer of the ball from left to right hand, and throw-down of the stumps at the bowler's end. Initially things continued to pick up after lunch, too, when Hayden was unlucky to get out. The scorecard tells you he was bowled by Flintoff, but the truth is he attempted to pull away from a rising ball which hit the bottom edge of his bat, bounced off his heel and rolled back on to the stumps. When Ponting was caught by substitute fielder James Hildreth, Australia were 100–3 and England sensed that they were clawing their way back into this Test match. The Australian captain, incidentally, still sporting a cut from Harmison's first-day bouncer, passed 7000 runs while compiling his 42, becoming only the seventh Australian to achieve such a mark.

Then came the downside of Pietersen's day, and arguably the pivotal moment of the whole game. Pietersen made it an unhappy hat-trick of dropped catches when he put down a seemingly straightforward chance at knee height from a Michael Clarke back-foot drive off the unlucky Simon Jones. What with his two earlier drops from Ponting and Lee the day before and a chance missed by Strauss off Warne as well, this was the fourth dropped catch by England, and by far the most significant. Australia were on 139–3 at the time.

The only real excuse Pietersen had was that Lord's, especially for the inexperienced, is a notoriously difficult ground on which to see the ball in the field. This, in part, is due to the slope, which when a fielder is standing on the higher, northern side can make balls flying low appear to come from the crowd. Clarke at the time was on 21. Blonde-streaked and just 24 years of age, Clarke was by some distance the baby of the Australian Test team. He began the Ashes series out of form with the bat. Indeed, in his previous two series against Pakistan and New Zealand, he had failed to get beyond 35 and looked out of touch in the One-Day Internationals against England the month before.

This time, energised by Pietersen's let-off, he took the Test away from England as he progressed towards what would have been the remarkable feat of scoring centuries on his Test debuts at home, away and in the Ashes. Giles, in particular, fell foul of Clarke's renewed vigour, being clouted for five an over and forcing Vaughan to play his still tired pace bowlers again before they had recovered from their exploits earlier on in the Australian innings. After tea Australia's fourth fifty of the innings came off just 47 balls, and the fifth fifty, off 54 balls. On 91, though, 70 on from being dropped by Pietersen, Clarke chopped a ball from Hoggard on to his stumps. By then he and Martyn had amassed a priceless 155-run partnership for the fourth wicket in 208 balls, the latter also passing 4000 runs in Test cricket.

England's fielding had dropped a notch or two during this heavy period of toil. Apart from missing that catch Pietersen also sent a shy at the stumps which ended with the ball clattering the boards behind the barrier. Hoggard then let the ball through his legs for four, and even Flintoff was deceived by an awkward bounce.

Clarke's dismissal was the start of a late flurry of Australian wickets. Four would go in the final nine overs

of the day. Martyn's fine Friday, after his sensational catch to dismiss Pietersen, continued with a thoughtful 65 before being trapped leg before by Harmison. Danger man Gilchrist was bowled by Flintoff, and Giles this time held on to a chance proffered by Warne from Harmison's bowling.

At the end of just the second riveting day of Ashes action, England trotted off the field in good spirits after their evening gains. In truth, however, the match was up. Australia ended Friday's proceedings on 279–7, already enjoyed a lead of 314 runs with three wickets in hand and three full days remaining, and appeared to be in business mode. On this Lord's pitch, judging by the clatter of wickets in just 48 hours, anything above 300 in the final innings was a huge ask. England's highest ever second innings total to win a Test match at Lord's was 282–3, a score they achieved in 2004 against New Zealand. Indeed, the highest score at Lord's by any Test team in that situation was 344–1, compiled by a Gordon Greenidge-inspired West Indies back in 1984. England

would have stood a much greater chance if their fielding had not turned so ragged during the afternoon session. Catches have always won matches. The old cricketing adage had never rung truer that evening.

Pietersen, as is his wont, remained positive and upbeat at the end of play. 'It is pretty even at the moment,' he insisted, a statement that redefined optimism. 'England have done well in the last couple of years chasing totals in the final innings and it looks like the wicket has evened out. We can definitely turn it round if a couple of our batsmen get in and play positively. We may well have two and a half days to get the runs, which is a lot of cricket. We're in a good position to go on and win this game and change history. The key is how we play Glenn McGrath when he takes the new ball. Surviving his first spell is so important because he is a great bowler who can do a lot of damage, as he showed in his first innings.'

On his own curate's egg of a performance Pietersen was happy to talk of his batting, and curiously blithe about the dropped chance from Clarke. 'It meant a lot to me to get that half-century today,' he said. 'I had enjoyed being out there on Thursday and really digging in, but today it was fun to have the freedom to smash a few. It's disappointing to drop the catch but that's just part of the game. No one goes through a career without dropping a catch at some stage. I've dropped lots of catches in my career, so I'm not going to get too het up about it. If I drop one tomorrow, so what?' Clarke saw it somewhat differently. 'I think we are in control now,' he surmised. 'It's going to be hard for them to get the runs. I think I owe Kevin a beer or two, though.'

Pietersen concluded by reinforcing his earlier point that 'all' England needed to do was knock over the last three remaining Australian batsmen in the Saturday morning session and England would be in business. He would be proved to be wide of the mark on both counts.

With all Pietersen's hero and villain act going on at Lord's, the day ended with the announcement that Graham Thorpe would be retiring with immediate effect from Test cricket after learning he would not be playing any part in the Ashes series. The 35-year-old had been clinging on to the hope that he would be recalled if one of England's top six batsmen suffered an injury, but the England selectors made it clear that he was now behind the likes of Kent's Robert Key and the uncapped Middlesex player Ed Joyce.

FACING PAGE The Lord's crowd celebrates a boundary, of which there were many in Kevin Pietersen's 57. BELOW Never a dull moment. Glenn McGrath enjoys putting Pietersen on the floor. OVERLEAF The great Australian bowler probably thought less of what happened here, though, as the ball sails from Pietersen's bat and into the members' section of the crowd.

'This is the best for everybody,' Thorpe announced. 'It draws the line under any speculation and it makes it clear for me as well. I said I was disappointed last week, but I totally accepted the way the decision went. I have no regrets on my career. It makes sense all round. The chance of an England comeback is pretty slim. For me, one door closes but another door opens. Now that England have overlooked me I can start another life.'

The chance of an England comeback from the current team's point of view looked pretty slim as well in this Test match as they ran on to the Lord's pitch on the Saturday morning intent on at least polishing off the three remaining Australian wickets to give them a shot at carving out a sensational victory.

Even this proved to be too stiff a challenge. If there were those who clung on to the grain of hope that England could still avoid defeat when the third day's play began, by the time Australia's second innings had come to an end the match was long gone. This was not entirely down to Australian supremacy, either, but rather to more cack-handedness from the English fielders as they allowed Jason Gillespie and Glenn McGrath to forge a further 95 runs in partnership with Simon Katich. The last-mentioned, as the senior batsman, scored most of these before falling to a Simon Jones catch off Harmison, but a 13 from Gillespie and an unlikely 20 not out from McGrath played crucial parts. What really sealed England's fate was a further three dropped catches, making it seven in the match. Flintoff, normally so reliable at slip, put down a looping chance from McGrath off Simon Jones, while the bowler's namesake, Geraint, spilled two relatively comfortable catches from first Gillespie and then McGrath. His Welsh colleague, Simon, was the unfortunate bowler on each occasion. For Geraint it was the start of a fierce examination of his skill behind the stumps, and a fierce debate over the merits of playing a batsman who could also keep wicket, as opposed to someone who first and foremost was a wicket-keeper – a subject that would dog him for much of the Ashes series.

Nobody could put their finger on why England's catching, usually so reliable in recent years, had been a shambles against Australia. With Pietersen's unfortunate hat-trick, Geraint Jones's brace, and two further lost opportunities courtesy of Strauss and Flintoff, England could not possibly hope to beat the best team in the world. The fact that they grabbed 20 wickets was no mean feat in itself, and one of only a few rays of light England could lay claim to afterwards, but the truth was,

in essence, they needed 27 dismissals to nail their opponents. By then the damage was irreparable.

England's reply began shortly after lunch. They would be required to score 420 runs to win or, to quantify this task, hit a world-record score in a fourth innings to win a Test match. The record stood at 418–3, achieved by the West Indies against Australia three years before thanks largely to the incomparable Brian Lara. The previous best by England stood at 332–7, achieved at the

| RIGHT Freddie Flintoff looks suitably unimpressed as Ricky Ponting and Damien Martyn begin the process of taking the game away from England. The pair put on 46 for the third wicket, Ponting passing 7000 runs in Test cricket in the process.

Melbourne Cricket Ground in 1928–29, and the previous best by England at Lord's was that 282 against New Zealand in 2004.

As if all this was not enough, England also had to do it against the two best bowlers in the world plus a more than useful supporting cast. Warne and McGrath, with nearly 1100 Test wickets between them, could not wait to get to work on a Lord's pitch on day three that would play into their hands.

For Warne, this really was his last chance to get his name up on that honours board. There was a hint of turn now in the tiring pitch, and the leg-spinner had already given notice before the start of the Test that he still possessed what he termed the 'X factor' when it came to bowling out sides. He was about to prove his point.

It took both pace and athleticism from Lee, however, to break what was beginning to look like a promising opening partnership between Trescothick and Strauss.

The pair had put on 80 before Strauss, on 37, tried to abort a hook. The ball remained in the air long enough for Lee to scramble down the pitch and dive to the ground to take the return catch. After Lee had bowled the out-of-sorts Vaughan for just four runs, Warne took over the proceedings, playing with the English batsmen like a cat does with a caught mouse. Hayden caught Trescothick with a fine effort at slip, and a bamboozled Flintoff could only edge the ball behind to Gilchrist. Perhaps the best example of Warne's teasing, probing trickery was in the manner he dismissed the hapless Bell.

So confused was the young batsman that having played and missed at so many, he left Warne's latest invention, the 'slider', padding up to a ball that suggested it would spin a great deal but actually continued straight on. The lbw was plumb and England found themselves at 119–5. Warne was especially grateful for that wicket, having seen umpire Aleem Dar turn down five good leg-before appeals off his bowling. The leg-spinner was close to self-combustion by the fifth refusal to raise the finger. 'Two or three of my lbw shouts were pretty close,' Warne insisted later. 'It's always frustrating when you think batsmen are out. It's a huge Test match for all of us, including me, because it's my last one here at Lord's. I am determined to make it a good one.'

By close of play England were in slightly better shape, thanks to Pietersen and Geraint Jones, but fighting what was plainly a lost cause. They had moved on to 156–5 at stumps, with Jones on six and Pietersen on 42, once again appearing to be the only England batsman capable of dealing with Messrs Warne, McGrath and Lee. And this, remember, was his Test match debut. Despite the odds against his team, Trescothick, at least, refused to concede defeat, even though there was little he could do about it, having been dismissed by Warne. 'We are not going to give this one up,' he insisted. 'We are on the back foot but there is still cricket to be played and we have to do our best. Who knows what could happen with Kevin Pietersen and Geraint Jones at the crease? It's important to fight hard in these situations.'

The reality was somewhat different. Four years previously, it had taken Australia three days and 16.1 overs to complete an emphatic eight-wicket victory over England at Lord's. This time it took them exactly six overs less to win by a whopping 239 runs. Only rain had been likely to save England. The forecast was indifferent, and when the rain came it held up play for two sessions. Far from frustrating Australia, however, it appeared only to galvanise them into finishing off England after tea.

It would take them only 7.4 overs to achieve this aim, and in this 42-minute spell England added just 24 runs. There were two extras, the remaining 22 runs all coming from the bat of Pietersen, who scored them in just 25 balls. Geraint Jones failed to add to his overnight score of six, caught by Gillespie off McGrath from a mistimed pull to mid on, and numbers eight to eleven on the England batting list all recorded ducks in the space of 36 deliveries. McGrath cleaned up most of them, accounting for Giles, who went second ball, Hoggard, who picked up a pair in the match, and Simon Jones. McGrath's four Sunday evening wickets came off 23 balls

LEFT Damien Martyn on the way to a second innings 65, during which he passed 4000 runs in Test cricket. FACING PAGE Ashley Giles is powerless to prevent Michael Clarke's progress.

and for just three runs conceded. Warne, meanwhile, took care of Harmison, trapping him leg before. Yet again only Pietersen stood up to the onslaught, remaining unbeaten at the end while his team-mates collapsed around him. His defiant 64 not out included six fours and two sixes, and meant that he left Lord's with an aggregate total of 121 runs and having been out once, to a quite stupendous catch by Martyn. It meant that he became the fourth England debutant to top-score in both innings. His performance coupled with Steve Harmison's match figures of 8–97 were just about the only rays of brightness in an otherwise predictable outcome that had all the hallmarks of previous Ashes tours. True, England had captured 20 Australian wickets for the first time in a live Ashes Test since 1997, but they had still been heavily beaten.

Two men, as in Pietersen and Harmison, could not beat an Australian team showing precisely why they had been the best in the world for nearly two decades. Two men, though, could beat an England team, it seemed,

especially when those two men were McGrath and Warne. The latter recorded second innings bowling figures of 4–64 and was cursing his colleague McGrath for wrapping up the England innings with the dismissal of Simon Jones, caught, ironically, by Warne himself. It meant that Warne, playing for the last time at the home of cricket, was stranded on four wickets yet again, and would never see his name up on the honours board.

Afterwards Australia's captain, Ricky Ponting, was predicting an easy summer for his team on the evidence of Lord's. 'The gap between the two sides in this game has been quite vast,' he said. 'We've got a very good chance of winning 5–0.' This series was supposed to be competitive, a string of five closely fought Tests in just seven illuminating weeks, but Ponting reckoned he had been here before. 'This Test match had a lot of similarities to the First Test of other Ashes series because England made lots of big mistakes at crucial times. To win so comprehensively is very satisfying but there are areas we can improve on, such as our top order who

summer. Hoggard's assertion before Lord's that Warne and McGrath were now too old had slapped him back full in the face almost immediately. Not only did the two ensure between them that the Yorkshireman failed to score a single run (besides hitting 60 runs themselves with only Warne twice out) but they also captured 15 of the 20 English wickets, with Warne taking six and McGrath, nine.

The latter revealed later how that Hoggard jibe had really struck a nerve. 'Past it?' he asked. 'I didn't feel past it at all. Matthew Hoggard's suggestion that I might be a bit long in the tooth gave us a laugh. I tried not to smile too much when Hoggy let one through his legs for four on day two. The bad news for England is that I feel there is plenty more still to come from me. My first target is to get past 519 wickets, the figure which the great West Indian Courtney Walsh retired on, to become the leading wicket-taker of all time among fast bowlers. Then I want to reach 1000 international wickets. I've got 508 in Tests now, plus 325 in One-Day Internationals. My aim is to take 600 in Tests, and 400 in one-dayers. If it all goes to plan I will knock off the Test wickets in the next Ashes series in Australia in 2006–07 and then complete the task by getting to 400 one-day victims at the 2007 World Cup.'

No hint of slowing down there, then, from a man who looked capable, on the evidence of Lord's, of providing no escape for the England batsmen throughout what was now looking like a steep, uphill task to give Australia a decent game of cricket.

England would have ten days to try and put wrongs right before the Second Test. They appeared to possess a stack of problems, starting with the captain's apparent inability to defend an off stump that was consistently being knocked out of the ground. Bell appeared like a frightened rabbit caught in the headlamps of an onrushing car. He seemed overawed, and against Warne a small boy receiving a harsh lesson from a teacher. Geraint Jones dropped two chances and failed to add weight to the arguments supporting his inclusion as a batsman/wicket-keeper. Flintoff's bowling looked to have affected his batting, Giles was easy meat to the Australian batsmen, and Hoggard caused few problems.

Australia, by contrast, were well set. Not only were their two bankers, McGrath and Warne, firing, but Lee, who had been recalled by the selectors after an 18-month absence, was back to his explosive best. Clarke, Katich and Martyn had all scored runs. Once Langer, Hayden, Ponting and Gilchrist really found their batting

didn't capitalise on good starts. We've gone a little way to breaking England's spirit but I think they are a better and stronger side than that.'

His dejected counterpart, Michael Vaughan, tried to remain upbeat. 'These are young players,' he explained, referring to his side. 'Give them a chance. They've lost one game. We have a bowling unit who are capable of bowling Australia out twice, as we proved. We created enough opportunities to bowl them out for 190 and, I believe, about 220 in the second innings. That is pretty hopeful. Australia have a knack of taking games away from you if you give them the opportunities. That's what we did.' Asked if England could still win the Ashes Vaughan's best answer was hardly convincing. 'There is a real opportunity to play some good cricket against them,' he said.

Ponting's prediction that Australia could go on to win the series 5–0 would go on to bite him later in the

LEFT Simon Katich scored 67 in Australia's second innings, in the process adding 95 invaluable runs with Gillespie and McGrath.
FACING PAGE Warne through. The leg-spinner celebrates having Andrew Flintoff caught by Gilchrist for three.

touch and Gillespie shook off the poor form that had continued in the First Test, an improved Australia would be untouchable.

As a team they complemented each other, both on and off the field. A varied collection of characters, they had pulled together to attain incredible success. Ponting, who has taken up the captaincy mantle vacated by Steve Waugh, is an interesting case. From Tasmania, he owns 30 greyhounds back in Australia and it is this love for the dogs, coupled with a penchant for cards, that has earned him the nickname 'Punter'. His other obsession is cricket bats, especially preparing them for battles ahead. His team-mates queue up to ask Ponting to regrip their handles, replace stickers or sand their blades. He has also come through a difficult personal time at the height of his career. Beaten up after a fight in a Sydney bar, Ponting admitted publicly that he had a drink problem. It was big news in Australia, and a pretty brave thing to do considering the macho environment he worked in, where being a heavy drinker was seen almost as a plus point, but Ponting had the courage not only to come clean but also to deal with and conquer his problems. By

the time Waugh stood down, Ponting was the natural choice to succeed him as captain. This was his first Ashes tour as Australian skipper, and he understood what this meant. 'It means everything,' he explained. 'The Ashes are so special and unique. They are set apart from any other series we play.'

Warne shares a love of cards with his captain and with team manager Steve Bernard. The three of them can often be found at the back of the team bus dealing out a pack. McGrath, or 'Pigeon' to his mates due to his chest, likes to play practical jokes on his team-mates when not throwing sweets at them or planning to learn the piano if his fast-bowling partner, Brett 'Binger' Lee, ever gets round to teaching him. Lee, whose nickname derives from the Bing Lee chain of electrical stores in Australia, has his own rock band, Six and Out, as well as a fashion label called 'BL'.

The Matthew Hayden Cookbook proved a big hit when published the previous year in Australia, as do some of the batsman's recipes with his team-mates on tour. His opening partner, Langer, is known as 'Schwarzenegger' because of his keen, bordering on obsessive interest in

Giles had had a torrid time in past years. Indeed, only 12 months earlier, he had sunk into the depths of a depression brought on by self-doubt and criticism of his performances. Described as a 'wheelie bin of a bowler' by radio commentators, the imagery cut deep, and when an order of mugs with the slogan 'Ashley Giles – King of Spin' for the Warwickshire club shop arrived sporting the misprint 'King of Spain', it only served to emphasise the now 32-year-old's sorry position. 'It got even worse than that,' Giles admitted. 'Someone sent an email into Sky Sports TV asking the question: "What is the point of Ashley Giles?" That really hurt. I'd hear people in the crowd shouting "Get him off" even before I'd bowled my first ball. It was terrible, and I was falling apart.'

An afternoon spent in a Nottingham coffee shop with England sports psychologist Steve Bull in the summer of 2004 did the trick. He started to write

body-building, martial arts and general fitness. And so the list goes on. Most knew each other and their game inside out, which, when they were thrown together, went a long way to explaining their unshakeable confidence and belief in their collective ability.

None of them had been forced to have the kind of rant that Ashley Giles uttered a couple of days after the Lord's Test. They would have been pleased, though, to have seen the post-match reaction of Giles, who, not for the first time, faced up to criticism from former players in the media following the First Test defeat. 'It feels as if ex-players don't want us to win the Ashes, either because they didn't achieve it themselves or because they were the last to achieve the feat,' Giles complained. 'That might be me being bitter, but that's the way it feels.'

Certainly some former England greats had had their say after Lord's. Ian Botham, for example, said, 'Some of the catches that went down were so poor they were almost criminal. A few of the top seven need to take a hard look at themselves, none more so than Geraint Jones.' Former captain Michael Atherton added, 'Old failings remain. Whereas England grope in the dark against Warne, the Australians played Ashley Giles with ease. Nor does the middle order inspire confidence.'

everything down in a diary, beginning with the compelling message: 'This has got to stop.' At the Trent Bridge Test match a few days later, he grabbed six second innings wickets and scored 45 as England cantered to a 3–0 whitewash against New Zealand. In the next Test, against the West Indies, he was voted Man of the Match after taking a nine-wicket haul. A further nine wickets fell to him in the following Test.

One year on, though, and Giles was feeling the heat again after that First Test defeat in the Ashes series. 'It feels like the end of the world,' he said. 'As a team we missed windows of opportunity, lost that game, and suddenly there are people saying "Get rid of your 'keeper" and "Get rid of your spin bowler".

'People seem to change their minds very quickly. Suddenly, everyone is on our backs again and it is quite offensive in a way. So there is a bit of anger and defiance among us. We have to stick together as a team, harness the feelings and say: "I'll show them".'

He had not enjoyed the best of times at Lord's. Giles did not bowl at all in the first innings dominated by England's pace attack, and then only bowled 11 overs in the second innings, going for an alarming 56 runs. He scored 11 and 0 with the bat. 'In the space of one game I haven't suddenly become a bad bowler again, so I find the reaction disappointing,' he said. 'I didn't get any runs, but not many people did.

'With this Aussie side you have to stand up and face them. I have worked bloody hard to get to the position I'm in now and to do what I've done for England. It's hard work, but I hope the majority of people are still backing me. There are four games left so, of course, we can still win the series. We can beat Australia at Edgbaston and go on from that. It is something we did in South Africa. We got murdered at Cape Town and came back to win the next Test. So it is possible. We've proved that.'

At least Giles would be returning home for the Second Test, to Edgbaston, the home of Warwickshire CCC where he is revered by the locals. His outburst had proved counter-productive. The Australian camp seized upon it as another sign of English fragility. First they had smashed him out of the bowling attack at Lord's. Now they were reading how persecuted the spinner felt.

'I can understand where Giles is coming from but there is nowhere to go for him,' explained a far from concerned Ricky Ponting. 'You are never going to win. From the way he's been speaking and all the speculation,

he is going to be under enough pressure without us having to change too much.' Giles, as far as the Australians were concerned, had just become their first victim. Test side after Test side had succumbed to Australian tactics over the years. When they announce that a 5–0 whitewash is on the cards, they may believe this to be true, but it is a statement designed in part to show the opposition how confident the Australian team feels, and also to prey on the opposition minds. It is a ploy that has worked for the best part of 20 years.

The England vice-captain, Marcus Trescothick, waded into the debate by offering words of support and comfort for his good friend Giles. 'It's been a tough week for Ashley, as you can imagine, but he's fine,' said the England opener, making it sound as if Giles had just been hospitalised by a career-threatening injury. 'He'll get a lot of support from his home crowd and, most of all, he'll get a lot of support from us. We'll talk to him over the next day or so to try to settle him down and make sure his mind is right for Thursday morning.'

There was a chance Giles might not play at all. Paul Collingwood, who had served England so well during

LEFT The Australians were in the dressing room until midnight, celebrating their First Test victory at the home of cricket.

As it turned out, Collingwood's obvious talents would not be required by England. The sun dried up the wicket, and England rightly decided to stick with their trusted XI. Besides, it was those players who had underperformed at Lord's. Now it was up to them to make amends at Edgbaston, a venue that had always been a happy hunting ground for England in the past.

The Australians had partied long and hard into the night on the day of their First Test win. Even after everybody bar one remaining security guard at the Grace Gates had left the ground, the Australian squad stayed in their dressing room, downing more than a few beers, with spinner Stuart MacGill the chief bartender, and enjoying both each other's company and the moment until midnight. The most famous ground in the world was now dark and desolate. Wrappers blew across the empty rows of seats. The square was engulfed by huge covers. Only a few dim lights shone, save for the dressing room, where they remained switched brightly on. Lord's that night belonged entirely to Australia, just as it had done for the previous four days. English cricket, beaten out of sight, had just handed over the keys of the ground to their great rivals. It was as if the walls of the citadel had come tumbling down.

In the England camp, the coach and captain, Duncan Fletcher and Michael Vaughan, sat down to plot the most unlikely of comebacks. 'It was crunch time,' Fletcher admitted. 'And it was a key meeting. If we waited for the Aussies to come to us after Lord's we would lose the series. We discussed the attitude of the players and how we could lift them. I didn't think we were intimidated at Lord's but we didn't play well and forgot to be positive. We'd decided all summer to be positive and take the game to Australia from that first Twenty20 game. We knew we had to be aggressive. I think we forgot that during the one-day series and we might have switched off during Lord's.

'It was a mental thing. I never thought we were in awe of the Aussies. It wasn't a question of telling the players not to be worried about failing in trying to have a go. The key was never to talk about or mention failure. The word "fail" was never used. We had to be positive and what Michael and I did was to offer a clear direction.' It proved to be the most significant conversation of the summer.

Over the five days that made up the Second Test at Edgbaston the Ashes series would suddenly catch fire, England would haul themselves back into the hunt, and the world of cricket would witness one of the most incredible Test matches ever played.

the one-day series and was enjoying sparkling form with the bat in the County Championship with Durham, had been drafted into the squad after storms, including a tornado that hit Birmingham and blew within 800 yards of the ground, had changed the nature of the Edgbaston pitch. As a seam bowler, Collingwood could prove to be a handful with the ball in hand as well. Hungry to get his chance, Collingwood declared, 'I'm a fighter and I always will be. That's what I bring to any side.'

ENGLAND V AUSTRALIA, 1st Test, Lord's
21, 22, 23, 24 JULY 2005

TOSS: Australia **UMPIRES:** Aleem Dar (Pak) and RE Koertzen (SA)
TV UMPIRE: MR Benson **FOURTH UMPIRE:** NG Cowley
MATCH REFEREE: RS Madugalle (SL)
TEST DEBUT: KP Pietersen (Eng).

Close of Play:
- **Day 1:** Australia 190, England 92-7 (Pietersen 28*)
- **Day 2:** England 155, Australia 279-7 (Katich 10*)
- **Day 3:** Australia 384, England 156-5 (Pietersen 42*, GO Jones 6*)

Australia 1st innings			R	M	B	4	6
JL Langer	c Harmison	b Flintoff	40	77	44	5	0
ML Hayden	b Hoggard		12	38	25	2	0
*RT Ponting	c Strauss	b Harmison	9	38	18	1	0
DR Martyn	c GO Jones	b SP Jones	2	13	4	0	0
MJ Clarke	lbw	b SP Jones	11	35	22	2	0
SM Katich	c GO Jones	b Harmison	27	107	67	5	0
+AC Gilchrist	c GO Jones	b Flintoff	26	30	19	6	0
SK Warne	b Harmison		28	40	29	5	0
B Lee	c GO Jones	b Harmison	3	13	8	0	0
JN Gillespie	lbw	b Harmison	1	19	11	0	0
GD McGrath	not out		10	9	6	2	0
Extras	**21**	(b 5, lb 4, w 1, nb 11)					
Total	**190**	(all out, 40.2 overs, 209 minutes)					

FoW: 1-35 (Hayden), **2-55** (Ponting), **3-66** (Langer), **4-66** (Martyn), **5-87** (Clarke), **6-126** (Gilchrist), **7-175** (Warne), **8-178** (Katich), **9-178** (Lee), **10-190** (Gillespie).

Bowling	O	M	R	W	
Harmison	11.2	0	43	5	
Hoggard	8	0	40	1	(2nb)
Flintoff	11	2	50	2	(9nb)
SP Jones	10	0	48	2	(1w)

Australia 2nd innings			R	M	B	4	6
JL Langer	run out (Pietersen)		6	24	15	1	0
ML Hayden	b Flintoff		34	65	54	5	0
*RT Ponting	c sub (JC Hildreth) b Hoggard		42	100	65	3	0
DR Martyn	lbw	b Harmison	65	215	138	8	0
MJ Clarke	b Hoggard		91	151	106	15	0
SM Katich	c SP Jones	b Harmison	67	177	113	8	0
+AC Gilchrist	b Flintoff		10	26	14	1	0
SK Warne	c Giles	b Harmison	2	13	7	0	0
B Lee	run out (Giles)		8	16	16	1	0
JN Gillespie	b SP Jones		13	72	52	3	0
GD McGrath	not out		20	44	32	3	0
Extras	**26**	(b 10, lb 8, nb 8)					
Total	**384**	(all out, 100.4 overs, 457 minutes)					

FoW: 1-18 (Langer), **2-54** (Hayden), **3-100** (Ponting), **4-255** (Clarke), **5-255** (Martyn), **6-274** (Gilchrist), **7-279** (Warne), **8-289** (Lee), **9-341** (Gillespie), **10-384** (Katich).

Bowling	O	M	R	W	
Harmison	27.4	6	54	3	
Hoggard	16	1	56	2	(2nb)
Flintoff	27	4	123	2	(5nb)
SP Jones	18	1	69	1	(1nb)
Giles	11	1	56	0	
Bell	1	0	8	0	

England 1st innings			R	M	B	4	6
ME Trescothick	c Langer	b McGrath	4	24	17	1	0
AJ Strauss	c Warne	b McGrath	2	28	21	0	0
*MP Vaughan	b McGrath		3	29	20	0	0
IR Bell	b McGrath		6	34	25	1	0
KP Pietersen	c Martyn	b Warne	57	148	89	8	2
A Flintoff	b McGrath		0	8	4	0	0
+GO Jones	c Gilchrist	b Lee	30	85	56	6	0
AF Giles	c Gilchrist	b Lee	11	14	13	2	0
MJ Hoggard	c Hayden	b Warne	0	18	16	0	0
SJ Harmison	c Martyn	b Lee	11	35	19	1	0
SP Jones	not out		20	21	14	3	0
Extras	**11**	(b 1, lb 5, nb 5)					
Total	**155**	(all out, 48.1 overs, 227 minutes)					

FoW: 1-10 (Trescothick), **2-11** (Strauss), **3-18** (Vaughan), **4-19** (Bell), **5-21** (Flintoff), **6-79** (GO Jones), **7-92** (Giles), **8-101** (Hoggard), **9-122** (Pietersen), **10-155** (Harmison).

Bowling	O	M	R	W	
McGrath	18	5	53	5	
Lee	15.1	5	47	3	(4nb)
Gillespie	8	1	30	0	(1nb)
Warne	7	2	19	2	

England 2nd innings			R	M	B	4	6
ME Trescothick	c Hayden	b Warne	44	128	103	8	0
AJ Strauss	c & b Lee		37	115	67	6	0
*MP Vaughan	b Lee		4	47	26	1	0
IR Bell	lbw	b Warne	8	18	15	0	0
KP Pietersen	not out		64	120	79	6	2
A Flintoff	c Gilchrist	b Warne	3	14	11	0	0
+GO Jones	c Gillespie	b McGrath	6	51	27	1	0
AF Giles	c Hayden	b McGrath	0	2	2	0	0
MJ Hoggard	lbw	b McGrath	0	18	15	0	0
SJ Harmison	lbw	b Warne	0	3	1	0	0
SP Jones	c Warne	b McGrath	0	12	6	0	0
Extras	**14**	(b 6, lb 5, nb 3)					
Total	**180**	(all out, 58.1 overs, 268 minutes)					

FoW: 1-80 (Strauss), **2-96** (Trescothick), **3-104** (Bell), **4-112** (Vaughan), **5-119** (Flintoff), **6-158** (GO Jones), **7-158** (Giles), **8-164** (Hoggard), **9-167** (Harmison), **10-180** (SP Jones).

Bowling	O	M	R	W	
McGrath	17.1	2	29	4	
Lee	15	3	58	2	(1nb)
Gillespie	6	0	18	0	(2nb)
Warne	20	2	64	4	

RESULT: Australia won by 239 runs MAN OF THE MATCH: **GD McGrath**

EDGBASTON

2ND TEST
4 AUGUST–7 AUGUST

FACING PAGE Kevin Pietersen and Michael Vaughan congratulate Andrew Flintoff, who has just dismissed Jason Gillespie lbw in Australia's first innings. RIGHT The England huddle at Edgbaston.

There is a very strong argument that the whole momentum and onus of the Ashes series swung thanks to a game of touch rugby and a loose cricket ball lying innocuously on the ground. As freak accidents go, what happened to Glenn McGrath must go down as one of the more unusual. As for its impact, never could such an incident prove to be so enormous in terms of its repercussions.

One hour before the start of the first morning's play at Edgbaston, and McGrath, the scourge of England during the previous Test, is limbering up with his Australian team-mates, enjoying a relaxed game of touch rugby. There was barely anyone sitting in their seats inside the Warwickshire cricket ground when the turning point of the whole series took place.

Ironically, the official Australian warm-up was due to begin in around a minute's time. McGrath was exchanging rugby passes with reserve wicket-keeper Brad Haddin, when he trod on a cricket ball, one of several placed in a line for fielding drills. He left the pitch in obvious pain in a groundsman's buggy, before being rushed to hospital for X-rays that confirmed that one of the most feared bowlers in world cricket had torn ligaments in his right ankle.

By the end of the first day's play McGrath was watching from the Australian dressing room on crutches, vowing that he would be back for the Fourth Test, and possibly even the Third Test at Old Trafford, which would begin three days after the scheduled end of the Second Test here at Edgbaston. At the time of the accident it appeared to those watching like a harmless slip on the ball, but McGrath knew better.

'I have done my ankle a few times and it has never been this bad,' he explained. 'At the time it felt like the

FACING PAGE AND RIGHT Australia's Glenn McGrath steps on a cricket ball during a game of touch rugby before the start of play and is ruled out of the Second Test with ankle ligament damage.

sole of my foot was pointing skywards. It all happened in a split second but I realised before I landed that I was out of this Test match. I knew straightaway that it would not be good, but I can deal with it.'

Most spectators were unaware of the news until Ricky Ponting announced at the toss that Michael Kasprowicz had been recalled in McGrath's place, news that was met by a resounding cheer from the Birmingham faithful, who make up the most partisan crowd in English cricket. Kasprowicz introduced some black humour to the incident by insisting, 'I didn't place the ball under McGrath's foot as some people might think.'

It was an extraordinary start to an extraordinary day's cricket in what would turn out to be the most extraordinary of Test matches. At the close of play England, having been put in to bat by Ponting, had raced along to 407 all out in just 79.2 overs, a total that included an incredible 157 runs in a frantic session between lunch and tea. The run rate for the day was 5.1 an over, achieved on a dull day and a slow pitch against the world champions. It was England's highest first-day score since the Second World War, and it was the most emphatic response to capitulation at Lord's. There was no doubt that the moment McGrath was stretchered off to hospital, England heads rose as Australian ones sank.

Nobody knows exactly at what point Ponting realised his folly, but it was evidently clear by the end of the first day that the Australian captain had made a huge mistake based on the theory that there was still a lot in the pitch for the bowlers after the torrential rains and storms earlier in the week. He might also have seen his decision to be a vote of confidence for Kasprowicz and his other bowlers after McGrath's injury. Clearly the plan had always been to bowl first, and to make a last-gasp change on the back of the injury would have sent out the wrong messages to his dressing room. Traditionally, too, Edgbaston has been a bowl-first pitch in Test matches.

Whatever his reasons, Ponting missed a trick, for sure. Instead of hammering home Australian dominance after Lord's by going after a big first innings score and asking England then to play catch-up cricket, he gave his opponents the chance to redeem themselves. There is no doubt that this Test match, and the Ashes series, swung on two outrageous pieces of luck, the McGrath injury and the Ponting decision – and neither of them had anything to do with England.

Still, the chance was seized as by a greedy man at a pantry. Trescothick and Strauss put on 112 for the first wicket, in double-quick time, too, to serve up precisely the right response to the Lord's reverse. From the

ABOVE Shane Warne drops Andrew Strauss at slip off the bowling of Jason Gillespie early on the first morning. FACING PAGE Marcus Trescothick takes the aggressive approach on his way to a first innings 90 from 102 balls.

moment the opening pair realised that Brett Lee was finding no deviation in the pitch, their eyes lit up and they went for it as if already in a run chase in a limited overs game.

Strauss did his bit with 48. The runs were useful, as was his contribution to the opening stand, but perhaps the greatest contribution from the Strauss innings was the way in which he set about Warne. In two Warne overs

Strauss hit three fours, delivering to the letter the message England coach Duncan Fletcher had sent out: 'Do not be fazed by Warne. Go after him.' Warne bowled his man out two runs short of a well-deserved half-century, but, as well as Strauss had performed, it was not the wicket Australia were looking for. Trescothick had been batting like a man on a mission, setting the tone for the day and, indeed, the rest of the series, with three fours off Lee's second over. He scored 77 before lunch and was finally out ten runs short of what would have been a maiden century against Australia, caught behind by Gilchrist off Kasprowicz. By then he had scored 15 fours and two sixes in a 90 that came off only 102 balls.

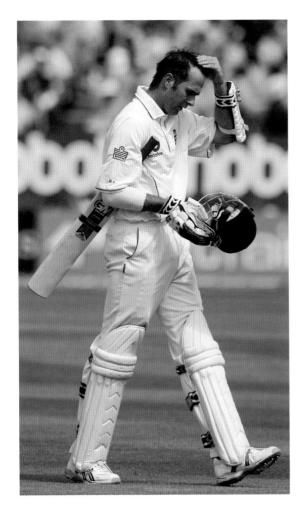

If the opening partnership was the first element of England's success, the fifth-wicket stand was the next. Before then, Vaughan had gone for 24 and Bell, playing at his home ground and still feeling his way into Test cricket at the sharp end, went the same way as Trescothick. At 187–4 there was a danger that all England's earlier good work would be in vain.

Kevin Pietersen and Andrew Flintoff had other ideas, though. Both received huge cheers from the full house at Edgbaston when they made their entrances, especially the latter. By Flintoff's high standards he had not enjoyed the best of starts in this Ashes series at Lord's, but the watching world and Australia, in particular, were about to discover why the man is one of the most exciting players in the game.

He began nervously, his first runs a lunge at Warne that skewed a foot over mid-off's hands for four. He then followed that up with an edge between his legs and survived a leg-before appeal that had Warne hopping about in frustration when turned down. Flintoff was on four at the time and Warne knew that this was a wicket, regardless of the England player's poor form, that Australia needed to claim quickly. His prolonged appeal, stamp of a foot, glare and, finally, hands thrown up in the air revealed this realisation. Then Flintoff settled in for his first proper partnership with Pietersen. This had been the dream ticket ever since Pietersen was selected for the Ashes series. To have two of the most destructive batsmen in world cricket in together was a spectator's fantasy, and a bowler's nightmare. There was a theory that the arrival of the extrovert Pietersen, with his bleached, striped hair and flurry of sixes, had stolen Flintoff's thunder and damaged his confidence. After all, the previous summer Flintoff had become a national hero after his superman performances with bat and ball against New Zealand and the West Indies. Since Pietersen had burst on to the scene, however, Flintoff had been unusually subdued. The afternoon of 4 August put paid to this idea.

Their century stand took only 66 minutes to complete, although even Pietersen, having initially matched his partner blow for blow in a slog-fest that had the spellbound crowd in raptures, had the good sense not to try and compete with Flintoff in the mood he was in at Edgbaston. Instead Pietersen became something of

a restraining influence, a statement that sounds ridiculous now, and true only in the context that his partner was Flintoff. While Pietersen struck 71 off 76 balls, and his third successive half-century in his first three Test match innings, Flintoff made him look like a batting sloth by comparison, hitting 68 off 62 balls in a knock that included six fours and five huge sixes. Their partnership of 103 battered Australia into afternoon submission, although when Flintoff fell, caught behind off Gillespie, shortly followed by Geraint Jones, also snapped up by Gilchrist, off Kasprowicz, England were still only 293–6 and their incredible start still looked in danger of petering out to a sub-350 total. For Gillespie, who endured another fairly wretched day's bowling, the Flintoff dismissal at least meant he had reached 250 Test wickets, a statistic that reminded the world of his former class. In achieving this mark, Gillespie became the fifth highest Australian Test wicket-taker of all time, surpassing Richie Benaud, who took 248.

It was a triumphant return to form for Flintoff, who, despite his proud Lancastrian roots, must wish he played at Edgbaston every day. A year ago he dismantled the West Indian bowling attack at this venue with a vicious 167, the whole summer and his own grounded attitude exemplified by his genuine joy and laughter out in the middle of a Test match pitch on seeing his father drop one of his sixes on the first deck of the Ryder Stand. 'He's been boring me all my life about how good a cricketer he was,' Flintoff said, famously, afterwards. 'Then he goes and drops me in front of millions on TV.' Over the winter, though, and at the start of the summer, Flintoff had batted like his younger self, indecisive and riddled with self-doubt. At Lord's there was nothing to suggest what was to come.

Nothing, except his obvious, huge talent and the fact that the beery, testosterone-filled gladiatorial arena at Edgbaston could rekindle the Flintoff fire. After his early scares against Warne he came to the decision, understandably, that he was not going to win a war of attrition with the great leg-spinner. And thus began the fireworks. The highlight of many was when having just been dropped by Kasprowicz off Lee, Flintoff responded to the predictable bouncer that followed with a six which he hooked virtually off his nose. 'There was more positive intent in the way I batted today,' Flintoff admitted that evening. 'I've not scored too many runs of late, and in the past week I've been trying to work out my best scoring areas. I wasn't reckless out there. I was just trying to hit the balls I could hit.' On the way England took the game to Australia, Flintoff insisted it just happened like that. 'It wasn't a premeditated way of batting,' he said. 'We just got off to a good start.'

Test matches, indeed whole series, can sometimes be measured by the finest of lines. Flintoff was a single foot

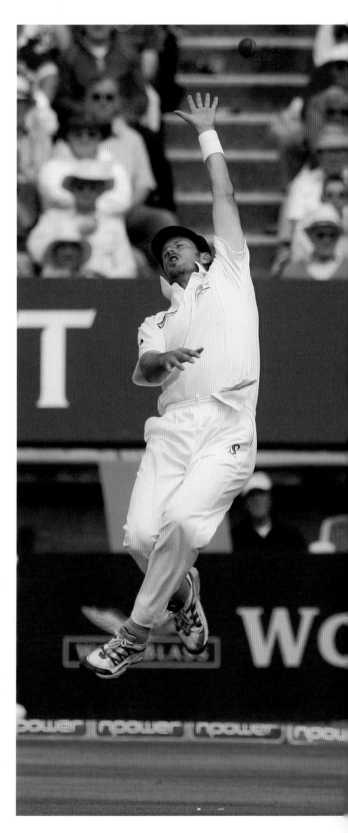

away from having the words 'caught Kasprowicz, bowled Warne, 0' next to his name. Instead he had 68 runs under his belt, and his Ashes series had taken off.

The England tail, which so often in the past had not been able to wag, this time continued the theme of the day with aplomb. Shepherded for a while by Pietersen, who managed 'just' the one six before holing out in the deep off Lee, batsmen eight to eleven all played their part in extending England's first innings total to 407, with Giles scoring 23, Hoggard 16, Harmison 17, and Simon Jones remaining unbeaten on 19, the latter two both striking a six apiece.

In total England struck ten sixes and 54 fours in all, or 276 runs out of their 407 in boundaries. The ten sixes is a record in one innings for England against Australia. It was exhilarating stuff, but was 407 enough? Had England's cavalier approach actually cost them a hundred runs on a pitch that turned out to be a superb batting wicket early on in the Test?

The only downside of an otherwise enthralling day's cricket came right at the end when a late shower prevented a few overs being bowled at the Australian openers. To grab a wicket or two in the little time available in what is always an awkward spell for batsmen really would have been the cherry on top of the icing on the cake, but perhaps the rain after a sticky day made everyone wake up from the dream they had been living for the previous six hours.

It made little difference to England come the morning of day two. By the seventh ball of the Australian innings, their bowlers were already making inroads. Justin Langer had survived a thorough working-over during the first over, delivered by Harmison. A tough, gritty customer, whose bouts of pre-tour boxing had toughened him up even further, Langer was hit on the

Vaughan, gratefully accepted the catch. Two wickets gone, and both as a result of quick-wittedness from England. In the over before lunch Damien Martyn, who has quietly amassed a Test average of close to 50, allowed himself to be run out by Vaughan on 20. Martyn only had himself to blame. Either he expected the ball to be fired at Langer's end, or he simply did not believe that Vaughan, who picked the ball up one-handed, swivelled and threw, would hit his stumps. Either way, there was a lack of urgency about the Australian number four as he ambled towards the crease at the other end.

FACING PAGE Kevin Pietersen hits out during his first innings 71.
LEFT Fans dive for cover as a Flintoff six descends into the stands.
BELOW England's middle-order destroyers give each other encouragement during their quickfire century stand.

helmet by the third ball of the day. Langer had made his disappointment known when he criticised the lack of concern from the England fielders after his captain, Ponting, was hit and bloodied by Harmison in the First Test. Now he was receiving the treatment, and it was noticeable, save for Ian Bell fielding close by, that the England players were hardly queuing up to enquire of his well-being. For good measure, the little opener was then winded by one in the stomach during Harmison's next over.

By then Australia were one down. Matthew Hoggard had Matthew Hayden caught by Strauss at short extra-cover after the opener had attempted a drive. It was the out-of-touch Hayden's first golden duck in his distinguished career, and a wicket cleverly plotted by the England management and captaincy, who had worked out that the batsman was vulnerable in that area early on. Ponting and Langer then began to repair the damage, the former surviving a run-out chance from Pietersen before scoring and then taking on the mantle of aggressor, the latter digging in obdurately. Advancing to 61, the Australian captain then swept Ashley Giles into a leg-side trap around the corner, where his counterpart,

ABOVE AND FACING PAGE Justin Langer was felled early in the first innings by a Harmison bouncer but went on to make 82.

Giles claimed his second wicket of the day after lunch when he had Michael Clarke, who had moved on to 40, caught behind by Geraint Jones. With Australia having reached 194–3, it was a crucial scalp for England. Fourteen runs later Simon Katich fell to Flintoff's reverse swing, something that would be repeated as the series wore on. Even with five down, Australia are dangerous, primarily because of the sight of Adam Gilchrist striding to the wicket. With Gilchrist the aggressor and Langer shoring up the other end, anything was still possible.

Simon Jones had other ideas, though. Jones had been desperately unlucky up to this point – his First Test figures and his bowling in Australia's first innings of the Second Test had not done justice to the way in which he had bamboozled the opposition with his reverse swing. But his dismissal of Langer was just as important as Clarke's dismissal by Giles. Langer had ground his way to 82 off 154 deliveries, constructing the kind of old-fashioned innings from an opener suited to a bygone era and entirely in contrast to the nature of the rest of this game. The Western Australian looked well set for a century when Jones's reverse swing did for him, the ball crashing into his pads in front of the stumps.

Australia still had Gilchrist at the crease, but the tail that had served their country so well in Tests over the years this time fell away. The four remaining batsmen compiled only 21 runs between them as Australia were dismissed for 308. Warne was first to go, advancing down the wicket to Giles with a horrendous slog that failed to

touch the ball as it made its way directly on to the stumps. Simon Jones put paid to the dangerous Lee, helped by Flintoff's catch, and then Flintoff himself, having not starred for at least half a session, finished off the tail with lbws from consecutive yorkers. Kasprowicz was the unlucky one to join Hayden as a member of the Primary Club, for those with a golden duck next to their name. Gilchrist, beginning to look ominous, was left high and dry on 49 not out. A big century from him might well have unlocked the shackles and shaken off the cobwebs for the rest of the series. Instead Gilchrist was left to return to the pavilion and put on his wicket-keeping pads, wondering what might have been.

At 262–5 Australia had looked set to emulate England's first-day total of 407. To amass 308 in less than a day is hardly slow going, but a first innings deficit of 99 runs looked big enough for England to start believing this match was theirs to win or to lose. It was, after all, the first time England had enjoyed a first innings lead over Australia in 22 Tests. The one area of doubt came at the end of the day's play, when Shane

with some success, and now England had in Flintoff and Simon Jones two bowlers who could produce it from both ends in tandem. Warne admitted afterwards that England had made the ball 'go' sooner than even the

ABOVE Joy for Ashley Giles, Kevin Pietersen and Michael Vaughan as spinner Giles sends back Michael Clarke for 40. RIGHT Panic as Marcus Trescothick decides against a run and drops his bat as he struggles to regain his ground at the start of England's second innings.

Warne bowled Strauss with a massive leg break that moved so far that comparisons were being made with Warne's famous 'ball of the century' that removed Mike Gatting in 1993. The delivery was not quite in that league but was pretty close. It also made Warne the first bowler in history to take 100 wickets in another country. How he loves bowling against the English! Still, at 25–1 at the close of play, with a lead now of 124 runs, and with McGrath on crutches, England were in the box seat – Warne permitting!

To dismiss Australia in just 76 overs on such a flat pitch was some achievement by England. Much of this was down to reverse swing, a technique that would take England far in this series. The great Pakistani all-rounder Wasim Akram was the first to reverse the ball both ways when nearly new. Darren Gough copied him

Australians, who began making it move after ten overs. This was an exciting and significant advance made by the English bowling attack. After so many years of being answerless on a flat pitch without a world-class spinner such as Warne, England could now dismiss well-set batsmen by reverse-swinging an old ball.

Although Jones picked up two wickets and deserved more, the day was a second one of triumph for Flintoff,

who finished with figures of 3–52, and one of satisfaction, too, for the much-maligned Giles, whose figures of 3–78 were the perfect riposte to his critics and to the Australian batsmen, whose plan was to smack the spinner out of the ground and out of the England bowling attack. Warne, in particular, showed almost contempt for the bowling of Giles, at least until he was bowled by the slow left-armer. Giles returned his best bowling figures since spinning out the West Indies the previous summer, endeared himself to a partisan home crowd even more, and won a new-found, grudging respect from the hitherto unimpressed Australians. After snaring Clarke, Giles returned to a far corner of the field to receive a standing ovation from seemingly the entire population of the Wyatt and Raglan Stands.

Perhaps he more than anyone else in the England side would have recognised the problems that lay ahead. The wicket had become dusty as it deteriorated, and the footmarks, created by both sets of fast bowlers, more menacing by the minute. It was the perfect environment for Warne to weave his magic, and weave it he did on a third day as riveting as the two that had preceded it.

In the First Test at Lord's Warne had taken six wickets. There he shared the responsibility of senior bowler with McGrath. At Edgbaston the onus was very much on his shoulders. It was during England's second innings at Edgbaston that Warne revealed just what a competitor he is, and how, as only the truly great sportsmen can, he could rise to the occasion. And it was in the same second innings that Flintoff matched the great bleached one for global sporting greatness.

England's overnight position of 25–1 soon became 27–2, then 29–3, and finally 31–4, as first Trescothick, who had had advanced rapidly to 21, wafted his bat wide of the wicket and nicked one to Gilchrist behind, then Vaughan lost his off stump again, and finally nightwatchman Hoggard was caught by Hayden. Vaughan, who would have been better advised to play forward, had been bowled for the third time in four innings in the series, having scored just 32 runs in the process. On his day he is one of the best batsmen in the world, but he looked seriously short of form and confidence. All three wickets were taken by Lee, who grabbed them in a spell of 11 balls costing four runs.

Worse was to befall England when Pietersen was adjudged out by the South African umpire, Rudi Koertzen, when Warne's delivery appeared to hit virtually everything except Pietersen's bat before dropping into the outstretched glove of Gilchrist.

RIGHT Fast bowler Brett Lee has an impassioned appeal for caught behind against Kevin Pietersen turned down. Evidence later suggested that Pietersen did get a touch to this, his first ball of his second innings.

Pietersen had finally come down to earth, his 20 signalling his first below-average score in Test cricket. Yet he had still managed to club two sixes, not bothering to score any fours in his short innings.

Flintoff strode to the wicket but could only watch as Koertzen raised his index finger again at Bell. The young batsman, after a horrendous start to his Ashes career at Lord's and then a first innings failure here, was just beginning to get the measure of it all, and had

who had enjoyed rich pickings in the past when operating together at the crease. For a while England's fortunes were picking up but, at 101, Jones fell to Lee, receiving just about the first lifter of the whole innings. Previous batsmen were largely at fault for their dismissals. Jones, unfortunately for him and for England, received a virtually unplayable ball. Ponting took the catch that looped up from the face of the Jones bat. As Warne's support bowler, Lee was magnificent in

advanced to 21 when he was given out, caught behind by Gilchrist off Warne, when, unlike in Pietersen's case, nothing had connected with the bat. They were two decisions that went against England, and they left their pre-innings plans of setting Australia an impossible second innings target of 350-plus in tatters.

All hopes seemed to rest on the seventh-wicket partnership between Flintoff and Geraint Jones, a pair

FACING PAGE 'Super Fred' crashes a four on day three during his 86-ball 73. ABOVE And this is what he was up against – a determined Brett Lee pounds towards the bowling crease.

this innings, as indeed he was throughout much of the Ashes series. In the first innings Trescothick, Strauss, Flintoff and Pietersen had set about the fast bowler so convincingly that he returned figures of 1–111 in only 17

overs. He delivered the perfect riposte in the second innings, finishing with 4–82.

Although Lee can take much of the credit for this, it is impossible not to see the influence Warne had. By spinning the ball three feet the night before to dismiss Strauss, Warne made sure that English minds were concentrated overnight on the threat the leg-spinner posed. Lee is no easy alternative, but England's batsmen early on took their eye off Lee, who responded by claiming three crucial wickets inside half an hour.

Flintoff remained resolute, producing an innings of contrasting strokes – forward defensives mingled with clubbed boundaries. Giles hung around for a while until deceived by Warne. The very next ball, Warne got the

FACING PAGE Ricky Ponting catches Steve Harmison first ball off Shane Warne. RIGHT AND BELOW Meanwhile the fans enjoyed themselves immensely. Many turned up in the now traditional fancy dress, among them a group of French onion-sellers, a batch of woopies, and a somewhat sinister black-clad pieman.

unfortunate Harmison, caught by Ponting first ball. The score read 131–9, and England's hitherto position of strength appeared to have been eroded. They held a lead of 230 runs, which, even to the eternal optimist, appeared at best no more than a par total to chase and, at worst, highly achievable.

Then came another twist in this Test match of twists and turns. Simon Jones – surely the world's best number eleven Test batsman – helped Flintoff put on a last-wicket partnership of 51 off just 49 balls. Jones did his bit, smashing three fours that amounted to his unbeaten score of 12, but for the best part of the next half an hour the Welshman had the best seat in the house to watch Flintoff at his most destructive. Freed from the shackles of responsibility with just one wicket remaining, the all-rounder was given the all clear to play with abandoned freedom. When this happens, teams around the world, even Australia, are made to suffer.

The scorecard tells you that Flintoff scored 73 off 86 balls, a relatively slow rate of runs by the big man's standards. What it fails to tell you is that most of those

ABOVE **Plaudits again for Flintoff, this time for for producing a brute of a ball to dismiss Australia's captain, Ricky Ponting, for a five-ball duck.**

balls came when Flintoff was in grown up, responsible mode, trying to defend his batting partners and easing the score along. Most of his runs, however, came when Flintoff returned to his natural game, and his natural game can produce carnage. The end result was a further six fours and four sixes. The capacity Edgbaston crowd began to chant 'Super Fred' as if at Wembley. This, after all, was English cricket's answer to David Beckham.

His destructive power was best exemplified when, in the middle of two overs in which England helped themselves to 38 runs – 20 off Kasprowicz, and then 18 off Lee – Flintoff smashed a ball from Lee back over the fast bowler's head and on to the roof of the pavilion. The Australian fielders were scattered around the boundary but were still left clutching at air. To achieve this when fully fit would have been remarkable. To produce such a knock when in evident pain from a problem in his left shoulder that first revealed itself when he attempted a cut off Warne when his innings had barely started was

incredible. Flintoff had hit 141 off 148 balls in two absolutely vital innings for England. His innings included nine of the sixteen sixes England slogged against Australia, amounting to one-sixth of their total runs. Those nine blows set a new record for the number of sixes scored by one batsman in an Ashes Test, beating the six sixes Ian Botham hit at Old Trafford in 1981. Flintoff more than anyone else had set England up for the most unlikely of comebacks. After the battering at Lord's, it was England this time who were on the front foot. And having shown his worth against the rest of the world, Flintoff had finally produced his best against the finest bowlers in the game. The last remaining question mark had been removed.

Flintoff finally fell to Warne, the leg-spinner deceiving him with a ball that clattered into his stumps. This was Warne's 599th Test dismissal, setting him up to create further history during the next Test at Old Trafford. He finished with second innings figures of 6–46 from 23 overs and match figures of 10–162. It was, in every sense, a huge performance. But would it be enough? And could Flintoff possibly produce any more magic after all his heroics?

Being bowled out for 182 in their second innings was not quite what England had in mind when they set out on the morning of the third day. But there was no doubt that the momentum, which had been with Australia when they had England struggling on 131–9, had switched back to England again after that last-wicket stand of over 50. The gloom that had been so tangibly evident in the crowd was replaced by joy. Jones and especially Flintoff trooped off to a standing ovation. Instead of walking on to the field 20 minutes later with the belief that they had thrown away a golden opportunity, the English players almost sprinted on to the green grass of Edgbaston armed with the utter conviction that they were close to completing the job.

England held an advantage of 281 runs when the Australian opening pair of Langer and Hayden emerged from the Edgbaston pavilion to begin the Australian second innings. The target they were chasing – 282 runs – was far higher than had ever been achieved before in a second innings of a Test match in Birmingham.

This was relatively unknown territory for Australia. Traditionally, they preferred not to go for hand-to-hand combat but to destroy their opposition from far afield. Since the turn of the century they had won 48 out of 64 Tests, losing only eight. Fourteen of these victories had been by an innings. By and large, they avoided close finishes.

In the past five and half years Australia had been asked to chase a target only five times. Twice they had succeeded, but on three other occasions they had failed. Twice they had capitulated to India – once in India after the hosts had been forced to follow on – and also once to England, in Sydney during the previous Ashes series. Perhaps, just perhaps, there was a chink here in the Australian armour.

It did not seem like this at first. Hayden and Langer put on 47 runs in 12 overs, their explosive start seeing off Harmison and Hoggard and forcing Flintoff, nursing his injured shoulder, back into the fray much earlier than he had anticipated. Having claimed Australia's last two wickets of the first innings with consecutive balls, he ran up to deliver his first ball in the second innings on a hat-trick. Langer dealt with it, and the riveted Edgbaston crowd, slightly on edge after seeing nine English wickets fall earlier in the day, sighed with disappointment. Five balls later they were chanting Flintoff's name after he had dismissed both Langer and Ponting, Australia's two highest scorers in their first innings. In two overs, spread out between the end of the first and the start of the second Australian innings, Flintoff had taken four wickets. He was especially pleased with that second over. 'It's probably the best opening over I've ever bowled,' he admitted later. First he bowled Langer for 28 off a tentative inside edge from the diminutive Western

Australian. Then he subjected Ponting to a horrendous sequence of early balls. The already old ball, ironically roughed up by Langer and Hayden early on, reverse-swung both ways at lightning pace, leaving the Australian captain in trouble every ball. Two good leg-before appeals came and went. After four balls a Ponting edge from a ball that moved away fell short. Off his fifth ball Ponting was put out of his misery, nicking a thin edge to Geraint Jones behind for nought.

Then Simon Jones got in on the act. He and Hayden had, of course, some history between them after the one-day rumpus that followed Hayden being hit by Jones's poor attempt at a run-out. It was an unsavoury incident, but at least the reaction from the English fielders in support of Jones had proved England's determination to meet Australia head-on, face to face.

Jones was fast becoming a revelation in this series. He had already contributed 31 unbeaten runs to the cause as a batsman. As a bowler he would enjoy better days and better games ahead in terms of taking wickets, but his role was every bit as crucial in this one. He could have taken a five-for in each innings had the Australian batsmen edged some of the very many deliveries they played and missed at. Even when Jones was not taking wickets he was placing the batsmen under so much pressure that they would fall at the other end.

Hayden, though, belonged to Jones. He set up the former holder of the highest individual score in Test cricket – 380 against Zimbabwe which was surpassed by Brian Lara's unforgettable 400 against England – with a series of inswinging deliveries. Then came the sucker punch. Jones bent the ball away from Hayden, the batsman was deceived and duly edged the ball, and Trescothick at slip did the rest with a breathtaking dive to his left. Jones was so elated with the manner in which he got his man (although the man he got and their recent history had probably something to do with it) that he showed Hayden exactly where the pavilion was as the batsman began the long walk away from the wicket. For his exuberance, Jones was later fined 20 per cent of his match fee, or around £1000, by the match referee, Ranjan Madugalle.

Damien Martyn felt the best way to reach the target was to attack. For a while this policy was looking to be a good one as the experienced number four batsman raced to 28 off just 36 balls, including five boundaries. When he then clipped to Bell at mid-wicket off Hoggard, this policy suddenly seemed anything but good. Yet another Australian had got out when seemingly well set.

Up stepped Ashley Giles. He had already done his bit in the Australian first innings by removing three key batsmen. Now he was at it again on the ground where he has played his cricket throughout his adult career. Simon Katich, although never one to empty the bars when batting, is nevertheless a sticky customer, and just the kind of player you might require when chasing a target with plenty of time at your disposal. He has the ability to stay in, which was precisely what Australia needed right then. Instead he fell to an arm ball from Giles, edging to the dependable Trescothick at slip. If that wicket was important, the next was vital.

BELOW Gillespie lbw Flintoff for the second time in the match.
FACING PAGE Michael Clarke and Freddie have words at the end of a Flintoff over.

In Giles's very next over he put paid to Gilchrist. In the first innings Gilchrist was left stranded on 49 not out as the tail folded around him. It was a classy innings from the wicket-keeper/batsman but not substantial enough for the man to completely find the kind of form that has at times single-handedly destroyed opposing Test teams. In the second innings, he never got going. After collecting a single run, Gilchrist went down the pitch to his fourth ball from Giles and drove straight to Flintoff at mid-on. With the kind of game Freddie was having, he was never going to put down a chance like that.

Still Flintoff had more to offer on the best day of his cricketing life up to that point. Jason Gillespie had not enjoyed either of the first two Tests with the ball in hand. As a batsman he had improved immeasurably and could, on occasions, prove to be infuriatingly stubborn. Not this day, however. Flintoff trapped the bearded bowler with a full ball that presented the extrovert New Zealand umpire Billy Bowden with one of the easiest leg-before decisions he will ever have to make. The crowd erupted on sight of Bowden's raised finger, and the sound of 'Super Fred' once more reverberated around the ground.

Australia had lurched to 137–7. Their old failings when set a target to chase had reappeared. England's old failing – namely lacking a killer instinct to finish off teams, especially Australia – had disappeared. It was possible the Second Test could be over inside three days.

Michael Clarke and Shane Warne had other ideas. Slowly the score crept up, past 150, 160, then 170. Warne had never scored a Test century but did have a 99 to his name, while Clarke had proved himself to be on form in this series and possessing a potential that suggested he would become one of the finest Test batsmen of his generation. These two could still win this match.

Steve Harmison had endured a quiet game. After his eight-wicket haul at Lord's, and his host of near unplayable deliveries that rattled so many Australian batsmen, he had been strangely off colour at Edgbaston on a flatter pitch. His stock ball was the awkward lifter, delivered at great pace. No batsman in the world likes a ball rising towards their nose, especially when sent down by a bowler as tall as Harmison. Just as the great West Indian Joel Garner used to do in the 1980s, Harmison despatches the ball from a height of close to ten feet. Yet he had been working on another ball which, in terms of delivery, could not be more contrasting.

The Harmison slow ball, when he gets it right, is becoming as feared as any of his rib-ticklers. Batsmen, preparing to cover themselves up on the back foot, tend to lose the slow ball bearing down on them from a great height. You have no time to play a Harmison stock delivery. A fraction late with your shot and the likelihood is you will hear the death rattle of the stumps or have the painful view of the umpire's extended finger after the ball has slammed against your pads.

The ball that saw the end of Clarke's resistance in the extra half-hour's worth of play was so slow that the

Australian middle-order batsman had time to look around the field to see where Michael Vaughan had placed all his fielders, twirl his bat and pick up some grass lying on the wicket before playing his stroke. This is an exaggeration, of course, but not by much. It was a pity from his point of view that Clarke did not carry out all those pre-delivery actions. If he had he may have hit the ball. As it was, he played his shot ages before the ball drifted past him and on to the stumps. It had taken Harmison a long time to develop this extra weapon in his already fearful armoury, but on occasions such as this all that extra time in the nets becomes worth it. Clarke had gone for 30, another batsman who had seemingly done the hard work of getting himself in, only to be dismissed when beginning to plan for a half-century. The wicket signalled the perfect end to another scintillating day's play and sent the predominantly partisan crowd home in happy mood. Seventeen wickets had fallen in yet another unforgettable day in what was fast becoming an unforgettable Ashes series. Australia were 175–8 and needed another 107 runs with just two wickets remaining. Warne and Lee, the latter due to begin his innings in the morning, were no mugs when it came to batting, but neither were they good enough to forge that kind of a partnership. Last man in Kasprowicz was a decent number eleven but no more than that. After all the histrionics of the previous three days of cricket at Edgbaston, day four would surely be an anticlimax, at least in terms of the drama served up. As it turned out, nothing could have been further from the truth.

How little Kasprowicz must have slept that Saturday night, knowing that he, as a batsman, might have to play a major part in this Test match and, indeed, in the Ashes series. And how little can he have known how big a part he would go on to play.

If you want to get an idea of how big an issue this game had become to the English sporting summer, then the figures go a long way to providing an answer. Edgbaston was packed to the rafters on the Sunday morning, while 4.1 million viewers tuned in to Channel 4 television. This, do not forget, was for a day's cricket that could, conceivably, have lasted two balls. Channel 4 had never seen anything like it before for their coverage of Test match cricket. The figure would be dwarfed as the series went on.

Levelling the series at 1–1 should, of course, have been a formality. The fact that England were so close to victory, however, coupled with the emotion of wanting the win so desperately, meant a significant change of tactics on the morning of the fourth day.

LEFT Steve Harmsion is ecstatic after his slower delivery thoroughly bamboozles Michael Clarke at the end of the third day and bowls him as the batsman plays too early.

After a brief go with Giles, captain Vaughan sent for the heavy brigade in Harmison and Flintoff. The previous day a line just outside off stump plus a normal length seemed to do the trick. Now they went for bodyline, laced with the odd yorker. Against tail-enders this is a traditional approach. Less accomplished batsmen are not supposed to cope with such tactics. But these Australians did. Far from being fazed by the aggression from the English bowlers, brought on by the understandable emotion of the day, they veritably fed off it. The more the kitchen sink was thrown at the Australian tail, the more they liked it. The runs began to flow, not just off the bat, but from a string of every kind of extra imaginable.

Warne, playing with the carefree abandon of a man knowing he had absolutely nothing to lose, led the way at first, batting in the only way he can. After the first four overs of the morning Australia had already put on 24 runs. No worries. England were still miles ahead. There was no way Australia could get the runs. Was there? Pietersen at cover might have been more concerned than most. He had seen Warne strike two centuries playing for their county side, Hampshire, earlier in the season. It had happened quite late in his incredible career as a spin bowler par excellence, but Warne was in danger of becoming a fully fledged all-rounder.

Just as it became clear that Warne was fancying his chances of becoming the ultimate hero, disaster struck for him. Flintoff had been peppering him with short-pitched deliveries which he had done well to fend off. With the score on 220, and after he had put on 45 runs with Brett Lee for the ninth wicket, Warne attempted a clip to leg but managed, instead, with a flick of his right heel, to tread on his own stumps. Out, hit wicket, bowled Flintoff, was one of the strangest ways Warne had been dismissed in his long career, and it could not have happened at a worse time.

Now, surely, the game was up. Australia needed a further 62 runs to tie the Test, and one further to win. They had just Lee and Kasprowicz left, and whereas Lee was looking settled, new batsman Kasprowicz, with an average of 10.5 in Test cricket, was there for the taking. And that's where the real, and at times almost unbearable, drama began. Few sporting occasions in recent years have been as compelling as what unfolded in front of an increasingly horrified English crowd and television audience. Twelve thousand miles away in Australia, a whole nation felt the necessity to stay up all night to watch two bowlers claw their way towards one of the greatest victories of all time.

The psychology of sport is always one of the most interesting and telling factors. Why does a tennis player having fought back from two sets down to all square at Wimbledon often go on to lose that final set? Why is 2–0 often regarded as a more dangerous scoreline in football midway through a game than 1–0? And why do tail-end batsmen score with absolute freedom until close to their target, when they forget how they reached this point and disappear into their shells?

This is what happened on the Sunday morning at Edgbaston in front of a crowd so frazzled by nerves that few knew where to look. England were always going to win this game, which is why Kasprowicz, and especially Lee, scored freely, knowing that they had nothing to lose. If Warne was in danger of becoming an all-rounder, then Lee, at the very least, was transforming himself into one of the world's quickest bowlers who could now, quite clearly, bat perfectly acceptably as well. He shepherded the less confident Kasprowicz expertly, pinching the strike whenever he could and frustrating the English bowling attack. He was made to pay for his innings, too. Lee took blow after blow to his person from the short-pitched bowling, the worst being one he received on the left hand from Flintoff from a delivery he would describe afterwards as the quickest ball he had ever faced in Test match cricket. But still he stayed at the crease.

The closer Australia edged towards their target, the more fidgety the crowd became. Vaughan revealed later that while he had had no shortage of advice from any number of English colleagues throughout the first three days of the Test, none was forthcoming on that final morning. The ball would not fall England's way. The edge was missed, fours were snicked, mishit shots saw the ball soar invitingly up into the air, only to fall in between the English fielders. Memories of the Melbourne Test in 1982 came flooding back. Then Australia got within four runs of an equally unlikely victory until Geoff Miller kept hold of a juggling catch to dismiss Jeff Thompson off Botham. Ironically, at the start of this Test England had rejoiced when McGrath's freak injury saw him withdrawn from the game. Without his bowling England knew they were in with a chance, and duly snapped it up. Now the whole of England yearned for McGrath the batsman to be out there in the middle instead of Kasprowicz.

Australia had got to within 15 runs of victory when an incident happened that could have haunted Simon Jones for the rest of his life. Kasprowicz edged Flintoff's rising ball down to third man. Jones needed to advance quickly from the boundary to reach it. He seemed to have done the hard work but then fumbled and dropped the catch as he dived forward. The Edgbaston crowd had their heads in their hands. The England players had their heads in their hands, too. And Jones, who trotted back to the boundary, felt terrible. 'When I spilled that catch at third man I thought: "Oh my God, I'm going to nailed for this,"' he revealed later.

The stakes had become so high by then that there was little doubt about what had happened. For all his heroics with bat and especially ball, and as harsh as it may sound, Simon Jones might well have become the man who had just dropped the Ashes. It would have been a tag that would stick to him like a leech wherever he went in life.

Flintoff, clearly distraught, then let fly with a ball so wild that it shot to the boundary for five byes. Australia needed just nine to win. Then Kasprowicz shuffled across his stumps to survive a huge leg-before appeal. The tension was becoming unbearable, not only for the England players and followers but now, and crucially, for the last two remaining Australian batsmen.

Up to this point, even, they had been out at the wicket putting up a brave fight. There was nothing more to it than that. Neither was expected to achieve what their specialist batsmen had failed so palpably to do the previous day. They were in the almost enviable sporting position of having nothing to lose. But now, suddenly, and to their obvious surprise, they had a great deal to lose. Being 107 runs adrift at the start of play was not a problem. Being 61 runs behind at the fall of the ninth wicket was not a worry. But being so close now to a win? Now this was a major problem.

If Australian stomachs were churning, then so, too, were English. This was a Test match they had dominated from the very first over of an enthralling game four days earlier. They had batted better than Australia and, for the most part, bowled better too. From day one they had been in control. Now England were about to lose a Test match. Worse, they were about to lose a game in just about the most terrible fashion. Most important of all, they were on the verge of going two down in two Tests in a best-of-five Test match series. Against the best team in the world, there would be no way back.

They tried to keep brave faces as they watched the horror unfurl from the field. 'The match had gone,' Ashley Giles confessed afterwards. 'I tried to be positive but I knew we'd blown it. And with it, most probably, the Ashes. It was a horrible feeling, and I felt powerless to stop it from happening.'

Australia now needed just four runs to tie, and five to win. Flintoff delivered what would be his last over of the game. This time his line was much better. His consistent off-stump deliveries yielded just one run to Lee, who kept the strike. Still, this was like watching a slow and painful death.

A serious-looking Harmison was thrown the ball. Somehow England needed a wicket, and fast. Instead England's opening bowler produced a full toss wide of the off stump. In a matter of a nano-second the whole of England froze as Lee launched into a drive and saw the ball head out towards cover. If it had split the field it would have been a boundary, and the Test match, and most probably the Ashes, would have been all over.

ABOVE It's all over. Michael Vaughan rushes to congratulate fast bowler Harmison, who has just had Michael Kasprowicz dramatically caught by Geraint Jones to bring England victory by the skin of their teeth.

Instead, and mercifully from an English point of view, it went to deep cover and only a single was taken. Lee must have relived that shot a thousand times since. In his dreams the ball would have crashed against the advertising hoardings a couple of seconds after leaving his bat, and Lee would have sprinted off the pitch to a hero's reception from his team-mates in the Australian dressing room and a grateful nation back home. He may never quite believe, battered and bruised though he was, that he missed out on such an opportunity.

Kasprowicz was now on strike knowing that only three runs were required to win. The omens were still looking exceptionally good for Australia, and terrible for England. Then came the moment of the summer.

Harmison decided to take a massive risk. Instead of tempting Kasprowicz with a well-pitched-up ball outside off stump, or even with the kind of slower delivery that had deceived Clarke the previous evening, he went for

broke. All morning Kasprowicz had been clubbing, shovelling or belting every short ball to leg but, with the match poised as it was, he opted for caution this time.

Michael Kasprowicz is a big man, and big men, especially if they are not accomplished batsmen, find it difficult to perform the perfect duck to evade a bouncer. The first part of this sequence went reasonably well. Kasprowicz got his head out of the way but, alas, not his glove. The ball looped high and wide down the leg side but sufficiently slowly for Geraint Jones to dive forward and to his left to gobble up the tumbling catch just inches off the turf. The ball seemed to be in the air forever, as if caught in time. Kasprowicz looked up

pleadingly to Billy Bowden, but the umpire who loves the show more than most was not going to miss out on this little piece of history. Up went the finger and down sank on to their haunches both Kasprowicz and a horrified Lee, watching from the non-striker's end. The time was 12.09 in the early afternoon of 7 August and the Ashes series had been set alight.

The differing emotions in evidence out in the middle at Edgbaston told their own story. While the rest of the England team first jumped in the air with joy and then went to mob Harmison, who had just grabbed the most important wicket of his life, Geraint Jones momentarily lost it. The Kent wicket-keeper, so heavily criticised during the first two Tests for his dropped catches and relative lack of runs, jumped up and down, shouted, punched and pointed towards a group of Australian fans who had been sledging him from the Wyatt Stand moments earlier. His namesake, Simon, meanwhile, bore a grin that went from ear to ear as he joined his team-mates from the third man boundary. After dropping that catch, he felt like a man on death row just reprieved.

Still there was time for one more moment of pure class from Flintoff. The man of the match had scored 141 runs in the game and taken seven wickets in a display that, quite rightly, brought instant comparisons with Ian Botham's incredible feats during the 1981 Ashes-winning series. Now, at this precise moment of English ecstasy, Flintoff had the presence of mind, and the understanding of what it had taken, to walk away from his own colleagues down the wicket and to crouch down to console a thoroughly dejected Lee.

It created arguably a snapshot of the summer. Flintoff and Lee had been at each other tooth and nail for four days at Edgbaston. Both had produced masterful performances. Flintoff recognised the draining effect of high emotion and massive effort inside Lee, because he had just lived through it himself. Now was not the time for triumphalism. Like a heavyweight boxer after 15 bruising rounds of slugging it out against his opponent, Flintoff placed his large paw of a hand on Lee's shoulder in consolation and congratulation.

The moment has been likened to one of the greatest shows of sportsmanship ever. The photo has already found its place up there alongside that of a shirtless Pele, all shiny with sweat, embracing the late and great Bobby Moore after the England captain had defended so well against the great striker during the 1970 World Cup. It

LEFT Andrew Flintoff makes his way across to a devastated Michael Kasprowicz and Brett Lee to offer congratulations and consolation after their heroic attempt to bring Australia home. The gesture exemplified the respect between the two sides and, in particular, between Flintoff and Lee.

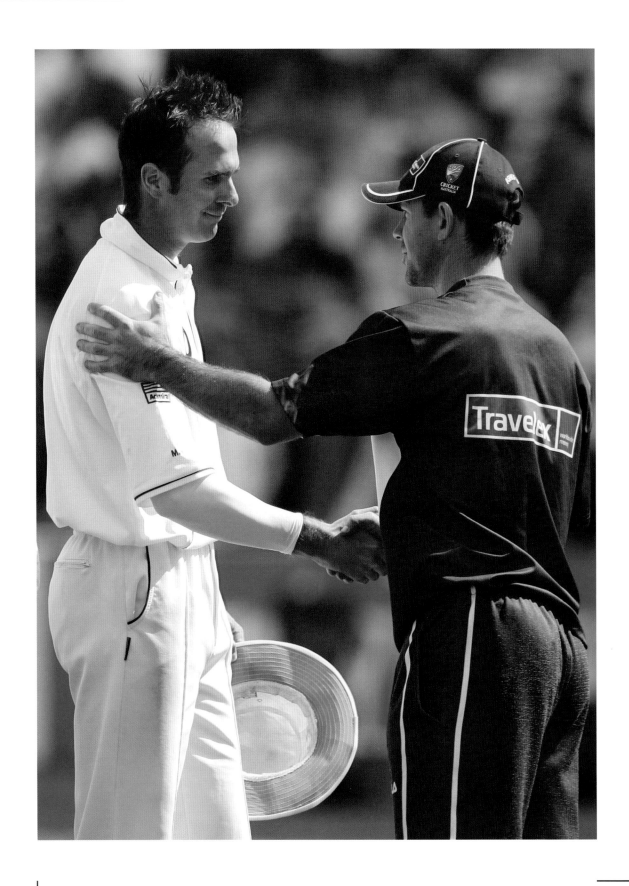

epitomised what this Ashes series was all about. The hardest of fights out in the arena but now a massive mutual respect back in the pavilion. It said a great deal about this Australian team that within moments of experiencing one of the most painful defeats imaginable, they were inside the England dressing room shaking hands and sharing a few bottles of beer.

A little afterwards it emerged that Kasprowicz should not, technically, have been given out. There was no doubt that Harmison's rising ball touched Kasprowicz's glove on its way to Jones behind the stumps, but television replays revealed that at the time of contact the Australian's hand was around three inches away from the handle. The laws state that the glove needs to be touching the bat for the batsman to be given out caught. For such a major decision, little was made of it. It was widely accepted that umpire Bowden could not possibly have seen this and had little option but to raise his finger at the unfortunate Kasprowicz. The Australians felt there was no cause for complaint after such an exceptional game of cricket.

The facts were these. England's two-run win was the narrowest by runs in Ashes history. It was the second narrowest in all Test cricket, behind Australia's one-run win over the West Indies in 1992–93. It was only England's second win in an Ashes series while the old Ashes urn was still at stake since 1989. And it had been the first time since 1981 that they had come from behind to level the series. This England team had guts. This, after all, was the sixth consecutive time that they had responded to Test defeat by winning the very next match. Unlike at Lord's, where England's fielders put down seven catches, only one chance went begging at Edgbaston, and that was the difficult chance to Simon Jones close to the end. Had there ever been a more exciting game of cricket? The sporting gods had decreed that, on this day, they would favour England.

The significance of it all was hard to quantify. Football, the all-conquering sport in England, would be under way the following week with the start of the new Premiership season. If England had gone two down,

FACING PAGE The captains shake after a wonderful Test match. BELOW The bowlers' union – Harmison, Flintoff, Simon Jones – stick together in the aftermath of the drama. OVERLEAF Andrew Flintoff, Man of the Match.

interest at home would have waned as eyes would have been diverted to Stamford Bridge, Highbury and the Old Trafford home of Manchester United. And Australia would have erased just about the only remaining question mark hanging over their incredible team. Yes, they could chase a fourth innings target, even when the cause appeared long lost.

The expression on the face of a mentally exhausted Michael Vaughan spoke volumes for the relief he felt. He knew the score. 'I don't think we would have come back from 2–0 down against a team like Australia,' he admitted. 'They are the number one side in the rankings, after all. It's fantastic to get back to one-all. To get over the line is a real boost. It sets the series up fantastically well. The most important thing now is to take this momentum into the Third Test and start well again at Old Trafford.'

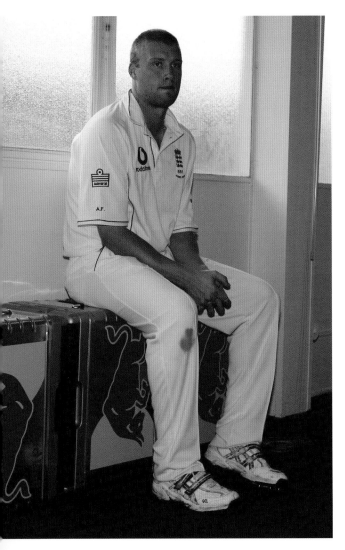

Ricky Ponting felt the same mental fatigue as his English counterpart but did the only thing he could do and tried to remain upbeat. 'It was probably the most nerve-wracking end to a match that I've ever played in,' he confessed. 'It's right up there with the World Cup semi-final against South Africa. [In 1999, Australia scraped through at, ironically, Edgbaston.] But we can take as much away from this as England can after the way we fought it out.' As for Flintoff, Ponting insisted his *Boy's Own* efforts did not surprise Australia. 'We've known about his talents for a long time now,' he said. 'You've only got to look at what he's done in international cricket to know that he's a very dangerous player.'

Australia's two heroes from the Test, Warne and Lee, spoke honestly after playing such a full part in the drama of the past four days. 'When we all sit down around a barbecue having a beer, this match won't be one I'm talking about,' Warne said, despite taking ten wickets. 'When you lose a game your bowling figures mean nothing.' Lee added, 'We knew we had to take a few balls on the body. I'd do it again to make sure we give everything we can to make Australia win. As much as we're hurting physically, it's good for cricket.'

Harmison, the man of the moment after finding the right ball to dislodge Kasprowicz, preferred to heap praise on his captain. 'Michael Vaughan was awesome with his bowling changes and his captaincy decisions,' he said. 'After Lord's the Aussies had a lot of momentum but now that has shifted and it is on our side.'

Indeed it was. The nation, let alone the two teams involved, would barely be allowed to recover from this high drama. Just four days after the Sunday lunchtime survival of English cricket, they would be at it all over again. The Third Test would begin on the Thursday at Old Trafford. And Old Trafford was the home of the country's new superhero, Andrew 'Freddie' Flintoff.

Flintoff remained endearingly down to earth after Edgbaston. Asked how good it felt to play in an Ashes series after a seven-year wait brought about by injury and poor form, he replied, 'Yeah, brilliant, innit.' Asked if England now had the psychological edge, his reply was pure Freddie. 'I'm not clever enough to get into psychology. We've won a Test match. We're happy. Dunno about them.'

The thought of playing Australia at Old Trafford, though, did get the man's eyes to shine a little more. 'It's going to be special,' Flintoff admitted. 'Walking through your home ground gate, knowing everyone, your family and your mates, will be there. I just can't wait.'

Neither could the rest of the sporting world. This Ashes series, whatever happened in Manchester, had already supplied more drama and action than anyone had envisaged. Surely there could be no repeat at Old Trafford. Could there?

ENGLAND V AUSTRALIA, 2nd Test, Edgbaston

4, 5, 6, 7 AUGUST 2005

TOSS: Australia
UMPIRES: BF Bowden (NZ) and RE Koertzen (SA)
TV UMPIRE: JW Lloyds **FOURTH UMPIRE:** AA Jones
MATCH REFEREE: RS Madugalle (SL)

Close of Play:
- **Day 1:** England 407
- **Day 2:** Australia 308, England 25-1 (Trescothick 19*, Hoggard 0*)
- **Day 3:** England 182, Australia 175-8 (Warne 20*)

England 1st innings			R	M	B	4	6
ME Trescothick	c Gilchrist	b Kasprowicz	90	143	102	15	2
AJ Strauss	b Warne		48	113	76	10	0
*MP Vaughan	c Lee	b Gillespie	24	54	41	3	0
IR Bell	c Gilchrist	b Kasprowicz	6	2	3	1	0
KP Pietersen	c Katich	b Lee	71	152	76	10	1
A Flintoff	c Gilchrist	b Gillespie	68	74	62	6	5
+GO Jones	c Gilchrist	b Kasprowicz	1	14	15	0	0
AF Giles	lbw	b Warne	23	34	30	4	0
MJ Hoggard	lbw	b Warne	16	62	49	2	0
SJ Harmison	b Warne		17	16	11	2	1
SP Jones	not out		19	39	24	1	1
Extras	**24**	(lb 9, w 1, nb 14)					
Total	**407**	(all out, 79.2 overs, 356 minutes)					

FoW: **1-112** (Strauss), **2-164** (Trescothick), **3-170** (Bell), **4-187** (Vaughan), **5-290** (Flintoff), **6-293** (GO Jones), **7-342** (Giles), **8-348** (Pietersen), **9-375** (Harmison), **10-407** (Hoggard).

Bowling	O	M	R	W	
Lee	17	1	111	1	(3nb, 1w)
Gillespie	22	3	91	2	(3nb)
Kasprowicz	15	3	80	3	(8nb)
Warne	25.2	4	116	4	

Australia 1st innings			R	M	B	4	6
JL Langer	lbw	b SP Jones	82	276	154	7	0
ML Hayden	c Strauss	b Hoggard	0	5	1	0	0
*RT Ponting	c Vaughan	b Giles	61	87	76	12	0
DR Martyn	run out (Vaughan)		20	23	18	4	0
MJ Clarke	c GO Jones	b Giles	40	85	68	7	0
SM Katich	c GO Jones	b Flintoff	4	22	18	1	0
+AC Gilchrist	not out		49	120	69	4	0
SK Warne	b Giles		8	14	14	2	0
B Lee	c Flintoff	b SP Jones	6	14	10	1	0
JN Gillespie	lbw	b Flintoff	7	36	37	1	0
MS Kasprowicz	lbw	b Flintoff	0	1	1	0	0
Extras	**31**	(b 13, lb 7, w 1, nb 10)					
Total	**308**	(all out, 76 overs, 346 minutes)					

FoW: **1-0** (Hayden), **2-88** (Ponting), **3-118** (Martyn), **4-194** (Clarke), **5-208** (Katich), **6-262** (Langer), **7-273** (Warne), **8-282** (Lee), **9-308** (Gillespie), **10-308** (Kasprowicz).

Bowling	O	M	R	W	
Harmison	11	1	48	0	(2nb)
Hoggard	8	0	41	1	(4nb)
SP Jones	16	2	69	2	(1nb, 1w)
Flintoff	15	1	52	3	(3nb)
Giles	26	2	78	3	

England 2nd innings			R	M	B	4	6
ME Trescothick	c Gilchrist	b Lee	21	51	38	4	0
AJ Strauss	b Warne		6	28	12	1	0
MJ Hoggard	c Hayden	b Lee	1	35	27	0	0
*MP Vaughan	b Lee		1	2	2	0	0
IR Bell	c Gilchrist	b Warne	21	69	43	2	0
KP Pietersen	c Gilchrist	b Warne	20	50	35	0	2
A Flintoff	b Warne		73	133	86	6	4
+GO Jones	c Ponting	b Lee	9	33	19	1	0
AF Giles	c Hayden	b Warne	8	44	36	0	0
SJ Harmison	c Ponting	b Warne	0	2	1	0	0
SP Jones	not out		12	42	23	3	0
Extras	**10**	(lb 1, nb 9)					
Total	**182**	(all out, 52.1 overs, 249 minutes)					

FoW: **1-25** (Strauss), **2-27** (Trescothick), **3-29** (Vaughan), **4-31** (Hoggard), **5-72** (Pietersen), **6-75** (Bell), **7-101** (GO Jones), **8-131** (Giles), **9-131** (Harmison), **10-182** (Flintoff).

Bowling	O	M	R	W	
Lee	18	1	82	4	(5nb)
Gillespie	8	0	24	0	(1nb)
Kasprowicz	3	0	29	0	(3nb)
Warne	23.1	7	46	6	

Australia 2nd innings			R	M	B	4	6
JL Langer	b Flintoff		28	54	47	4	0
ML Hayden	c Trescothick	b SP Jones	31	106	64	4	0
*RT Ponting	c GO Jones	b Flintoff	0	4	5	0	0
DR Martyn	c Bell	b Hoggard	28	64	36	5	0
MJ Clarke	b Harmison		30	101	57	4	0
SM Katich	c Trescothick	b Giles	16	27	21	3	0
+AC Gilchrist	c Flintoff	b Giles	1	8	4	0	0
JN Gillespie	lbw	b Flintoff	0	4	2	0	0
SK Warne	hit wicket	b Flintoff	42	79	59	4	2
B Lee	not out		43	99	75	5	0
MS Kasprowicz	c GO Jones	b Harmison	20	60	31	3	0
Extras	**40**	(b 13, lb 8, w 1, nb 18)					
Total	**279**	(all out, 64.3 overs, 307 minutes)					

FoW: **1-47** (Langer), **2-48** (Ponting), **3-82** (Hayden), **4-107** (Martyn), **5-134** (Katich), **6-136** (Gilchrist), **7-137** (Gillespie), **8-175** (Clarke), **9-220** (Warne), **10-279** (Kasprowicz).

Bowling	O	M	R	W	
Harmison	17.3	3	62	2	(1nb, 1w)
Hoggard	5	0	26	1	
Giles	15	3	68	2	
Flintoff	22	3	79	4	(13nb)
SP Jones	5	1	23	1	

RESULT: England won by 2 runs MAN OF THE MATCH: A Flintoff

OLD TRAFFORD

3RD TEST
11 AUGUST–15 AUGUST

FACING PAGE Shane Warne watches as Adam Gilchrist catches Marcus Trescothick in England's first innings to make the Australian leg-spinner the first bowler to take 600 Test wickets. RIGHT A cheerful Freddie Flintoff at Old Trafford on his 50th Test appearance.

The last time England came from behind to win the Ashes was in 1981 when Ian Botham did then what Andrew Flintoff was promising to do now. It may have been a case of straw-clutching, but comparisons were already being made between the two years of 1981 and 2005. Prince Charles, for example, was married in 1981, as indeed he was in 2005. Liverpool won the European Cup then and now. And so on. The portents, so an English public in love with the game again believed, were looking good.

Michael Vaughan remained calm amid the frenzy, just as he had on that last morning at Edgbaston when he refused to panic and backed Flintoff and Harmison to finish the job. 'We lost the First Test at Lord's as a team and now we've won the second as a team,' he explained. 'The most important thing is that we go to Old Trafford and try to reproduce the Edgbaston performance. Can we do it again starting on Thursday? I'm sure we can.'

Unlike the Australians, Vaughan had bent over backwards not to talk his England team up too much.

Insisting that they could win in Manchester was about as bullish as Vaughan gets. He had seen how predicting 5–0 whitewashes had come back to hit Australia full in the face. Yet he prepared for the Third Test full of hope. 'I think we can keep producing performances,' he said. 'I asked them whether we could bounce back from Lord's. It's fantastic that we have. Now I'll ask them before the next game whether we can reproduce that performance. If we can, then we can keep putting Australia under a lot of pressure.'

Australia were feeling the pressure all right, the more so because they faced the possibility of having neither McGrath, recovering from his ankle ligament damage, nor Lee available for Old Trafford. The former was rated as having no chance of making Old Trafford after treading on that infamous cricket ball just six days previously at Edgbaston during the warm-up. Yet, with 48 hours to go before battle recommenced in Manchester, the Australian tour party were refusing to rule their man out just yet. The latter, fresh from his near match-winning innings on the Sunday morning, was, in many ways, in a worse state that McGrath. Lee had spent the Monday and Tuesday nights in hospital on an intravenous drip and was planning to rise from his hospital bed in the hope that a workout in the nets the day before play began would be enough to pass him fit. The fast bowler had grazed his knee badly while diving in the field at Lord's. The area was aggravated again during the Second Test and infected hairs then carried the bug into the fleshy part of his knee.

Merv Hughes, he of the famous moustache and put-downs to opposing batsmen during his playing days, was the Australian selector who would have faced a hideous dilemma. His two other seamers, Kasprowicz and Gillespie, had both suffered a loss of form and had been clattered to all points of the boundary by England's rampant batsmen. In reserve Hughes could call on the fast but raw Shaun Tait or Stuart Clark, a barely known seam bowler who had just returned to Middlesex. Clark was summoned up the motorway to Manchester to join the squad just in case the news was bad. He arrived in time to join his new team-mates as they went to a football match. They could have chosen Manchester United, who were playing in the qualifying round of the Champions League that night, but instead they chose Altrincham versus Bangor. The reason? The Australian team bus driver, Geoff Goodwin, also happens to be the Altrincham chairman. He laid on the coach that Aston Villa had used in their 1960 promotion season to transport the players to the game.

Lee rose from his sickbed after all, came through the Wednesday net session, and declared himself fit and raring to go. McGrath, as he predicted all along, was also passed fit, a testament to the Australian physio, Errol

FACING PAGE Brett Lee rises from his sickbed to participate in practice before the Third Test, watched by Australian physio Errol Alcott and Glenn McGrath, also not 100 per cent fit. ABOVE Jason Gillespie, who had struggled for form throughout the tour, got the nod as third seamer ahead of Michael Kasprowicz.

Alcott, otherwise known as 'Hooter'. Formerly in rugby league down under, Alcott was so unused to the ways of cricket that when he first joined up with the Australian squad he asked one of the bemused players when the hooter sounded at the game. The name stuck. The nickname may be gently mocking, but the respect and gratitude his players felt for him after steering McGrath's unlikely recovery was heartfelt.

Over in the England camp all was looking good, too. Well, almost. Vaughan's captaincy in the Second Test had been impressive, but his batting was a real concern. In his four Ashes innings so far he had amassed the worrying total of just 32 runs, with an average of 8. This was after a two-hour session with England coach Duncan Fletcher before the Second Test to iron out a few flaws that had appeared in his technique. It seemed to have worked when Vaughan scored a century in a Totesport 45-over match for Yorkshire in between the two Tests, but at Edgbaston he went for 24 and 1. The 30-year-old was one of the most respected batsmen in the world, as far as the Australians were concerned. The last time these two sides had played for the Ashes, in 2002–03, Vaughan smacked three centuries. They were big ones, too. Scores of 177, 145 and 188 saw him soar to the top of the world batting rankings, a list that included the likes of Sachin Tendulkar and Brian Lara. Since then,

apart from a 156 against South Africa two summers before, Vaughan had not come close to regaining the dizzy heights of the Australian tour. Now, like so many of his predecessors, the burden of being England captain meant that he was paying a price with his batting. His fall from grace, at least as a batsman, was being analysed to the 'nth' degree in the media. Much more of this and there was a danger that the rest of the England team would be carrying their captain.

That was the theory, in any case. By the end of the first day's play at Old Trafford that particular theory looked in tatters. Vaughan began the day by being awarded an honorary doctorate from Sheffield Hallam University. Then he won his first toss of the Ashes series after three attempts. He ended his day, five hours later, with a mammoth 166 to his name scored at a breakneck pace. It was the Vaughan of old and it was much needed. Not only did he score a large hundred – and indeed the first century of this Ashes series – but he produced a

FACING PAGE Andrew Strauss's off stump is removed by a Brett Lee slower ball. ABOVE England skipper Michael Vaughan is bowled by Glenn McGrath on 41, having been dropped by Gilchrist off the previous delivery. Australian celebrations were cut short by the sight of umpire Bucknor's outstretched arm, signalling a no-ball.

leader's innings. At close of play on day one, England, having won the toss and elected to bat, were in the healthy position of being 341–5.

Watching in the Old Trafford crowd was the Manchester United captain, Roy Keane. He would have been impressed by the determination, guts and pure leadership qualities Vaughan revealed out there. On the surface Vaughan has the demeanour of a vicar. Deep down, as was already clear by the way he had forged his men into a team capable of beating Australia, Vaughan has the heart of a lion. Keane's United team-mate, Gary Neville, the England right back, could have told him this. Neville and Vaughan have been lifelong friends.

LEFT One of the most elegant sights in world cricket. An in-form Michael Vaughan caresses the ball through the off side on his way to a first innings 166. **FACING PAGE** Six hundred up. Warne has Trescothick caught by Gilchrist to reach the magic milestone.

Vaughan got his chance to prove his critics wrong early on. Lee bowled Strauss for just six with an inswinging yorker that clattered in to the off stump, a rare failure for the Trescothick and Strauss opening partnership. It was some feat by Lee, too. A couple of days in a hospital bed seemed to have done him the power of good. Against Strauss he produced a brilliant series of balls straight out of the Steve Harmison

masterclass that had put paid to Michael Clarke at Edgbaston. First, down came the short ball to soften Strauss up. Then followed the slower ball which did for him. Clarke, incidentally, was off the field virtually from the off with recurring back problems. Substitute fielder Brad Hodge replaced him for a long day spent mostly close to the boundary.

Lee could and should have had more success early on, too. Trescothick had made only 13 when Gilchrist fumbled a textbook edge to his left. After that the Somerset opener continued his rich vein of form, hitting 63 in his customary rapid style before helping to create some more cricketing history.

It was Trescothick's demise that had given McGrath his 500th Test wicket at Lord's. Now it was the same man who handed Shane Warne his 600th Test wicket. Trescothick was looking good again but, once more, failed to convert a half-century into three figures. Given a wonderful opportunity to do so by the Old Trafford groundsman, Peter Marron, who had prepared a batting wicket for the first day as good as any you are likely to see, Trescothick fell instead after an attempted sweep shot off Warne saw the ball hit his glove, his arm, then the back of his bat and, finally, Gilchrist's knee before the Australian wicket-keeper claimed the catch.

Warne had been promising all summer that his Hampshire friend and colleague, Kevin Pietersen, would be his 600th victim. Instead it was Trescothick who obliged, although Warne admitted later it was not the prettiest way to reach the magical 600 mark. 'It was a pretty scrappy wicket,' he said. 'But I'll happily claim it. It's never a bad thing to get Marcus Trescothick out.'

Warne got his chance because the new ball had been tamed on a surface so true in pace and bounce. He had to work hard for it, too. But, then again, Warne is hardly averse to working hard. When Fred Trueman, the great English fast bowler of the 1950s and 1960s reached 300 Test wickets, then a record, the thought of surpassing even that figure seemed enough of a challenge. 'If anyone beats it they'll be bloody tired,' Trueman remarked at the time.

Well, Warne had not only beaten it, he had doubled it. If it were not for two operations on his shoulder and spinning finger, he would most probably have passed 700 wickets by now. Still, 600 would do. The Test came to a halt as Trescothick departed and Ian Bell made his entrance. In this time the Australian team had rushed to Warne to offer their congratulations, and Warne had made a point of kissing a white wristband on his right

hand, a present given to him by his daughter back home in Australia. To a spectator, the Old Trafford crowd rose to their feet in acclaim. Warne may have been an Australian, he may have just robbed them and Trescothick of a possible century, and he would no doubt have a major part to play in the eventual outcome of the Ashes, but they stood in recognition of seeing the best spinner of all time ply his trade for the last time at the famous ground.

Bell, understandably, took his time to get going. Vaughan, by contrast, was in the groove. Aggressive, stylish, confident, the England captain was back to his best. Moreover, he was lucky, too, as every good batsman needs to be. On 41 he was dropped by Gilchrist high to his right off McGrath. Shane Warne standing at first slip would probably have taken the catch with his eyes closed. Instead Gilchrist attempted to poach the catch with an instinctive dive. This was the wicket-keeper's second spilled chance of the morning. So enraged was McGrath

that he threw everything into his next ball and bowled Vaughan through the gate. Off a no-ball! Thus followed a few seconds of mayhem as Gilchrist ran towards a celebrating McGrath, and Trescothick screamed at his captain to run for byes, aware that umpire Steve Bucknor's arm was outstretched, signalling the no-ball.

Reprieved, Vaughan went on to reach his fifty and then his century, to rapturous applause from a Lancastrian crowd for once grateful for the white rose of Yorkshire. The Ashes nightmare for Jason Gillespie continued. In trying to avoid giving Vaughan width, the lanky pace bowler instead gave the England captain ample opportunity to work him through the on side, including one glorious shot that saw the ball fly over mid-wicket and into the stand for six.

On 141 Vaughan was dropped again, this time by Matthew Hayden off the tireless Warne. It was one of five chances that went begging as the pressure told on Australia. Of those five, only one could be considered a

half-chance. The other four would have been gobbled up by the Australia of old.

In the end Vaughan's dismissal was so soft it bordered on the ridiculous. Having seen off everything Lee, McGrath, Warne and Gillespie could throw at him, the captain fell victim to Simon Katich, an occasional spinner. Katich threw up an unintentional, inviting full toss and Vaughan smacked the ball straight down McGrath's throat out in the on-side deep. McGrath kept both hands clasped around the ball as he ran towards his team-mates, as if to remind them that this was the way to catch a ball.

To his credit, while seemingly everyone else was questioning whether he could ever return to the batting glories of his Ashes tour down under, Vaughan had remained confident in his ability. 'I was on a bit of a bad run, that's all,' he explained. 'I knew it wouldn't last. I wasn't happy about it, but neither was I losing sleep. You don't become a bad batsman overnight. Today I just played by instinct.'

Vaughan was furious with himself, however, for being dismissed with 14 overs of the day remaining. So, too, was Kevin Pietersen when he latched on to a speculative short ball from Lee. Sporting a new blue rinse to his hair to mark the occasion, Pietersen had once again set off like a runaway train and suggested a late flurry of fireworks. Instead he could only watch as his pull shot picked out substitute fielder Hodge on the square-leg boundary. Lee followed this up by knocking over nightwatchman Matthew Hoggard's off stump with the last ball of the day.

At 341–5 it had been another good day for England, and especially for Vaughan, but with the capture of his wicket, and then both Pietersen and Hoggard, Australia left the field with a sniff of a chance. They were back in the match, just when it looked as if England would put themselves in a winning position after the first day's play. And with the new ball due early the following morning, Australia had every right to be hopeful.

England, though, had plenty to be upbeat about, too. Apart from another half-century from Trescothick and Vaughan's brilliance, the other major plus point from the day was an impressive and unbeaten 59 from Bell. It was an innings very much of two halves. Beginning slowly and cautiously, the Warwickshire batsman seemed determined to hang around long enough this time to build an innings. After such a memorable start to his Test match career against the West Indies the previous summer, when he scored 70, followed by another half-century and then a huge hundred against Bangladesh, Bell had found playing

Test match cricket with the really big boys to be quite a challenge. Up to this point he had not succeeded in meeting it, but his 59 was seen as a coming of age for a man expected to enjoy a long and prosperous Test career. He failed to score off 120 of his 146 balls. He spent 37 of these balls stuck on 18, a spell that saw McGrath fail to hold on to a return chance offered from his bowling, but eventually Bell's confidence rose and he began to display a wide array of more attacking strokes. The hope was that he could follow this up in the morning by completing what would be a memorable century against the world champions.

That was the hope. The reality was somewhat different. Bell fell without adding to his overnight score, caught behind off the consistently impressive Lee, attempting an unnecessary pull. Unhappily for Bell, television replays proved that his bat had not connected with the ball. It was another umpiring error, this time from the popular Steve Bucknor. Nevertheless, with Flintoff and Geraint Jones at the crease, England's hopes for a score of 500-plus looked intact. The pair put on 87 effortless runs for the seventh wicket, matching each other with their albeit differing styles as both raced in to the 40s. Flintoff was all straight drive and clubs, Jones more cuts and slices. Between them they peppered the boundary at all points.

Warne remained at his belligerent best. Refusing to yield to Flintoff when all around him were toiling in the field, he finally coaxed a skier from the all-rounder to Justin Langer on the boundary. It was a good moment

FACING PAGE AND RIGHT **Shane Warne enjoys the adulation of his team-mates and of the crowd on reaching 600 Test wickets.**

ABOVE Kevin Pietersen, out late the previous evening, watches from the balcony as England rack up **444** in their first innings.
FACING PAGE Andrew Flintoff hooks during his **46** on day two.

for Warne, and for Langer, who had been subjected to largely good-natured banter from the predominantly English-supporting section of the stand behind him. Ridiculed for slipping to concede a four, he caught Flintoff and then, later, produced a wonderful chase to deny Steve Harmison a boundary to third man, flipping the ball behind his back to Brad Hodge. Gillespie produced a rare good ball to skittle Geraint Jones, and Warne cleaned up the tail by removing Giles and Simon Jones for ducks, the former caught by Hayden at slip and the latter bowled.

Although conceding 444 runs was hardly something to be delighted about, and it was enough in England's account to avoid defeat, Australia would have been pleased to capture the last five English wickets for just 103 runs. Lee and Warne shared the honours, both taking four wickets apiece. McGrath, bowling clearly under par, had no wickets to his name. Gillespie, now drinking at the last chance saloon, had been given the nod over the unfortunate Kasprowicz. He replied with first innings figures of 1–114 off just 19 overs. England, for their part, would have liked a total nearer or beyond 500. That said, they would have settled for 444 on Thursday morning, and would be relieved to see

Vaughan, Bell and Geraint Jones all score runs after two pretty fruitless previous Tests.

When Australia began their reply Old Trafford expected wickets from one of the opening bowlers, Harmison or Hoggard. When this did not happen, Vaughan summoned Flintoff, but Justin Langer and Matthew Hayden appeared ominously comfortable as they raced to a fifty partnership.

The man who put a stop to it was the same man who had emerged from his post-Lord's depression to make such an impact at the Edgbaston Test. Ashley Giles, resplendent in his shades, removed both openers, before later delivering the ball of the day to end Damien Martyn's resistance. He had much to thank Ian Bell for, though, for his first wicket. The ball flew to the right of Bell via an inside edge and a rebound off the Langer pads, but the fielder, acting on pure instinct, somehow clasped it brilliantly at short leg. It was a catch that vied with Damien Martyn's diving effort in the deep to dismiss Pietersen at Lord's as the catch of the series to date. Hayden followed shortly after, pinned in front of his stumps by Giles, and when Simon Jones forced Ponting to lob the ball tamely into the grateful hands of Bell again, this time at point, Australia were 82–3. England's 444 looked a long way off on a perfectly suitable pitch for batting. Like that of just about everyone else in the Australian batting line-up, Ponting's form had deserted him. Jones had struck once more with a ball that stopped on Ponting, forcing the airborne drive to Bell. He had made just seven.

Then came a moment Giles is unlikely to forget in a hurry. Martyn was, once more, looking reasonably set, having advanced to 20. He, like his colleagues in the Australian team, had changed their view of Giles from one of nonchalance to respect, but they still failed to believe he could turn the ball much. That was until they witnessed Martyn's dismissal. Twelve years previously, Shane Warne had produced his 'wonder ball' to bowl Mike Gatting, a delivery talked about today as the best ball in Test cricket ever. Giles's ball was not quite in that class, but it was close. Bowling from the same Brian Statham End as Warne did back in 1993, Giles produced a slow left-arm delivery that pitched outside the leg stump, turned viciously and bounced before brushing the outside of the off stump just enough to dislodge a bail. Martyn had taken a huge stride out to cover his wicket with his pads, and appeared completely bemused at ending up bowled. Australia had been reduced to 133–5. It was, by common consent, the finest ball of Giles's colourful career. Flintoff followed this up shortly afterwards by bowling Simon Katich, the Australian number five misreading an inswinger and leaving a ball that knocked his off stump over.

Nobody at this point could complain about England's performance. They had rattled up a first innings score that virtually guaranteed avoidance of defeat, and now had Australia lurching towards the ignominy of being asked to follow on. If there is an occasional criticism of this England team, however, it is the inability still on occasions to hammer home their advantage. The Australian dog was lying down, but England failed to kick it.

In some respects they got lucky. They dropped Adam Gilchrist twice, which normally serves as an invitation to the destructive batsman to pulverise the opposition. During a fiery spell from home boy Flintoff, Gilchrist prodded to point when on 12. Bell, who had already caught both Langer and Ponting, threw himself to his left, managed to get both hands to the ball but failed to hold on to the chance. It was a difficult one, but a chance, nonetheless, for England to press home their advantage. Three balls later England, and Pietersen, did it again. Flintoff was bowling a fine over. Even Gilchrist was noticeably ruffled by the England bowler's pace and bounce. Pushing uneasily forward, Gilchrist directed the ball low and into the path of Pietersen at cover point. Pietersen, who had caught three Australian batsmen in the Twenty20 international, had since managed to drop three chances at Lord's. Old Trafford made it four when he fumbled Gilchrist's offering down by his ankles.

Fortunately for England Gilchrist failed to make them suffer. Simon Jones managed to find the edge of the Australian wicket-keeper's bat when he was on 30, having Gilchrist caught behind by his opposite number, Geraint Jones. Once again Simon Jones had enhanced his image as a critical impact player. After a useful sixth-wicket partnership of 53 between Gilchrist and Warne, Australia were 182–6. This became 197–7 when Clarke spooned a Simon Jones delivery straight to Flintoff at mid-off. Clarke had spent virtually the whole two days cooped up in his hotel room lying on his damaged back. Such were Australia's concerns, however, as wickets continued to tumble, that the management team summoned Clarke back to Old Trafford. He arrived at the ground in a tracksuit 20 minutes before he walked out of the pavilion, down the steps, and on to the pitch.

Hampered clearly by his back, Clarke put up only minimal resistance before holing out to Flintoff. Warne, finishing on an unbeaten 45, and Jason Gillespie saw off the remaining few overs to leave their side on a precarious 210–7 at stumps. Australia had lost six wickets in a disastrous final session of play after tea.

Flintoff, on his home ground, had an average day for him. Average, that is, if you call taking the wicket of Katich and catching Clarke average. And average only compared to the superhero exploits of Edgbaston. Still, there was no better place for the all-rounder to celebrate winning his fiftieth Test cap than at the home of Lancashire CCC.

'It's a ground special to my heart,' Flintoff reiterated. 'I love playing here. I know everyone from the gateman to the dressing room attendant. I have the same peg in the dressing room for this Test. My corner of the

BELOW Skipper Michael Vaughan sets his field in Australia's first innings. FACING PAGE Australian number four Damien Martyn finds himself on the wrong end of a short one.

dressing room is usually a disgrace, it has to be said, particularly my locker. I've got everything from pads to helmets, caps and blazers there. But it's home.'

Giles was in a much happier frame of mind now than after the Lord's defeat. 'We held our composure and the guys bowled well,' he said. 'We're in a good position and have a chance to finish them off quickly in the morning, although Shane Warne is batting well. I wouldn't say we've got them on the run. There's a long way to go in the series but we have played good, aggressive cricket in the last two matches. Simon Jones bowled beautifully today and got wickets at the right times. He used his reverse swing well and deserved his wickets. As for me, I've done quite well in the past two weeks by concentrating on my cricket. It's worked out nicely.' As for the ball that deceived Martyn so much, Giles called it one of his best. 'Getting Brian Lara out at Lord's last summer was fantastic and I got Chris Cairns out with a similar one at Trent Bridge. But it's certainly up there. I don't bowl those deliveries every day.'

While Flintoff was painting his blissful picture of home, sweet home, and Giles was enjoying talking about the positives of his cricket, John Buchanan was trying to come to terms with another day in the Test series in which his side had come off decidedly second best. The Australian coach had already been regretting his words earlier in the series in which he blasted England's fielding and suggested that few of England's batsmen would cause Australia many problems. After the second day's play had ended he likened Giles and Simon Jones to rabbits emerging from a magician's hat. 'It was bloody terrible,' he said. 'Everyone talks about Flintoff and Harmison, but then these two rabbits come in and do that. Giles troubled the left-handers throughout the day and Jones seems to have the knack of picking up wickets almost every time he is brought on. England are taking wickets at key times and that means the next player is not as free to play in the way he'd like. But as we saw at Edgbaston, there is quite a lot of fight in this Australian team and we have three days to turn it round.'

For Jones, one of the more interesting characters in the England team, all the miseries of his previous Ashes experience were being erased. A common feature in the gossip columns, where he is forever linked with various models and other girlfriends, Jones is confident enough in himself and a body which he has pummelled long and hard in the weights room to strip naked and pose for charity in *Cosmopolitan* magazine. Yet as he lay on a Brisbane field three years previously, all this seemed a distant dream.

It was the first morning of the first Ashes Test in Brisbane in November 2002. Jones, then 23 and overwhelmed with excitement at the prospect of taking on the Aussies, attempted a sliding stop on the relaid outfield at The Gabba. He had made his debut for England during the previous summer against India, suffered a rib injury, but fought his way back into the Ashes team. At the time of the accident he had already taken Justin Langer's wicket. As he lay writhing on the ground the Australian supporters sitting closest to him in the stand hurled abuse. One even threw a can of drink at him. The Welshman had torn his anterior cruciate ligaments, the kind of injury that, even just a few years before, would have ended his career there and then. 'I was lying on the ground in so much pain with my right knee twisted and broken that I was ready to punch anyone who tried to touch it,' Jones recalled. 'I was asking myself: Is that it? Is that my career over?'

It was not, although it took a great deal of rehabilitation and inspiration gleaned from the Lance Armstrong autobiography, which tells of the seven-time Tour de France winner's successful battle against cancer and his triumphant return to the saddle. Jones endured an operation and then a knee brace for six weeks. The physiotherapy that followed made him weep with pain. As he improved, so he worked on his bowling action with former Australian wicket-keeper Rod Marsh and England's specialist bowling coach, Troy Cooley, at the National Academy. In March 2004, he claimed the wicket of Brian Lara after just 13 balls back in Test cricket. 'Let me tell you, it was an extremely emotional moment for me,' Jones admitted. Although he went on to achieve his first Test five-wicket haul in the Caribbean, uncertain form meant that until this Ashes series, Jones was still seen as the fourth pace option at best, behind Harmison, Hoggard and Flintoff. His father, Jeff Jones, was also a fast bowler for Glamorgan and England. Now Jones junior was cementing his place in this ever-improving England side.

He, and the rest of England, would be frustrated by the following day's play. Saturday was the day, with a little slice of luck, that England would take the final three wickets of the Australian first innings and hopefully a good number of wickets in the second innings, too, having asked the visitors to bat again. The plan was in tatters, though, thanks to two components English cricket has had no answer to over the years: rain and Shane Warne.

Actually, there was another element. More missed chances. In the solitary hour's play that the inclement weather allowed on the Saturday, England missed a further three, with the beleaguered Geraint Jones responsible for two of them behind the stumps.

Play fell into two short stints in the afternoon. For much of the rest of the day the England players were trying, and failing, to come up with an answer to what Andrew Strauss referred to as 'demon spinners' from seamer Matthew Hoggard at indoor cricket in the

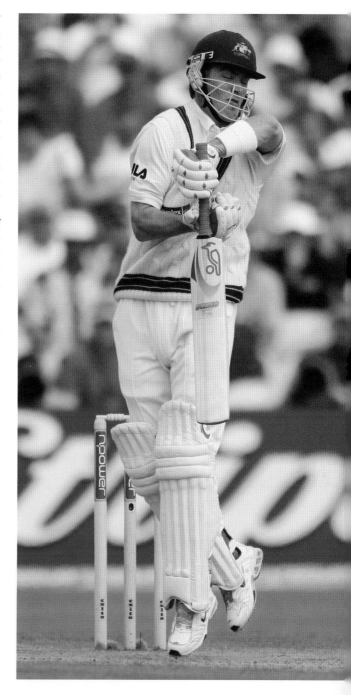

English dressing room. In the morning Australia had added a further four runs to their total without facing a ball. Umpire Steve Bucknor had failed to signal four byes off a Simon Jones no-ball on the Friday night. The mistake was rectified the following morning. Between lunch and tea the rain stopped long enough for Australia, or rather Warne, to save the follow-on by

adding 31 runs to their overnight total. After tea a further six overs were possible. Australia finished the disappointing day on 264–7, 20 runs past the follow-on target of 244. Of those 54 runs, Gillespie added three to his overnight score while a belligerent Warne smacked 31 to end the day on 78 not out. Having captured his 600th wicket on the first day at Old Trafford, Warne was now making plans to score his maiden Test hundred in the same match. Already he had made his highest Test score against England and, once again, he had shown some of his batting betters in the Australian team how to resist a rampant England. Not content with bowling England out as the leading wicket-taker in the series, he was also becoming one of the leading run-scorers for Australia.

His short innings in between the showers was hardly error-free. Off consecutive balls from Giles, Warne offered first a fierce return catch to the bowler, and then a fairly regulation stumping to Jones. The ball did bounce above the stumps, but other than that there was no reason why Jones should not have whipped off the bails. Warne was on 55 at the time. Thirteen runs later,

he was reprieved for a second time when he edged an especially quick delivery from Flintoff straight to the wicket-keeper. Inexplicably, the chance was put down.

The magnifying glass was now firmly pointed towards Geraint Jones. He had endured some stick already in this series for his wicket-keeping gaffes and failure to produce a big score with the bat. Wicket-keepers are not normally under pressure to supply a pile of runs. Wicket-keepers picked ahead of others because of their batting ability are, though. In the five Tests against South Africa during the winter, he had missed four catches, and then another two at Lord's against Australia. He had character, though. In abundance. Born in Papua New Guinea and raised in Toowoomba, a country town in Queensland, and then Brisbane in Australia, he has a father from Blaenau Ffestiniog whose

FACING PAGE Simon Jones has Michael Clarke caught by Andrew Flintoff for seven, one of the Welshman's six wickets in Australia's first innings. BELOW A WG Grace lookalike features in a Channel 4 promo during the Old Trafford Test.

first language is Welsh. He qualified for England under the four-year residency regulation. Jones was hardened to life's knocks when he lost his mother to cancer when he was just 12 years of age. After coming to Britain he played local cricket first for Clevedon, near Bristol, earning money by putting up fences and playing as, believe it or not, a fast bowler. He then worked, famously,

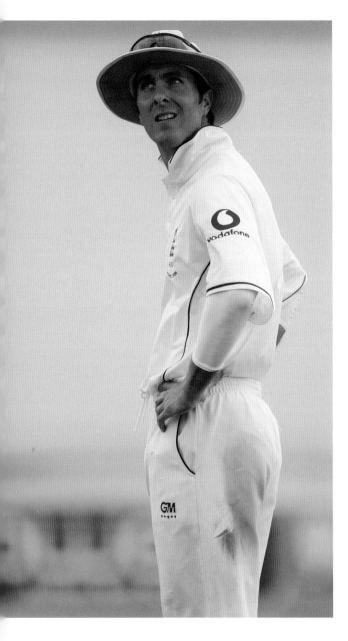

in a chemist's in Abergavenny while playing cricket for a Welsh club. As recently as 2000 Jones was good enough to captain Abergavenny but was only the second-choice 'keeper. He borrowed the chemist's wife's car to attend a trial at Kent that ended his time as a pharmacy assistant and began a new career as a professional cricketer.

The day of his mother's death was shattering. 'She went into hospital that morning without me even knowing she had cancer,' he recalled. 'My mother went in for an operation and died on the operating table. She was cancer-ridden. You can imagine what that's like, as a 12-year-old, to come home to that news. As kids we all had to grow up pretty quickly and I learnt to look after myself. After the funeral I decided to play cricket that afternoon. I guess it was the best release for me.'

When Jones scored his maiden Test match hundred in 2004 against New Zealand his first thoughts were for his parents. 'I just looked up at the sky. I was thinking of my mother, Carol, and my father, Emrys. I called him up later and he'd listened to my whole innings on the Internet. He said that his yell as I reached the century woke up all the neighbours.'

His selection ahead of Chris Read had incensed Rod Marsh, the ECB National Academy coach who was one of the greatest wicket-keepers of all time for Australia. It was just another hurdle for Jones to clear. He was suffering right now from his various fielding blips and lack of runs, but nobody underestimated his ability to come through. 'I'm pretty tough because of what life has thrown at me so far, and it helps at times such as this,' he said. He had the support of the England dressing room, for sure. 'Nobody's questioning Geraint in our dressing room,' was Flintoff's defiant retort to the brickbats being hurled at his friend. And he had the support of the most important man of all. It was coach Duncan Fletcher who replaced Read with Jones, and he was not in any hurry to perform a selection U-turn.

'Adam Gilchrist has dropped two chances in this match and I've seen Mark Boucher [South Africa] and Kumar Sangakkara [Sri Lanka] drop many,' Fletcher insisted. 'Most of the sides these days go for a batsman who can keep wicket and if you go for that policy you have to expect a couple of chances to go begging from time to time.' As for the day's cricket, or lack of it, Fletcher was understandably disappointed. 'We thought we had built up a nice momentum on Friday evening, so to sit around all day has been frustrating. It was not easy to go out there and switch on.'

Failing to force Australia to follow on was something of an irrelevancy, however. Would England really have fancied chasing a target of 200 in the fourth innings on the final day of the Test with Shane Warne bowling into the rough? The truth was that England never had any plans to enforce the follow-on. 'We weren't sure how this

wicket is going to pan out,' Fletcher confirmed. 'It's still very important to have as many runs as we can so that then you don't have to bat for as long.'

The forecast was much better for the Sunday, but England would have to move fast. Not only did they need to knock off Australia's last three remaining wickets before lunch – and this meant probably preventing Warne from completing his hundred – but also to score enough runs in the remainder of the day to set Australia too steep a target to attain, and provide enough time for the English bowlers to claim ten Australian wickets. The odds were for Australia to achieve the draw, followed by an English win.

Nothing particularly changed these odds, either, after England took just 15 overs to wrap up the

Australian first innings. Simon Jones doubled his wicket tally from three to six in the process, trapping Gillespie leg before for a stubborn 26, having the dangerous Lee caught in the slips by Trescothick for 1, and getting Warne, finally, caught by Giles for 90. The look of anguish on Warne's face said it all. He knew that this was a golden opportunity to finally make that maiden Test match century. Few in the Manchester crowd would have begrudged him this. Jones lived up to his impact billing yet again, bouncing Warne out with just his second delivery of the day after attempts from previous bowlers had fallen flat. Warne could not have hit the ball more firmly, nor found Giles at deep square leg more directly. Lee fell to the kind of bowling he had been dishing out for much of this series, a bouncer that put him firmly on the back foot, followed by a pitched-up outswinger that did the rest.

Jones finished with Test best figures of 6-53 as Australia were bowled out for 302. They were the best figures, in fact, by an Englishman against Australia at Old Trafford since Jim Laker took all ten wickets in the 'Laker Test' of 1956. England held a lead of 142 runs which they needed to increase at a rapid rate of knots.

Sunday was the day that Andrew Strauss, to borrow one of coach Fletcher's favourite sayings, came to the party. It was not as though he had suffered a poor series up to this point. By his high standards, however, and

judging purely on the amazing start he had made to Test cricket the previous summer and then during the winter tour to South Africa, Strauss had not done himself justice in this Ashes series.

Had his honeymoon period ended? Apparently not. First, though, came the usual array of strokes from

Trescothick, who once again was a man in a hurry. Of the opening partnership of 64, the Somerset player scored 41 before being bowled by McGrath. Trescothick had

BELOW Sunshine, and a rainbow, after the rain at Old Trafford. Only 13 overs' play was possible on Saturday, the third day.

LEFT AND BELOW LEFT Australia's frontline pace bowlers, Brett Lee and Glenn McGrath, both struggling for fitness coming into the match, feel the strain as they try to stem the flow of England runs on Sunday afternoon. FACING PAGE Ian Bell climbs into a Shane Warne delivery. With two half-centuries in this Test, Bell began to look the part against the world champions.

passed 5000 runs in the process, in his sixty-fourth Test match. Only Jack Hobbs, Walter Hammond, Len Hutton and Ken Barrington had reached that milestone in fewer matches, and that, in anyone's language, is an impressive list of cricketing talent.

Vaughan came and went quickly. In trying to rush the innings along he was caught by substitute fielder Brad Hodge off Lee's bowling for 14. Before then he had been lucky to survive, when Hodge, fielding at mid-off, refused to claim a low catch that was marginal enough for the umpires to debate. It was another example of sportsmanship amid the searing heat of this Ashes series. Shortly afterwards Hodge caught the same batsman, his fair play vindicated in the best possible way. In came Bell for an invaluable partnership with Strauss worth 127 runs. The opening batsman had been targeted by the Australian attack from the very first day of this Ashes series. Warne, in particular, had made it public, via his newspaper column, that he was out to get a man who had earned mass respect from the world of Test cricket for the weight of runs he had scored so early in his career. The century that Strauss hit against Australia at Old Trafford in the second innings was not only vital to England's chances of winning the match but was also carved out in difficult circumstances. His form coming into this game had been patchy. He, alone of the top six batsmen, had failed to register a half-century in this series. Before he had even scored, Strauss had taken a cut on the left ear from a vicious Lee bouncer. Lee, ironically, is a former grade cricket team-mate of Strauss's in Sydney. Then, having scored just one run, Strauss edged the same bowler straight between Warne and Ponting in the slips. Warne had taunted Strauss in his column by stating that the England opener had no plan against him. It was ironic, therefore, that in this second innings Warne bowled down 25 overs without claiming any English wicket, let alone Strauss's.

The morning had begun with rumours abounding that Warne and Ponting had engaged in a huge row after Edgbaston, with Warne finding his captain's decision to ask England to bat first reprehensible. The allegations were vehemently denied by the Australian camp, but the Warne–Ponting axis was looking decidedly frosty after both had watched Strauss's edge fly between them.

Strauss went on to score 106 before being caught by Martyn off McGrath. The innings included nine fours and two sixes, including one off Lee in response to the

ear-splitting bouncer earlier in the day. Removing his helmet and raising his bat to receive the plaudits at making his ton, Strauss revealed a bloodied dressing clasped to his left ear, a mark of the character shown by a man who, by scoring his sixth Test century, had rediscovered his form. Understanding this, both Warne and Lee made a point of shaking the opener's hand.

'It's been frustrating in the first couple of Tests, getting in and then getting out, so it was personally satisfying to get through that and reach three figures,' Strauss said afterwards. 'It was hard to begin with but, given the situation of the game batting got a lot easier. Against a side like Australia you've got to be satisfied with a hundred.'

As significant for England was a second, and this time more fluent, half-century from Bell. The successes of Pietersen and now Bell ended any arguments about Graham Thorpe's omission from the Test team. Bell was now looking the part against the very best. If his first innings 59 was all about patience, his second innings 65 was more about flair. The highlight was a straight six off McGrath, a shot that would have done him the power of good. McGrath got his man, with help from a Simon Katich catch, but this was the innings in which Bell proved that he could score runs at the highest international level, and not only against the lesser teams in world cricket.

By this stage Pietersen had fallen first ball to a low McGrath full toss fired towards his legs. Pietersen would have been looking to rush the score along but instead found himself almost falling over from the impact of the ball slamming against his pads. McGrath bowled Flintoff

BELOW Andrew Strauss reverse-sweeps during his maiden Ashes century, a 158-ball 106 as England sought quick second innings runs. FACING PAGE High spirits among the Old Trafford crowd as England's golden summer of Ashes resurgence continues.

soon afterwards for four to finish with the surprising figures of 5–115 off 20.5 overs. 'Not one of my best five-fors,' he conceded later. 'But I'll take it, just the same.' Despite his haul it was clear that McGrath had been fast-tracked back into the team when not fully fit. It was a testament to him that he could still cause damage, but Australia's action was indicative of their growing anxiety.

Ordinarily, to lose Pietersen and Flintoff for four runs between them would have represented a disaster for England, but by then the job was almost done. It was left to Geraint Jones to redeem his first innings errors behind the stumps slightly by smacking an unbeaten 27 off just 12 balls, with two fours and a couple of huge, cross-batted sixes off McGrath into the deep mid-wicket seating. McGrath's final three balls went for 16 runs alone. It was nothing more than a cameo, but it explained why Jones continued to get the selection nod over his rivals. With Jones in the side and scoring runs, it allowed England to field five key bowlers and bat Flintoff at number six. With 20 wickets required to win a Test match, this was a vital element in England's run of five Test series wins coming into the Ashes. The misery Jason Gillespie had experienced virtually throughout

this tour was complete. In England's second innings he was permitted just four overs, which went for 23 runs. As he was then exiled to the nether regions of the outfield, Gillespie knew his last chance to redeem himself had come and gone.

England declared on 280–6 scored off just 61.5 overs. Once again the crowd had been delighted by

scoring more in keeping with a limited overs game than a Test match. This was achieved despite Australia's thinly disguised attempts at time-wasting. Eventually umpire Bucknor, who is renowned for the amount of time it takes for him to make a decision, issued an official warning against them. England set Australia an unlikely 423 runs to win. To put this into perspective, the highest ever fourth innings total to win a Test match in the history of the game was the 418–7 the West Indies had produced to beat Australia a couple of years before in Antigua. The largest fourth innings winning score Australia had ever produced was the 404–3 against England at Headingley in 1948. Now they would have to break a world record, let alone their own, to win the Third Test.

They had one ray of hope. The Australian opening partnership of Langer and Hayden survived a tricky 30-minute end-of-day spell in the Manchester gloom on the

They were not so inclined to produce an innings to save a match. They knew how to win games. Did they know how to save them? Strauss was not so sure. 'There are going to be enough balls to be misbehaving to take ten wickets,' he predicted. The ever-confident McGrath saw it another way. 'We only need to score at four runs an over to win,' he stated. The old man was refusing to go down without a fight.

After the last-day histrionics at Edgbaston, interest in this final day's play was unprecedented, no doubt

Sunday evening to finish on 24 without loss. The requirement was now a further 399 runs in a maximum of 98 overs. There was nothing to reveal Australia's intentions in that final half-hour on Sunday. Langer and Hayden were intent simply on survival against a twin spin attack of Giles and Vaughan, the latter opting to bring himself on instead of a quick bowler to prevent Australia from claiming bad light.

The challenge that lay ahead was an interesting one. Australia were well versed in forcing other teams to cave in under the unbearable pressure placed upon them.

encouraged by the generous last-day admission fee of just £10 for adults and half that figure for children. Queues began forming outside the Old Trafford gates at six in the morning. Some people had even camped outside overnight as if they were attempting to gain a Centre Court seat at Wimbledon for the men's final. Twenty thousand managed to cram into the ground. An estimated 20,000 more were turned away at the gates. The nation had quite clearly contracted Ashes fever.

The Third Test will be remembered for a number of reasons, most notably the way in which it ended in yet more high drama. But it was also the game when both captains, under pressure because of their own poor form with the bat, stood up and came to the mark. Vaughan's 166 in England's first innings was final proof of the old sporting adage, that form is temporary whereas class is permanent. He had never doubted himself, even when most around him did.

Ponting's 156 in Australia's second innings, achieved on the final, gripping day at Old Trafford, was possibly even more impressive. The Australian captain was facing defeat and a 2–1 deficit with two to play in the series. No Australian had lost the Ashes for 16 years. His country had grown used to previous captains Allan Border, Mark Taylor and Steve Waugh retaining the old urn. Was Ponting going to return to Australia as the captain who lost the Ashes?

Not, it seemed, without a great deal of resistance, and an even greater show of character that was called upon from the eighth ball of the day. One ball earlier Matthew Hoggard had induced a slight edge from Langer to Geraint Jones. After his 82 in the first innings at Edgbaston, Langer had proved that he was the most stubborn batsman in the Australian line-up. It was the perfect start for England.

More success could have followed had England set a more attacking field. Hayden twice edged through a gaping hole where a third slip would have gratefully received the catch before Vaughan plugged the gap. In the end Flintoff accounted for Hayden by clean bowling him for 36, by which stage Australia had advanced to 96. Damien Martyn was unlucky to be given out leg before to Harmison by umpire Bucknor, who was having an incident-packed game. Replays revealed that the batsman had clearly got a thick edge on to his pad. His thunderous face as he returned to the pavilion told its own story. Flintoff, steaming in now like an express train, then removed Katich once more, caught by Giles, and then Gilchrist, for the third time in the series, for just four. For a while Michael Clarke, in tandem with Ponting, halted England's progress. Revealing commendable control, the young batsman progressed to 39 before becoming the victim of another inspired piece of bowling from Simon Jones. The Welshman set Clarke up expertly with a series of reverse swingers, enough to encourage him to leave his off stump exposed sufficiently for Jones to find the target. When Gillespie fell leg before to Hoggard, thus completing another Test match he would care to forget, Australia were stumbling on 264–7.

FACING PAGE Cricket is king once again. Fans wait for Old Trafford's gates to open on the morning of the final day. ABOVE RIGHT Andrew Flintoff makes a suggestion. RIGHT Adam Gilchrist gains his ground safely as Australia fight to save the game.

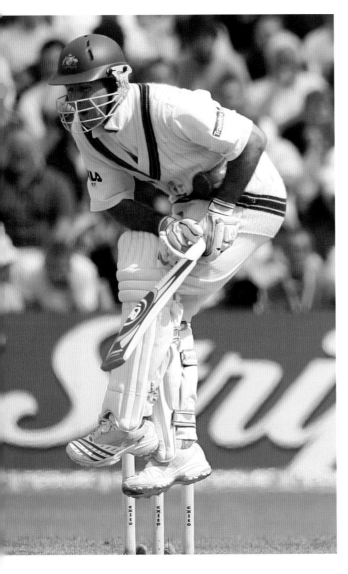

Then, as in the previous Test, the Australian tail wagged. Warne, continuing his consistently good form with the bat, added 34 runs to his first innings score of 90 before Flintoff induced an edge indirectly to Geraint Jones behind the stumps. Jones, continuing his rollercoaster Ashes series, pulled off a brilliant reflex catch after the ball had bounced off Strauss at second slip. Warne should have departed seven overs earlier when he clipped Simon Jones to mid-wicket, where Kevin Pietersen dropped his fifth catch of the series. Not one chance had stuck. For all Pietersen's brilliance with the bat, his increasing number of dropped catches was becoming expensive. Dropping Clarke at Lord's went a long way to ensuring Australia set too big a target for England to reach. Spilling his friend Warne at Old Trafford cost England seven overs. Warne and Ponting had put on 76 for the eighth wicket, with absolutely no evidence of any hostility between them. The potential enormity of Warne's wicket was not lost on Flintoff. Momentarily he lost his sanity on seeing Warne safely held by Jones behind. Flintoff first launched into a break-dance routine, falling on to the pitch and then back-flipping up again, before slinging Hoggard over his shoulder like a rag doll.

Amid such euphoric celebrations, Ponting remained. He had long passed his century and had dug in for the day. As foolish as he looked after predicting a 5–0 whitewash for Australia after the First Test win at Lord's, and as stupid as his Second Test decision to ask England to bat first at Edgbaston now appeared, it was clear that the man was not lacking in gumption. He had asked his

LEFT Spirit of Australia. Ricky Ponting is struck by a lifter from Flintoff during his captain's 156 that eventually kept England at bay. BELOW Poor Kevin Pietersen puts Shane Warne down as England strive for the vital breakthrough. RIGHT Flintoff strikes. Warne is caught by Jones the Gloves via Strauss at slip for 34.

batsmen before the match to stop squandering their good starts and convert them into big scores. Now he was leading by example. He batted for close to seven long hours and faced 275 balls for his 156. While his fellow batsmen once more failed to deliver, it was the captain, and the captain alone, who stood above the parapet under intense fire. For a while the unlikely prospect of Australia actually winning this Test match was alive. When he finally fell, caught off the glove down the leg side by the vastly improved Geraint Jones off a Harmison delivery that climbed suddenly, Australia still needed to survive four final overs, with just their last pairing left. Ponting departed from the fray looking like a man who had just lost a Test match, rather than someone whose brilliant 411-minute innings had probably saved one.

Or had it? It was down to Brett Lee, no mug with the bat, and Glenn McGrath to save the day. McGrath's batting had improved during this series, but England sensed blood. Lee, meanwhile, was lucky to still be there. Just a couple of overs before the Ponting dismissal, England's substitute fielder, Stephen Peters, had missed the stumps by an inch with a shy that would have left Lee well out of his crease.

Now just 24 balls remained. The win had long gone for Australia. It was evens between a draw and an English win. Lee shepherded McGrath as much as possible, farming the strike and easing singles as late in the over as he could. But come the start of the final over of the match, McGrath, whose comeback from injury to play in this Test was of near Lazarus proportions, was on strike to Steve Harmison.

ABOVE Flintoff's break-dance routine celebrating the wicket of Warne culminates in a back-flip. FACING PAGE The whole of England goes up as Ponting gloves a leg-side ball from Harmison to Geraint Jones.

It is reasonable to say that the result of this Test was then decided by a centimetre. That was the difference between Harmison's ball striking McGrath's off stump and missing it in that final over. English hands shot to English heads, both out on the field and in the packed stands of Old Trafford, at 6.30 pm on the fifth day of the Third Test. An old-fashioned slip cordon of seven fielders surrounded McGrath, who, in the face of the kind of treatment he has meted out so many times before, came through the ordeal, even taking a single. Harmison's final ball of the match slipped harmlessly down the leg side and Australia had survived to draw.

England had won just about every session of the match and, but for the rain on Saturday, would most certainly have been 2–1 up in the Ashes. As it was, Australia had hung in there and would start the Fourth Test still, and miraculously, on level terms.

While McGrath remained relatively impassive, no doubt aware that his much-vaunted team had escaped another defeat by the narrowest of margins, both Lee and his watching team-mates on the Australian balcony went berserk with relief. The Australian players had become so nervous watching yet another nail-biting end to a Test that they remained rooted to their seats until the final ball had passed. Any player who attempted to move was immediately ordered to stay put for good luck.

Lee had ended the previous Test match slumped in despair. After his brave but ultimately unsuccessful resistance at Edgbaston with an unbeaten 43, this time he had come through still smiling at the end after a rearguard lasting nine overs. 'They say things come in threes and I pray that doesn't happen again because it's so nerve-wracking,' he confessed later in the evening. 'The difference between today and Edgbaston was that there I was talking a lot with Kasper [Kasprowicz] to keep us pumped up. Today Glenn [McGrath] didn't want to know. He just kept ignoring me and walking away.'

It might have made the difference if Lee had not recovered from the knee infection that saw him leave a Birmingham hospital 24 hours before the start of the Third Test after receiving antibiotics through a drip. 'It wasn't the best preparation for a Test to have a two-hour drive up here, train and then play the next day, but I bowled 40 overs and it feels like I haven't bowled a ball.'

His heroic captain, Ponting, was honest enough to admit that his side had been let off the hook. 'We have been outplayed for four days so we just had to dig deep today and we did just that,' he said. 'We've come away with a draw after being outplayed so there's a good mood in the changing room right now. It doesn't feel like a win but it feels like we've worked very hard and snuck away with a draw. It was a long, hard and tough day of Test cricket.' As for his match-saving innings of 156, Ponting was a proud man. 'It was one of my best knocks,' he considered. 'I tried to play instinctively and it is satisfying to put your hand up when it matters as a batsman and leader.'

His English counterpart, Vaughan, was not too disheartened by the outcome, despite so nearly winning

consecutive Ashes Tests. 'It was another great game and it had everything,' he pointed out. 'Hundreds, sixes, a 600th wicket, a close finish, the lot. This series has been fantastic to play in and it sounds like it's been fantastic to watch, too. It has been played in a great spirit and there are a lot of players with great ability in the two sides. It's great that cricket is getting a lot of coverage and a lot of people are talking about it again.'

Although Australia were the team celebrating as the light faded in Manchester, Vaughan insisted that they had not gained the psychological advantage. 'It was not a psychological victory for Australia,' he argued. 'We

were one wicket away from being 2–1 up in the series and I am extremely proud of how the team have responded to losing the opening Test. I don't think the fact that they have hung on for a draw will matter one iota come Trent Bridge in nine days' time. We can take a huge amount out of this game. We have dominated for four days against the number one team in the world. Three weeks ago we were being completely written off. Now we are at 1–1 in the series and more than matching Australia.'

Had England blown a golden chance to take the lead? The answer was probably yes, although there was little more that they could have done, save for the

BELOW **Well done, partner. Brett Lee and Glenn McGrath hold out for the draw at Old Trafford, leaving the series poised at 1–1. Attention now switched to Trent Bridge, and the Fourth Test.**

catches that went begging. Would Australia, reprieved, strike back in the Fourth Test to win and retain the Ashes? All they needed to do, after all, was draw the series to keep the urn. A draw may not have been in their minds after Lord's, but after defeat at Edgbaston and this huge scare at Old Trafford they realised that one win in the next two Test matches, or no more defeats, would be enough to accomplish their mission.

The Ashes series had just produced two incredible matches. The difference between the two sides was the thickness of a cigarette paper. Edgbaston and Old Trafford had just witnessed epics.

In nine days' time the Fourth Test would begin at Trent Bridge. Amazingly, a third epic in a row would commence, and a nation's fingernails would be chewed down to the bone.

ENGLAND V AUSTRALIA, 3rd Test, Old Trafford
11, 12, 13, 14, 15 AUGUST 2005

TOSS: England
UMPIRES: BF Bowden (NZ) and SA Bucknor (WI)
TV UMPIRE: NJ Llong **FOURTH UMPIRE:** JH Evans
MATCH REFEREE: RS Madugalle (SL)

Close of Play:
- **Day 1:** England 341-5 (Bell 59*)
- **Day 2:** England 444, Australia 214-7 (Warne 45*, Gillespie 4*)
- **Day 3:** Australia 264-7 (Warne 78*, Gillespie 7*)
- **Day 4:** Australia 302, England 280-6 dec, Australia 24-0 (Langer 14*, Hayden 5*)

England 1st innings			R	M	B	4	6
ME Trescothick	c Gilchrist	b Warne	63	196	117	9	0
AJ Strauss	b Lee		6	43	28	0	0
*MP Vaughan	c McGrath	b Katich	166	281	215	20	1
IR Bell	c Gilchrist	b Lee	59	205	155	8	0
KP Pietersen	c sub (Hodge)	b Lee	21	50	28	1	0
MJ Hoggard	b Lee		4	13	10	1	0
A Flintoff	c Langer	b Warne	46	93	67	7	0
+GO Jones	b Gillespie		42	86	51	6	0
AF Giles	c Hayden	b Warne	0	11	6	0	0
SJ Harmison	not out		10	13	11	1	0
SP Jones	b Warne		0	7	4	0	0
Extras	**27**	(b 4, lb 5, w 3, nb 15)					
Total	**444**	(all out, 113.2 overs, 503 minutes)					

FoW: 1-26 (Strauss), **2-163** (Trescothick), **3-290** (Vaughan), **4-333** (Pietersen), **5-341** (Hoggard), **6-346** (Bell), **7-433** (Flintoff), **8-434** (GO Jones), **9-438** (Giles), **10-444** (SP Jones).

Bowling	O	M	R	W	
McGrath	25	6	86	0	(4nb)
Lee	27	6	100	4	(5nb, 2w)
Gillespie	19	2	114	1	(2nb, 1w)
Warne	33.2	5	99	4	(2nb)
Katich	9	1	36	1	

England 2nd innings			R	M	B	4	6
ME Trescothick	b McGrath		41	71	56	6	0
AJ Strauss	c Martyn	b McGrath	106	246	158	9	2
*MP Vaughan	c sub (Hodge)	b Lee	14	45	37	2	0
IR Bell	c Katich	b McGrath	65	165	103	4	1
KP Pietersen	lbw	b McGrath	0	3	1	0	0
A Flintoff	b McGrath		4	20	18	0	0
+GO Jones	not out		27	15	12	2	2
AF Giles	not out		0	4	0	0	0
Extras	**23**	(b 5, lb 3, w 1, nb 14)					
Total	**280**	(6 wickets dec, 61.5 overs, 288 minutes)					

DNB: MJ Hoggard, SJ Harmison, SP Jones.

FoW: 1-64 (Trescothick), **2-97** (Vaughan), **3-224** (Strauss), **4-225** (Pietersen), **5-248** (Flintoff), **6-264** (Bell).

Bowling	O	M	R	W	
McGrath	20.5	1	115	5	(6nb, 1w)
Lee	12	0	60	1	(4nb)
Warne	25	3	74	0	
Gillespie	4	0	23	0	(4nb)

Australia 1st innings			R	M	B	4	6
JL Langer	c Bell	b Giles	31	76	50	4	0
ML Hayden	lbw	b Giles	34	112	71	5	0
*RT Ponting	c Bell	b SP Jones	7	20	12	1	0
DR Martyn	b Giles		20	71	41	2	0
SM Katich	b Flintoff		17	39	28	1	0
+AC Gilchrist	c GO Jones	b SP Jones	30	74	49	4	0
SK Warne	c Giles	b SP Jones	90	183	122	11	1
MJ Clarke	c Flintoff	b SP Jones	7	19	18	0	0
JN Gillespie	lbw	b SP Jones	26	144	111	1	1
B Lee	c Trescothick	b SP Jones	1	17	16	0	0
GD McGrath	not out		1	20	4	0	0
Extras	**38**	(b 8, lb 7, w 8, nb 15)					
Total	**302**	(all out, 84.5 overs, 393 minutes)					

FoW: 1-58 (Langer), **2-73** (Ponting), **3-86** (Hayden), **4-119** (Katich), **5-133** (Martyn), **6-186** (Gilchrist), **7-201** (Clarke), **8-287** (Warne), **9-293** (Lee), **10-302** (Gillespie).

Bowling	O	M	R	W	
Harmison	10	0	47	0	(3nb)
Hoggard	6	2	22	0	
Flintoff	20	1	65	1	(8nb)
SP Jones	17.5	6	53	6	(1nb, 2w)
Giles	31	4	100	3	(1w)

Australia 2nd innings			R	M	B	4	6
JL Langer	c GO Jones	b Hoggard	14	42	41	3	0
ML Hayden	b Flintoff		36	123	91	5	1
*RT Ponting	c GO Jones	b Harmison	156	411	275	16	1
DR Martyn	lbw	b Harmison	19	53	36	3	0
SM Katich	c Giles	b Flintoff	12	30	23	2	0
+AC Gilchrist	c Bell	b Flintoff	4	36	30	0	0
MJ Clarke	b SP Jones		39	73	63	7	0
JN Gillespie	lbw	b Hoggard	0	8	5	0	0
SK Warne	c GO Jones	b Flintoff	34	99	69	5	0
B Lee	not out		18	44	25	4	0
GD McGrath	not out		5	17	9	1	0
Extras	**34**	(b 5, lb 8, w 1, nb 20)					
Total	**371**	(9 wickets, 108 overs, 474 minutes)					

FoW: 1-25 (Langer), **2-96** (Hayden), **3-129** (Martyn), **4-165** (Katich), **5-182** (Gilchrist), **6-263** (Clarke), **7-264** (Gillespie), **8-340** (Warne) **9-354** (Ponting).

Bowling	O	M	R	W	
Harmison	22	4	67	2	(4nb, 1w)
Hoggard	13	0	49	2	(6nb)
Giles	26	4	93	0	
Vaughan	5	0	21	0	
Flintoff	25	6	71	4	(9nb)
SP Jones	17	3	57	1	

RESULT: Match drawn MAN OF THE MATCH: RT Ponting

TRENT BRIDGE

4TH TEST
25 AUGUST–28 AUGUST

FACING PAGE Andrew Flintoff raises his bat in acknowledgement of the applause for his first Ashes hundred. RIGHT Andrew Strauss gets the Flintoff hoist treatment after taking a sensational catch off the all-rounder's bowling to get rid of Adam Gilchrist.

ngland stuck with the 11 men who did them so proud at Edgbaston and so nearly repeated the feat at Old Trafford when they named the team for the Fourth Test at Trent Bridge. It had become their most settled side since, tellingly, they last won an Ashes series back in 1987. 'Our real examination as selectors was after the First Test match,' explained the chairman of selectors, David Graveney. 'We were outplayed and there was a lot of media speculation about whether this was the same old England and were we going to lose 5–0. That was the time when we had to hold our nerve and as a group we decided the squad we selected for that First Test hadn't become bad players overnight. We decided to give them another chance, they've taken that chance and they've played some great cricket as a group over the last two Tests.'

Australia, meanwhile, were facing up to the news that, for a second Test match in four, they could be without Glenn McGrath. This time his ankle was not the problem. The scourge of England pulled out of Australia's net session the day before the first day of the Test with an unspecified problem with his right elbow that was painful enough to have him rushed off to hospital for a scan. McGrath's first spell at Lord's had destroyed England. Absent at Edgbaston, McGrath could only watch his team-mates lose. At Old Trafford he had taken a second five-for in the Ashes series, and then stood resolute with the bat to earn Australia a draw. Now it was looking increasingly likely that he would be missing from Trent Bridge. Matthew Hoggard's pre-Ashes comments questioning whether the Australian old guard could survive such a packed series of Test matches were ridiculed when said. Now they were looking more prescient by the day.

If McGrath failed to make it then Michael Kasprowicz would be recalled. Jason Gillespie, by contrast, knew his series was over. The 22-year-old fast bowler Shaun Tait would be replacing him and making his Test debut. With its low, slinging arm and crumpled follow-through, Tait's action was a throwback to the days

FACING PAGE Australian coach John Buchanan and skipper Ricky Ponting get their heads together during the tour match against Northamptonshire, which preceded the Fourth Test. RIGHT While Australia's pace-bowling problems continued, England's attack remained unchanged, with reverse-swing specialist Simon Jones a key component.

when Jeff Thompson terrorised English batsmen in tandem with Dennis Lillee. Tait was quick, too. And Australia, shaken up by the fire and brimstone thrown down at them by Messrs Harmison, Flintoff and Jones in particular, needed to answer back with some lightning of their own. Tait had been waiting for his chance. 'I've seen things out there I think I can do,' he said of the past three Tests. 'You see the reverse swing and the blokes getting lbw and bowled, and that's probably my whole game. I'd love to get out there and do the same.' And what of the awkward scenario of replacing Gillespie? 'Dizzy and I are great mates and we help each other out all the time so it won't be an issue at all.' Certainly Justin Langer knew all about Tait's pace. The opening batsman was hit agonisingly in the groin during the final net session by a high Tait full toss. Angry words were exchanged. With reserve wicket-keeper Brad Haddin taking a blow on the knee from a reversing London taxi the night before, Australians were falling like ninepins.

Andrew Flintoff, the man who more than any other English cricketer had taken on and beaten Australia, was back in town after a break with family and friends on the French Riviera. He had returned full of vim and vigour. 'The thrilling cricket, the media interest, the crowds. It's all new ground for us,' he said, wide-eyed with excitement. 'There is pressure on us because people now believe we can win the Ashes. We won't let that interfere with the way we've been playing, which is with enjoyment and not the fear of failure. That approach is the main reason for our success over the past two years, so I can't imagine it's going to change now. Our original plan for the series was to compete with Australia, the best side in the world. We didn't do that at Lord's, except for a session or two. But now we've beaten them once, and almost for a second time at Old Trafford, our expectations have gone up as well.'

Had, in his opinion, Australia underperformed? 'It's not so much a case of Australia showing themselves to be vulnerable, more us showing how much we've improved. We've taken confidence from two years of beating everyone and now the final challenge is Australia. We've gone into this backing our ability rather than worrying about theirs. Winning at Edgbaston was massive but even after Lord's we realised that we could bowl them out. With runs behind us, we knew we could get them under pressure, which is exactly what we've done since and hope to do again over the next few days.'

Michael Vaughan remained at his confident, but still level, best on the eve of the Fourth Test. News of Tait's inclusion in the opposing side did not appear to concern him too much. 'We'll need to be wary of him early on but he's bound to be nervous on his debut,' Vaughan said. 'We hear Tait's quick, but the boys have played Brett Lee pretty well. He's probably the quickest in the world right now, so we're not worried about the pace factor.'

As for his team's chances, Vaughan could only go on what had already taken place in this incredible Ashes series. 'We've started very, very well in the last two games and managed to put Australia under pressure early,' he added. 'The team that starts best will have an advantage and that has been proved in this series. Australia are like any team in the world if you get on top of them, but it's a matter of trying to make the advantage count. In the last two games we've had we've managed to keep our concentration levels over a period of time and that's the way to beat good teams.'

Ponting could not be faulted for his honesty. The post-Lord's arrogance had been replaced by a large dose of reality. 'It's been very rare that we've been well and truly outplayed for the majority of two matches in a row and found ourselves under pressure for long periods,' Australia's captain admitted. 'We're basically suffering from what normally other teams face against us. It's almost as if we've become these opposition teams, and England have become Australia.' It was a telling analogy.

At the end of day one, for just about the only first day in the series so far, there was relative parity. It was a punctured day of stops and starts after rain allowed just 60 overs to be bowled. In that time England, who won the toss yet again, elected to bat and ended the day on 229–4. It was a decent total given the lack of time at their disposal, but after being 105 without loss and then 137–1 they would have been marginally disappointed. The dominant start designed to place Australia immediately under the cosh had failed to materialise, despite the first morning withdrawal of McGrath with an inflamed elbow.

That England would fail to reach that sought-after position of early superiority seemed unlikely after the

customary good start they made. Under unexpected clear, blue skies and facing an Australian side lacking their chief pace destroyer, and showing a propensity for no-balls, Trescothick and Strauss made hay. The no-ball situation had gone beyond a joke for Australia. On the Thursday they delivered 22 of them, 18 before lunch. For the third time in successive Tests an English batsman was out to a no-ball, this time Trescothick being bowled by Lee after the fast bowler had overstepped the mark.

In a pre-lunch scoring spree that saw England hit 129 runs from just 29 overs, the only casualty was Strauss, and that was down to ill-luck on his part. Having enjoyed a 105-run opening partnership with Trescothick, Strauss was happy to let his partner be the boisterous one. With his second innings century at Old Trafford safely tucked away in his pocket, Strauss was confident enough to ease himself along to 35, when an attempted sweep off Warne rebounded from his foot into the waiting hands of Hayden at slip. The referral to

television replays and the third umpire sealed Strauss's fate. It was another twist in this unbelievable story.

Unperturbed, in came Vaughan to carry along England's scoring rate. Trescothick passed his half-century and was suggesting that, at last, and after a 90 and a 63 in the previous two Tests, he was about to hit his first Ashes century. Shaun Tait begged to differ. Looking like a seasoned campaigner rather than a young, nervous debutant, he had already gained true pace with his slinging, swinging action when he sent Trescothick's middle stump flying with a late, inswinging ball. Just short of yorker length, it came back late into the left-hander at speed to bowl him through the gate. Trescothick departed for 65, and England found themselves on 137–2. The knock took Trescothick past South Africa's Jacques Kallis to become the highest run-scorer in Tests in 2005 and on to 924 runs, although he had feasted on the gifts continually presented to him by Bangladesh. The 65 he scored also took him past Trevor Bailey's record of 875 runs against Australia without scoring a century, although this was not a record he would have been so proud of. During his innings Trescothick wore a black armband in memory of Stuart Dove, a youngster he met at the Twenty20 international at the Rose Bowl who had just died from cancer.

Of Tait, Trescothick later said, 'He was OK to start with,' adding, 'I had my eye in when he came on first change but he did take a lot of watching closely because the ball does disappear behind him before it slings back out so you have to remain focussed and give yourself a bit of time to see it. It's a different sort of pace to Brett Lee in that it varies with the effort and is a little bit inconsistent whereas Brett is quick all the time.'

Tait, whatever else he may achieve in cricket, will not forget Trescothick's wicket. 'The guys talked to me about the best moments in your first game: the presentation of the baggy green cap and your first wicket. I can tell you that the wicket was the better feeling. I was a little nervous and being uptight meant I didn't let myself go much. I bowled better after that.' Indeed he did.

The score rapidly became 146–3 after Bell, seemingly in a better frame of mind after his two half-centuries at Old Trafford, nicked the ball to Gilchrist off Tait, who knew about Bell's perceived weakness outside the off stump and probed it incessantly until he got his man. Bell lasted just five balls, scoring three runs.

The mini-slump of three wickets falling for 41 runs was halted by Vaughan and Pietersen. By then play had been interrupted twice by prolonged rain breaks and the previously fine batting conditions had been replaced by a moist pitch, a slower outfield and a heavier, danker air.

Vaughan, though, was looking good. Gone were the days earlier in the series when he was struggling to buy a run, or defend his off stump. The world-class batsman had returned. So, too, had his luck. On 30 he was dropped by Hayden at deep gully off Kasprowicz. It had not been a happy tour for Hayden. Along with his one-day contretemps with Simon Jones and his consistent inability to convert useful starts into scores, he had also put down more than his fair share of chances. Dropping Vaughan merely added greater weight to his already burdened shoulders.

When Vaughan reached and passed his half-century, Hayden must have feared the worst. Then came an extraordinary piece of luck for Australia, and an instance, yet again, of the strange quirks of cricket. On 58, Vaughan, instead of crashing the ball off the back foot to the cover boundary, nudged part-time bowler Ponting to Gilchrist. While his Australian counterpart celebrated his good fortune, Vaughan left the field mortified. It was one of the rare occasions where Ponting actually got the better of the England captain. To put the likelihood of this happening into perspective, the last time Ponting had taken a Test wicket was back in the last century. In fact, all four of his Test wickets, which had come in 80 overs, fell before the Millennium. At Trent

Bridge Vaughan had completed the hard work by seeing off the high-velocity bowling of Lee and Tait. Ponting with his dibbly-dobblers, which struggled to reach 70 mph, should have been easy meat. Instead he bowled down six overs for a miserly nine runs, including two maidens and, crucially, the wicket of Vaughan after the England captain fenced at a ball that found a little extra bounce outside the off stump. There were just five overs to go before close of play, enough time for Flintoff to announce himself with two sweetly struck fours.

At the other end remained Pietersen, who had moved, by comparison with his usual rate of knots, slowly on to 33 not out. It had taken him 89 balls. The slogger, not for the first time in this series, had become almost workmanlike, although after his golden duck at Old Trafford it was understandable. On the Nottinghamshire ground where he began his career in England after moving from South Africa disillusioned with the system that he felt gave him little chance of breaking through, Pietersen got lucky, twice. First Kasprowicz dropped a return chance drilled at him by the South African-born number five. In fairness to the fast bowler, the way Pietersen went for the ball suggested that it would come flying back to Kasprowicz at double the speed it had left his hand a split-second earlier. The fact that it looped back instead caught him off guard. Then, on 23, Hayden's shy at the stumps missed when Pietersen was stranded mid-wicket after a mix-up with Vaughan. Besides their century partnership at Edgbaston, the Pietersen–Flintoff dream ticket had not quite exploded into life yet in this Ashes series. The whole of England was hoping it would the following morning, including Marcus Trescothick.

'The morning session will be crucial,' he said. 'If they get going Freddie and KP will score at a good rate and we'll probably add another one hundred before lunch. That would put us well on our way to the 400 mark. But if they get a couple of early wickets we'll be really struggling. I think we've probably just got our noses in front but we have to go well tomorrow to give ourselves a chance.'

Australia's coach, John Buchanan, remained pretty upbeat, too. 'I'm always reminded about Bill Lawry's quote about adding two wickets and then assessing the state of the game,' he said. 'If we did that on a pretty good batting wicket it's evenly poised at the moment.'

Maybe it was, but not by the end of day two of what would become another enthralling encounter at Trent Bridge. By then England had more than doubled their score to be bowled out for 477, and then finished the day in perfect fashion by pinning Australia down to 99–5.

The chief architects of yet another big first innings score from England were not Pietersen and Flintoff, as everyone would have imagined, but Flintoff and Geraint Jones. It seemed as if everything had been set up nicely for Pietersen on a ground he knew so well. He began quickly enough, adding a quick 12 to his overnight score, but was then undone by a full-pitched delivery from Lee, edging to Gilchrist behind for 45. Australia had begun to realise that this was a possible weak area in Pietersen's armour, and this wicket went some way further to proving that theory.

Enter Geraint Jones. He had ended the Old Trafford Test much better than he had started it with the gloves, but still the runs had not been forthcoming. At least until now. Whereas the Pietersen–Flintoff dream ticket had

LEFT Another close shave for Pietersen, who dives to make his ground as a shy passes just wide of the stumps. FACING PAGE Ricky Ponting is on top of the world after inducing Michael Vaughan to nick one to Adam Gilchrist. PAGES 150–151 Trent Bridge, soon to be the scene of one of cricket's great dramas.

was out shortly afterwards, leg before to new boy Tait, hitting across the line, for 102, but by then his work had been completed.

Flintoff's ton turned him, in the eyes of the traditionalist, into a bona fide all-rounder. For the first time in his Test career his batting average, now standing at 33.35, had risen higher than his bowling average of 32.77. Apart from his six – a casual, nonchalant swat off Warne into the new stand – Flintoff was a respecter of every ball. Virtually his only bad shot was the one that proved to be his last, an attempt to force Tait with a heave towards mid-wicket.

His partner in crime was, for the most part, Jones. This was the fourth time that the pair had amassed a three-figure partnership, and the 177 they produced between them this time was the biggest partnership of the whole Ashes series. An odd couple they may be, with one hewn from the north and the other the rather more exotic environment of Papua New Guinea, but their differing styles complemented each other and the pair had an understanding.

It was not probably lost on Jones that he was playing at the Nottinghamshire home of his biggest rival for the England wicket-keeping gloves, Chris Read. Due a big score in this series, Jones duly delivered, playing Warne particularly well by pushing and cutting him through the covers. He had reached 85 with the help of eight fours, and looked poised to complete his first century against Australia, when he instead ballooned the ball up off his bat and then pad to the bowler, Kasprowicz. It was not a simple chance, though. Kasprowicz, for a big man in the throes of his follow-through, did well to dive full-length to his right and grasp the ball inches above the ground. The disappointment Jones would have felt in falling 15 runs short of that ton would be eased by the knowledge that he and Flintoff had all but ensured that the game would not be lost. Even better, he had repaid all the faith the selectors, and coach Fletcher, had shown in him when he faced a torrent of criticism for his earlier Ashes misdemeanours.

With Jones back in the pavilion, the last three English wickets fell for 27 runs, with Warne taking the lot to end up with figures of 4–102. He was trawling in the wickets at an incredible rate of knots now, and disappearing away from his nearest challenger in this series on either side. He pinned Giles leg before for 15 and had Hoggard caught behind for 10, but by far the most comical wicket was his last. In what appeared to be

not yet really got going, the Flintoff–Jones partnership had already proved to be remarkably successful at six and seven in the batting order. When Jones arrived at the crease the score was a worrying 241–5. When Flintoff departed, having hit an impressive 102, the score had raced away to 418–7, and the partnership had produced 177 invaluable runs.

This was rapidly turning into Freddie's Ashes series. After his heroics with both bat and ball at Edgbaston, and another massive contribution at Old Trafford, here he was at Trent Bridge, knocking the stuffing out of Australia with his fifth, and best, Test match century. Best because it was not all about biff and bang from the Flintoff bat. Coupled with the aggression – and that meant 14 fours and a towering six – was patience and maturity as he dragged the game away from Australia just when the opposition were closing in. The only time he looked in trouble was when he was stuck on 99 facing Warne. The master leg-spinner had Flintoff poking and pushing uneasily for the best part of two overs as the full house at Trent Bridge were reduced to a hushed silence. When Flintoff finally dabbed a single out to square leg, the whole ground erupted in a cacophony of noise. He

pure slapstick, Harmison attempted to smack Warne over the mid-wicket boundary for six, ended up falling flat on his back, and watched as Gilchrist stumped him. The dependable Simon Jones added a further unbeaten 15 to his growing tally of runs and increasing average as England ended their innings on 477. So confident a batsman was Jones becoming in the 'no lose' haven of batting last that he lofted Warne over long off for four, then drove him through extra cover for a second boundary off consecutive balls.

If England had scored just two more runs it would have been their biggest total against Australia since they last held the Ashes. Nobody was complaining inside the England dressing room, though. Thanks to Freddie again, and his trusty lieutenant, Jones, England had posted another huge total and the message to a battered and bruised Australia was clear: Chase that if you can.

Judging by Australia's initial response, the answer was that they could not. Flintoff had done more than his

bit in this Test series to date. So, too, had Trescothick's numerous scores, the impact wickets of Simon Jones, the hostility of Harmison and the centuries from Vaughan and Strauss. But the main reason this England team had come so good over the past two years was that they were, first and foremost, a team. Whenever a key performance was needed, somebody had always produced the goods. Now, a little belatedly in this series, it was the turn of Matthew Hoggard.

The popular Yorkshireman needed to prove himself to no one. England's best bowler during the winning winter series in South Africa, he had captured more Test wickets than either Harmison or Flintoff. Yet in this current Ashes series he had served as nothing more than

FACING PAGE AND BELOW Examples of the contrasting but complementary styles of Geraint Jones and Andrew Flintoff, as the Kent wicket-keeper/batsman slots the ball through the off side while Freddie clatters Warne over square leg for six.

an occasional wicket-taker. All this was about to change. Hoggard was about to have the kind of influence on an Ashes Test he would only have dreamt about.

Up to this point his bowling figures for the Ashes series had read seven wickets at 33. His captain, Vaughan, had only allowed him 56 overs, a reflection in part on how well the others had been bowling but also on how below par Hoggard had been in comparison.

Shaggy-haired and full of figure, he had appeared mortal in the company of some seemingly superhuman team-mates.

Yet he came out after tea on the second day at Trent Bridge to take three crucial wickets and blow a gaping hole in Australia's attempt to reach parity on first innings scores. In an 11-over spell Hoggard reduced the tourists to 58–4 with figures of 3–32, bowling with renewed confidence at a swing-friendly venue which he knew would best suit his bowling. Since the construction of the new stand, the idiosyncrasies of Trent Bridge had been helpful mostly to Hoggard's brand of swing.

Hayden, formerly one of the most dominant batsmen in world cricket, looked totally lost out there against Hoggard. He had been in, stumbling and stuttering, for 40 minutes and 27 balls for his seven runs before Hoggard got him leg before as he almost fell over an inswinger. The wicket was always going to come, although Hayden may have felt himself unlucky as the ball appeared to hit his pads high.

Simon Jones got in on the act soon afterwards, dismissing Ponting. The man who had saved Australia's neck in the previous Test with an imperious seven-hour 156, this time perished leg before after just six balls for a solitary run. His face was as dark as a thundercloud. He believed he had edged the ball on to his pad from a forward prod, and the snickometer used on television backed him up on this. Damien Martyn survived for even less time at the crease. Hoggard trapped him leg before as well, after just three balls and for one run. Replays showed that Martyn, for the second successive time, had also got an inside edge on to his pads. This time it was umpire Aleem Dar's turn to make the mistake. England had got lucky just when they needed to.

Justin Langer was watching all this from the other end. With Martyn's questionable dismissal, Australia had slumped to 22–3. It needed another show of obduracy from the remaining opener. For a while Langer produced just that but, on 28, Ian Bell struck again with his safe hands to catch Langer from an inside edge on to his pads from Hoggard's swinging delivery. Hoggard might have grabbed a fourth wicket when Bell put down a stiff chance at short leg which would have seen Simon Katich dismissed first ball. Katich and Michael Clarke then put on a useful 41 before Harmison trapped the rather carefree Clarke leg before for 36. It proved to be the last ball of a day England had dominated totally, and, for a second successive Test, Harmison had ended a day's proceedings by dismissing Clarke.

It left Australia in a precarious position. The follow-on target of 278 appeared a lifetime away, let alone England's now gargantuan first innings score of 477. With just five first innings wickets remaining, and with a new batsman at the crease the following morning, the odds heavily favoured England now to win the match.

That new batsman, however, was Adam Gilchrist, and he possessed enough of a threat for England to assume nothing. On the other hand, Gilchrist knew that

he and his team-mates were once more under the cosh. 'It's been demanding mentally,' Australia's wicket-keeper/batsman admitted at the close of the second day's play. 'England are doing to us what we've been doing to other teams for years. They've got the best attack I've faced in my Test career. They are working together and hunting as a pack. England have again come out and played consistent cricket for two days while we haven't. That sees us in another challenging position and we'll have to work hard to get out. We are facing the ultimate challenge at the moment and we are under pressure. We have to believe we can get it right some time and before the end of the series and do enough. What with missing the odd chance, as well as umpiring decisions going against us, it feels like we're in a vicious circle. Even if we lose and go to The Oval 2–1 down, we will not lose belief. We are not suddenly bad cricketers.'

FACING PAGE The Australians appeal unsuccessfully for a catch against Matthew Hoggard. Simon Katich is the fielder. RIGHT Gone for 102. Flintoff leaves the field after his magnificent century.

As for Flintoff, there was no keeping him down. 'We're doing all right, aren't we?' he said, with a huge grin. 'It was a tremendous effort from the bowlers. Matthew Hoggard did very well and then the last wicket by Steve Harmison has put us in the box seat. There's not a great deal in the pitch, but Brett Lee showed what can be done if you put the ball in the right place. We're in a great position but we're not daft. We know they have fine players who can come back at you, but we just have to stay disciplined.'

He had no doubt that he had just produced the best innings of his life. 'That ton was up with my best ever and the timing was very good. We needed the runs and Geraint and I managed to take the score up past 400. We complement each other very well with the bat and our average per partnership is about 79. We score in different areas and that means the bowlers have to bowl in different places.'

LEFT Langer, caught Bell, bowled Hoggard. BELOW The Fanatics, Australia's support on tour, cheer an Adam Gilchrist six. FACING PAGE Andrew Strauss (centre) has just taken a wonder catch at slip to return Gilchrist to the pavilion.

Strauss spoke for the team when he talked of the contributions of Hoggard and Geraint Jones. 'We're all particularly pleased for both Matthew and Geraint tonight, as they have once again proved their doubters wrong,' he said. 'The reason why this team has been so successful in the past two years is not because of superstars, but because all 11 players have contributed at important times, and today was no different.'

As long as Katich and Gilchrist stayed at the crease, though, England's chances of winning the Test remained far from secure. For much of the morning of the third day the pair hung around, scoring surprisingly freely as England forsook cutting off runs in their attempt to capture wickets. Australia had added 58 runs for the sixth wicket and were beginning to suggest that they would dig themselves out of a hole they had created for themselves, when they then proceeded to lose four wickets for just 18 runs.

If Hoggard had been the hero with the ball in the latter half of the previous day's play, then Simon Jones took over the mantle on the Saturday morning. As ever with the Welshman, he had to wait his turn. When he finally marked out his run-up, ten overs of the morning had passed and the runs Australia required to avoid the follow-on had been reduced to 121 with five wickets still standing. The weather forecast for the remaining two and half days in Nottingham was not good, either, so it was imperative for England to press home their advantage, and equally important for Australia to hang in and force England to bat third. They had almost done enough against the odds at Edgbaston. And they had succeeded in a backs-against-the wall rearguard at Old Trafford. Were they about to do it again?

Jones made sure they did not. Katich fell to a wide delivery from the Glamorgan man, directing his shot straight into the grateful hands of Strauss at gully. Warne emerged in the unusual position of being, at least statistically, Australia's third best batsman on this Ashes tour. He would return to the pavilion just one ball later, having spooned a catch to the dependable Ian Bell at extra cover after Jones's delivery had turned Warne inside out and ricocheted off the face of his bat. A total of 157–5 had suddenly become 157–7. Six runs later, Australia's eighth wicket fell to the catch of the series.

It was the most important wicket, too. Once again Adam Gilchrist was beginning to threaten. He had moved on to 27 and was beginning to hint that the big score everyone feared but expected was about to transpire. Suddenly he was leaving for the pavilion, shaking his head in consternation after seeing Strauss fling himself full length and snatch the ball out of the air with his outstretched left hand at second slip after Gilchrist had slashed at a ball from Flintoff that had risen more than he had anticipated. When Strauss

caught the ball his body was horizontal. The Martyn catch at Lord's to dismiss Pietersen was special. The Bell reaction at Edgbaston to remove Langer was extraordinary. But Strauss's catch to remove Gilchrist was out of this world. His England team-mates recognised the fact immediately. Before he knew it, Strauss found himself hoisted upon the shoulders of three of the other fielders. 'I was exceptionally pleased to catch Adam Gilchrist,' Strauss said later. 'It was pure instinct. See it, dive and, thankfully, it stuck. I'm not sure I'm capable of taking a better catch than that.'

Back came Simon Jones, pumped up after seeing a forlorn Gilchrist trudge back to the pavilion. In the next over he swung the ball around a defensive push from Kasprowicz to clatter his stumps. Australia were teetering on the edge at 175–9. Not for the first time Brett Lee the batsman proved to be an irritant. At Edgbaston he so very nearly masterminded an epic victory. At Old Trafford he was there at the end with McGrath to deny England. Now, with just the inexperienced Tait to partner him, he let fly. In no time he had raced to 47, a score that included three sixes, two pulled off Harmison into Hound Road and a pull-driven blow off Simon Jones that dented the Nottinghamshire chairman's car bonnet. The latter, like the rest of English cricket, breathed a sigh of relief when Bell snared another catch from the bowling of Jones. Australia were all out for 218, still 60 runs short of the follow-on target, and Jones, carrying on from his six-wicket first innings haul at Old Trafford, had finished with figures of 5–44.

In Manchester, even if the rain and Shane Warne had permitted, England had no intention of enforcing the follow-on. In Nottingham circumstances were very different. Michael Vaughan knew that it would mean chasing a target in the fourth innings against Warne's leg-spinners, but the plan was to ensure that the target was too small for Warne, or anyone else for that matter, to prevent England from achieving their aim. Quite rightly, Vaughan enforced the follow-on. Australia still trailed England by 259 runs.

This really was unknown territory for the beleaguered Australians. Certainly for this particular team, in any case. It had been 191 Tests since the last time Australia were invited to follow on, and that was in Karachi back in 1988. They went on to lose the Test and the series to Pakistan.

Jones was given the new ball for a change. This was normally the territory of Harmison and Hoggard, but Vaughan felt that he should ask Jones to continue his progress against the Australians from the morning's play, in which he had wrapped up their first innings. The move backfired. It became obvious from early on in the second innings that he was struggling with fitness. After just four overs he left the field with an ankle injury. Jones would not appear again in the day.

It was left to a three-pronged pace attack of Harmison, Flintoff and Hoggard, plus the spin of Giles, to do the donkey work. Langer and Hayden had put on exactly 50 in their opening partnership when Giles clung on to a catch at second slip off Flintoff to remove Hayden. Once again Hayden, with 26, had failed to deliver having seemingly done the hard work of settling in. His opening stand with Langer saw them fall only eight short of their highest of the whole series. Having managed to restrict Langer and Hayden, hitherto the best opening partnership in the world, to a highest stand of 58 was one major reason why England had fared so well. Hayden's scores in this Ashes series had thus far read: 12, 34, 0, 31, 34, 36, 7, and 26.

Still, Australia were making a much better fist of it second time round, aided by the fact that the ball was not swinging anywhere near as much as it had in the first innings. Langer and Ponting put on 79 for the second wicket, a partnership broken up by Giles, who produced enough turn to have Langer caught by the safe hands of Bell at short leg. Langer had scored 61, which, in normal circumstances, would have been good news for Australia. On this day it was not enough. He had been fortunate, too. On 37 he gave Strauss a chance. It was easier than the one he took to remove Gilchrist – although any chance would have been easier than that – but Strauss put it down. It could have been vital. Instead it cost England a further 24 runs. The onus was now on Ponting to reproduce his epic century at Old Trafford if his country were to stand any chance of saving this Test match. Instead the Australian captain became embroiled in one of the major moments of controversy of the series.

He had been going well. His 48 had appeared both fluent and untroubled. Then his partner, Damien Martyn, called for a quick single to the Durham player Gary Pratt, who was on the field as a substitute for the injured Simon Jones. Ponting would have been well within his rights to send his partner back but instead

took the gamble. Pratt hit the stumps with a direct hit and it was clear that a scurrying Ponting was in trouble.

As the Australian captain awaited the decision of the third umpire, he exchanged words first with umpire Aleem Dar, then with the England players, who were confident they would soon be celebrating another wicket. Once the wicket had been confirmed, Ponting walked towards the pavilion furious with the manner in which he had been dismissed. Climbing the pavilion steps, he looked upwards towards the England dressing room and shouted a few expletives in the general direction of England coach Duncan Fletcher.

This kind of incident was likely to come. Australia had been growing more and more frustrated with the way in which England regularly used their substitute

FACING PAGE Brett Lee opens up during his 47 in Australia's first innings. RIGHT Ashley Giles in action on the third day.

fielders, often exchanging their frontline bowlers in the process. The Australians believed that the players went off for nothing more than a rest, and not for any injury. Their argument was that this was not in the spirit of the game. On this occasion Ponting was quite clearly in the wrong. Pratt was on the field because Simon Jones had gone to hospital for scans on his injured right ankle. It was an interesting show of emotion from Ponting, which said more about the state he and his team were in than the rights or the wrongs of the substitute issue. This, incidentally, was the fourth time England had run out an Australian batsman in this series. Australia, by contrast, had failed to make their mark yet. It was yet another fact to underline England's supremacy.

Martyn, no doubt distraught after playing such a part in the dismissal of his angry captain, and struggling to find his touch, sent a fine edge to Geraint Jones behind off Flintoff and was gone for 13. It was just 13 balls after he had run out Ponting. Clarke and Katich managed to avoid any further wickets falling before the close of play, putting on an unbeaten 61 for the fifth wicket to end the day with Australia 222–4, still 37 runs behind England's first innings total. It could and should have been worse for Australia. Just when you thought Geraint Jones had erased the mistakes from his game, he missed a simple stumping chance off Giles when Clarke was on 35, in the deepening gloom that finally put paid to the day's events early. As for Katich, he had a day he would have hoped would not occur. In the morning he had emerged from the dressing room to try and thwart England as Australia lurched towards a sub-standard first innings total. Then, in the evening he was hanging on again, but this time in the second innings, as others around him fell.

Afterwards Ponting tried to explain his actions, as well as offering a fulsome apology for an incident that not only soured the day but was also not in keeping with the good-natured, sporting spirit the series had been played in. 'I am very disappointed with my dismissal, given that it was at a crucial stage of the game and I had worked very hard to get to that position,' he said. 'I no doubt let myself down with my reaction and for that I apologise to those who see me as a role model. My frustration at getting out was compounded by the fact that I was run out by a substitute fielder, an issue that has concerned us throughout this series.'

Coach Fletcher attempted to defuse the situation. He claimed, for example, not to have heard the words Ponting directed at him. 'I could not hear because of all the noise,' he insisted. 'He was mumbling something. I

FACING PAGE **A forlorn-looking Matthew Hayden makes his way back to the dressing room, caught by Giles off Flintoff as Australia follow on.**

think it was directed at us. We had to have a substitute on for Simon and if someone wants to take a single to cover point and is run out, whose fault is that? There is a lot of pressure building up in this series and it's a question of who can handle the pressure best.' As for the use of Gary Pratt, Fletcher had no reason to apologise. 'Gary is a good cricketer,' the coach said. 'We try and get hold of fielders from a county having a rest. We've been doing it for five years. Players have to drink a lot of fluids and have to relieve themselves. It's something that's not going to change in the modern game.'

Justin Langer was refreshingly unbiased when asked his view of the soured atmosphere. 'I think most of Ricky's reaction stems from the frustration of being run out,' said the Australian opening batsman. 'It's a cardinal sin in Test cricket, and in a game that is as important as this that is why he was frustrated. He was batting well and getting some momentum going. The substitute issue has come up throughout the series. I don't want to delve too deep but cricket has a great tradition of 12th men being bowlers. Generally the English have been smarter than the Australians and, in this day of professionalism, I suppose it's just another way of getting the best out of your resources available within the rules. As for the game, I'd be surprised if there isn't another twist in it yet. We're hanging on by the skin of our teeth.'

To cap another good day for English cricket against their oldest and greatest rivals, England's women's cricket team reclaimed their version of the Ashes after 42 years with their first Test win over Australia since 1984. After the First Test was drawn, England won the Second Test at New Road, Worcester, by six wickets.

Glenn McGrath, so confident at the start of the series, was being forced to change his view. Unable to do anything else but watch from the team dressing room, even he had to concede that England were getting a great deal right. 'There is no escaping the fact that, so far, we have let ourselves down in crucial areas and at vital times,' he admitted. 'England have played really well and they've come at us hard. Apart from the First Test at Lord's, they have dominated the series and we have not been able to turn the tide. I can't recall many other occasions when we have been tested like this and there is no denying that our response has not been what we would have liked or expected of ourselves as a team.'

And so to Sunday – day four of the Fourth Test. This was the day when England were supposed to wrap up the Australian second innings and knock off the relatively small total required to win the Test and go 2–1 up in the series with just one match remaining. After everything that had taken place before, all the drama of Edgbaston and Old Trafford, it would be Trent Bridge's turn now to come up with another thriller to leave the viewing public either on the edge of their sofas, or hiding behind them.

Australia started the day steadily enough. Thirty-seven runs behind, Clarke and Katich soon took the tourists past England's first innings total and, for the first time in the match, Australia were ahead in terms of runs. England's bowlers were starting to toil, and hopes were sinking fast as the tourists served up attritional cricket.

Had Australia made it to lunch without losing a wicket, the psychological metronome might have swung again. They nearly did, too, until Clarke, having made 56, wafted at Hoggard to give Geraint Jones a simple catch.

England's lot improved immeasurably shortly after lunch, when Gilchrist also fell to Hoggard, this time leg

before. Hoggard had collected two wickets in Australia's second innings to add to the three in the first. Five wickets in a Test match is good rather than spectacular, but each of the five Hoggard claimed were absolutely crucial to England's cause, not only in the personnel he dismissed but in their timing. A score of 261–4 had now become 277–6.

Over the years one of Australia's many strengths has been their inability to recognise defeat, even when it is staring them full in the face. They had been pounded mercilessly in the Second, Third and Fourth Tests, but still they clung on, even if their fingernails were beginning to slide down the cliff face.

One of their most obstinate factors now played its part once more. The Australian tail, and in particular Messrs Warne and Lee, who had already contributed so much to their country's cause with the ball, now piled on some vital runs for Australia, and nerve-wracking runs for England. First, though, came the removal of Katich, who was beginning to match Langer for his adhesiveness at the crease. The number six had reached 59, when he

FACING PAGE An unhappy Ricky Ponting walks off, having been run out by substitute fielder Gary Pratt. ABOVE A glum Shane Warne watches Australia struggle from the dressing room balcony. RIGHT An incandescent Simon Katich leaves the field after getting a questionable lbw decision.

was the victim of a harsh leg-before shout off Harmison. Once again the umpire was Aleem Dar, and once again Australia had some justification in feeling hard done by. Nevertheless, none of the Australian top six had gone on to make a major score, yet another telling factor behind their struggles.

In came Lee to join Warne, and both agreed to have some fun. Warne, especially, decided to have a swing and, largely, proved successful. Never recognised as anything more than a useful number eight, Warne had been just about Australia's most consistent batsman in the Test series, besides the fact that he stood head and shoulders above everyone else from either side in the bowling department. Eventually he went for one too many and was stumped by Geraint Jones off Giles. Still, Warne had added a further 45 runs. At 314–8 the Australian resistance appeared to be close to an end.

This was not quite the case, although England made it hard for themselves. In hindsight, wrapping up this Test match should have been a doddle. Nerves would not have been frayed, fingernails not bitten down to the bone, and years not taken from people's lives. All it needed was for England to have taken at least one of the three chances offered them by Lee before he had scored.

The two culprits were the ones, on the evidence of the series so far, you would have put money on to err. If Pietersen's sixth straight dropped catch out of six attempts was bad enough – and still the new find of English cricket had failed to cling on to even one chance so far in the Ashes – the two missed by Geraint Jones

were bordering on criminal. First he dropped an edge that was flying at a comfortable height to Trescothick at first slip. It was the action of a man eager to make amends for his earlier missed stumping. Then he managed to knock a bail off with his glove as Strauss attempted to run Lee out with a shy at the stumps. The bad was as frequent as the good with Jones in this series.

Kasprowicz hung around long enough to become a real nuisance, just as he and Lee had in all but winning the Second Test at Edgbaston. Harmison finally tempted a nick behind to Jones, who this time held on to the catch, and Kasprowicz departed for 19. He and Lee had put on a useful 31 runs. Now only Shaun Tait remained to join Lee. If Tait's bowling was relatively unknown in England, then his batting was a complete non-subject. The fact that he was Australia's eleventh batsman, however, suggested not too much was expected of him.

LEFT Australia's number eleven Shaun Tait wanders across his stumps and is bowled by Harmison, ending both his innings and his team's. ABOVE Kevin Pietersen and the injured Simon Jones look apprehensive on the England balcony as their team set off in pursuit of 129 runs to win.

Lee certainly felt that way, farming the strike and nicking singles off the last ball of the over. A further 14 runs were added for the last wicket, each one applying extra pressure to England, until Tait, inexplicably, moved right outside the line of his off stump, partly to avoid Harmison and partly to spoon the ball out on to the leg side. The end result was predictable. Harmison's yorker left Tait's stumps splattered and Lee, stranded on 26 – yet another decent score for a number nine batsman – less than amused by the rash shot just executed.

Australia were all out for 387, having added a further 165 runs to their overnight score for the loss of six wickets. It was, ironically, their highest innings score of the whole series. Harmison just nudged ahead of the others to be the pick of the English bowlers with 3–93, but Hoggard, Flintoff and Giles all played their part in collecting two wickets apiece. It left England just 129 runs to win the Fourth Test, and the chance to do to Australia what they had done to England at Lord's. England did not just want to win now, they wanted to hand out a fearful beating in the final session of day four.

What happened instead was theatre at its darkest and most enthralling. The fact that it turned out like this should have been, on the premise that England's task appeared relatively simple, a major surprise. The fact that it was not a surprise was because by the end of the Fourth Test it had become official – this really was the greatest Ashes series ever.

If they thought their cause was lost, Australia certainly did not show it when they all but sprinted out of the Trent Bridge pavilion and on to the pitch. Lee, in particular, was pumped up, while Warne had a happy smile etched all over his face. He had seen enough cricket in his time to know that he was in the midst of something special and, Warne being Warne, he wanted to make sure he played a central part in the proceedings.

Trescothick and Strauss gave little hint of what was to come. The former started aggressively, intent on knocking off the runs as quickly as possible. He may have been facing one of those nasty, pressure-filled little totals – and the history of Test cricket is riddled with such targets not being met – but he saw no reason to change the approach that had brought him so much previous success in the series. The opening partnership had raced to 32, with Trescothick making 27 of them in just 22 balls, when Shane Warne decided to grab the limelight.

ABOVE Michael Vaughan begins the long trudge back to the pavilion, having been taken at slip by Hayden to become Warne's second victim of England's second innings. FACING PAGE Brett Lee produces a thunderbolt of a ball to burst through Andrew Flintoff's defences.

First to go was Trescothick off Warne's first ball, pushing forward to provide a bat-pad chance to Ponting at silly point. By his standards he had just failed, but Trescothick did not seem unduly concerned. England only needed another 98 runs, with nine wickets standing. It should be a piece of cake.

Make that 94 runs with eight wickets. Vaughan attempted a drive to leg but was caught out by a ball from Warne that turned out of the rough. Hayden did the rest at slip and the England captain had gone for a duck, having lasted just six balls. The first seeds of doubt had been sown.

Strauss and Bell appeared to be steadying the ship, though. With Strauss looking settled, England seemed safe. The opener had scored that vital second innings century at Old Trafford, and he had the ability to dig in or play with flair, depending on what was required.

Then Warne struck again, luring Strauss into a tiny, leg-side tickle that was snapped up by Clarke at leg slip. Strauss stood his ground until television replays confirmed the ball had carried to the catcher. The opener had gone for 23 and the score read 57–3. Surely England were safe, though. They may have been making hard work of it, but they only needed a further 72 runs and had seven wickets in hand.

For all his undoubted potential, and despite his two half-centuries at Old Trafford, perhaps it was asking a little too much of Ian Bell to be the man to steer England through the troubled waters that had swelled up around them. No run had been added to England's score when Bell, more through nerves than bravado, top-edged his attempted hook off Lee straight to an advancing Kasprowicz at long leg. 57–4. It was beginning to look as if all England's hard work could be undone.

Time, then, for sensible play from an unlikely pair. English cricket had dreamt of Pietersen and Flintoff murdering the opposition attack all summer. Few would have foreseen both of them having to bat so calmly and

maturely, quelling their natural fires in the process, to ease England towards victory. This, though, is precisely what happened, although Warne's penetrative bowling, in which the leg-spinner used every sinew in his body to conjure another wicket, helped to keep the pair in check.

Slowly the England score rose. When Flintoff lofted a four off Warne over wide mid-on, the release of tension was palpable. It seemed two stand-out characters in the England team would see them home. But then came the final few twists in this unbearable drama. Channel 4 reported that by this stage over eight million television viewers had tuned in to watch the last rites of this match. It was a figure unimaginable at the start of the summer.

Pietersen and Flintoff had put on 43 invaluable runs when Brett Lee intervened. Steaming in off his long run and breaking 95 mph, he induced a snicked drive from Pietersen through to Gilchrist. Pietersen had made 23 and the score had crept on to 103–5. The success visibly lifted the pace bowler. Eight runs later he produced the ball of the day, an express delivery that kept low and nipped back late into Flintoff's off stump. 111–6, and

Flintoff was gone for 26. He would win the Man of the Match award for another sterling all-round effort, but right this moment Flintoff would have swapped the award for his wicket. By now Ponting was calling for group huddles after every wicket. It was quite evident that Australia believed they could pull off the most incredible victory. If they succeeded, they would not only win the Test but, by going into the Fifth and final Test at The Oval 2–1 up, they would have retained the Ashes.

This was not going well for England. Not well at all. The hitherto boisterous crowd had become strangely muted by all the goings-on. Only the far smaller section of the stand filled with Australian supporters was making any noise. The fact remained, however, that England needed only 18 runs, with four wickets remaining, to finish what had become a hard job.

FACING PAGE Cometh the hour… England's batting heroes Ashley Giles and Matthew Hoggard. RIGHT AND BELOW Giles pushes Warne into the leg side for two and the England balcony erupts. England are 2–1 up in the Ashes with one match to play.

They had added a further five runs to the cause when Geraint Jones, looking to finish the job in style, attempted to hit Warne over the top for four. Revealing the growing tension and disbelief inside the heads of the England camp, he succeeded only in sending a skyer straight to the safe hands of Kasprowicz. Jones became Warne's fiftieth Test victim of the year, and England found themselves wobbling and stuttering now on 116–7. They only needed 13 runs to win. Right now it looked more like 113.

A betting man would probably have put money on first Flintoff, and then Pietersen to be the hero of the day. That is how the great sporting scriptwriter would have had it. Or maybe Vaughan, the captain, leading his men home. But Ashley Giles and Matthew Hoggard? It became the kind of script that would have been ripped up and ridiculed inside a Hollywood producer's office.

It is fair to say that when Hoggard, his tousled, blonde hair jutting out from the sides of his helmet, ambled out on to the pitch, few watching the drama would have been filled with hope. He had the look more

of a hapless farmer than of a determined international cricketer. Giles, who has known Hoggard longer than most, put it this way later. 'Hoggy was trying not to show it, but I could tell he was shitting himself.'

Yet both produced the most sensible batting of the whole English innings, playing the percentages and hitting only the bad balls. A cover drive from Hoggard brought England two runs. 'I hadn't seen Hoggy hit a cover drive in six years of batting with him,' Giles also pointed out later. A no-ball from Lee was met with a rapturous cheer from the crowd. Giles added another two runs, then Hoggard drove an off-side full toss from Lee through extra cover for four. The shot, coming from a man who had not registered a decent total all series, was close to textbook. 'Whether it was a full toss or not, at that pace, with that much reverse on it, to get it through that gap, and so technically sound, something fell in our favour there,' Giles said. On the England dressing room balcony Trescothick leapt to his feet and punched the air. Pietersen chewed nervously on a mouthguard as the ball trickled over the boundary rope just in front of a pursuing fielder.

Now four runs were needed. Hoggard clipped Lee off his legs to square leg and scampered another two runs. The Trent Bridge crowd had spent the previous two hours not knowing whether to laugh or to cry. Now they were beginning to laugh.

Up stepped Warne for the denouement. He sent down a leg-side full toss. Giles's eyes lit up, he got himself into position, and smacked the ball to leg. A watching Michael Vaughan punched the air, then sank back to his seat in despair. Giles's forceful shot had hit Katich fielding close in at silly mid-on. Warne and Ponting smiled at the ridiculous level this Ashes series had reached. Both knew that should have been that, both knew they had got lucky, and both knew they still, just, were in with a chance. Back in the England dressing room Steve Harmison was padded up but praying his questionable batting skills would not be required. After him there was only the injured Simon Jones left, and he could barely walk.

Warne trundled in again. Giles pressed forward and the whole of the Australian team went up, shouted, and then placed their hands on their heads. Giles had misjudged one that turned, and was powerless as the ball spun past his bat and, crucially, his off stump. Australia had been within an inch of claiming their eighth wicket.

Two balls later Warne sent down a leg-side half-volley. Giles may have been tempted to hit it into the crowd. Fortunately, control beat off excitement. Instead he middled a push out in to the largely vacant leg side, scampered the first run with Hoggard, and then raised his bat in triumph and relief during the midst of the second, winning run. Warne had grabbed a further four wickets, and Lee three, but none of this seemed to matter as both sank to their knees in despair.

The English balcony went ape. The Trent Bridge crowd went ape. And Giles and Hoggard simply stood in the middle of the wicket hugging each other as if saying a final farewell. It was 6.30 on a Sunday evening, and cricket had just witnessed another truly incredible ending to another truly incredible Test match.

'To go out there and get the winning runs was awesome,' a mightily relieved Giles explained when it was all over. 'I've never been so grateful for a chip through mid-wicket. None of us thought it would be easy. For one thing Australia are not in the habit of surrendering. And we make a habit of finishes like this.

As we lost wickets I was thinking: "This can't be happening to us. We don't deserve this." These games are so tough. We have all aged ten years in the past three weeks. You don't sleep well. Every minute of the day you are thinking about cricket. You wake up in the middle of the night and still you're thinking about cricket. It's not healthy, but that's the Ashes for you.'

His captain, Vaughan, tried to calm things down. There was still one more match to go, after all. 'We realise we're on the brink of something special,' he admitted. 'I'm just delighted we got over the line. To go 2–1 up in an Ashes series hasn't been the case for a long, long time. But we have to be exactly how we have been for the past four weeks. We didn't change a thing after

Lord's, and we won't change a thing now. I'm sure The Oval will be an epic like the last three.'

Ponting's summing-up was spot-on. 'The first two days of this game cost us the Test match,' he assessed. 'We fought hard and played some good cricket over the past couple of days but when you're that far behind you have to play exceptional cricket to win. We got close today, closer than we should have got, if I'm honest.'

As for the final chapter of this remarkable series, one could tell that Ponting, far from shirking, was almost looking forward to it. 'We have to turn things round quickly to hold on to these Ashes,' he concluded. 'It's as simple as that. There's no other option now.'

No other option at all. After four Test matches and more twists and turns than an Agatha Christie novel, it had all boiled down to this: England needed simply to avoid defeat at The Oval to win the Ashes for the first time in 18 years. Australia needed a win, and nothing less, to maintain what had become a shaky grip on the old urn.

English cricket had never witnessed anything like this. National interest in the sport had reached sky high. Tickets for The Oval became nuggets of gold. And the country waited in nervous anticipation.

This would be quite possibly the biggest sporting occasion on British soil since England won the football World Cup in 1966. Could England finish the job? Could they douse the world champions' fire? Or would the dying breed that was this Australian team make one, final, concerted effort before accepting the inevitable? All eyes turned to The Oval.

BELOW Ashley Giles and Matthew Hoggard explain how they brought England home at a press conference the day after the dramatic three-wicket victory at Trent Bridge. After three successive epics, what would the decider at The Oval bring?

ENGLAND V AUSTRALIA, 4th Test, Trent Bridge
25, 26, 27, 28 AUGUST 2005

TOSS: England **UMPIRES:** Aleem Dar (Pak) and SA Bucknor (WI)
TV UMPIRE: MR Benson **FOURTH UMPIRE:** IJ Gould
MATCH REFEREE: RS Madugalle (SL)
TEST DEBUT: SW Tait (Aus).

Close of Play:
- **Day 1:** England 229-4 (Pietersen 33*, Flintoff 8*)
- **Day 2:** England 477, Australia 99-5 (Katich 20*)
- **Day 3:** Australia 218 and 222-4 (Clarke 39*, Katich 24*)

England 1st innings			R	M	B	4	6
ME Trescothick	b Tait		65	138	111	8	1
AJ Strauss	c Hayden	b Warne	35	99	64	4	0
*MP Vaughan	c Gilchrist	b Ponting	58	138	99	9	0
IR Bell	c Gilchrist	b Tait	3	12	5	0	0
KP Pietersen	c Gilchrist	b Lee	45	131	108	6	0
A Flintoff	lbw	b Tait	102	201	132	14	1
+GO Jones	c & b Kasprowicz		85	205	149	8	0
AF Giles	lbw	b Warne	15	45	35	3	0
MJ Hoggard	c Gilchrist	b Warne	10	46	28	1	0
SJ Harmison	st Gilchrist	b Warne	2	9	6	0	0
SP Jones	not out		15	32	27	3	0
Extras	**42**	(b 1, lb 15, w 1, nb 25)					
Total	**477**	(all out, 123.1 overs, 537 minutes)					

FoW: **1-105** (Strauss), **2-137** (Trescothick), **3-146** (Bell), **4-213** (Vaughan), **5-241** (Pietersen), **6-418** (Flintoff), **7-450** (GO Jones), **8-450** (Giles), **9-454** (Harmison), **10-477** (Hoggard).

Bowling	O	M	R	W	
Lee	32	2	131	1	(8nb)
Kasprowicz	32	3	122	1	(13nb)
Tait	24	4	97	3	(4nb)
Warne	29.1	4	102	4	
Ponting	6	2	9	1	(1w)

England 2nd innings			R	M	B	4	6
ME Trescothick	c Ponting	b Warne	27	24	22	4	0
AJ Strauss	c Clarke	b Warne	23	68	37	3	0
*MP Vaughan	c Hayden	b Warne	0	8	6	0	0
IR Bell	c Kasprowicz	b Lee	3	38	20	0	0
KP Pietersen	c Gilchrist	b Lee	23	51	34	3	0
A Flintoff	b Lee		26	63	34	3	0
+GO Jones	c Kasprowicz	b Warne	3	25	13	0	0
AF Giles	not out		7	30	17	0	0
MJ Hoggard	not out		8	20	13	1	0
Extras	**9**	(lb 4, nb 5)					
Total	**129**	(7 wickets, 31.5 overs, 168 minutes)					

DNB: SJ Harmison, SP Jones.

FoW: **1-32** (Trescothick), **2-36** (Vaughan), **3-57** (Strauss), **4-57** (Bell), **5-103** (Pietersen), **6-111** (Flintoff), **7-116** (GO Jones).

Bowling	O	M	R	W	
Lee	12	0	51	3	(5nb)
Kasprowicz	2	0	19	0	
Warne	13.5	2	31	4	
Tait	4	0	24	0	

Australia 1st innings			R	M	B	4	6
JL Langer	c Bell	b Hoggard	27	95	59	5	0
ML Hayden	lbw	b Hoggard	7	41	27	1	0
*RT Ponting	lbw	b SP Jones	1	6	6	0	0
DR Martyn	lbw	b Hoggard	1	4	3	0	0
MJ Clarke	lbw	b Harmison	36	93	53	5	0
SM Katich	c Strauss	b SP Jones	45	91	66	7	0
+AC Gilchrist	c Strauss	b Flintoff	27	58	36	3	1
SK Warne	c Bell	b SP Jones	0	2	1	0	0
B Lee	c Bell	b SP Jones	47	51	44	5	3
MS Kasprowicz	b SP Jones		5	8	7	1	0
SW Tait	not out		3	27	9	0	0
Extras	**19**	(lb 2, w 1, nb 16)					
Total	**218**	(all out, 49.1 overs, 247 minutes)					

FoW: **1-20** (Hayden), **2-21** (Ponting), **3-22** (Martyn), **4-58** (Langer), **5-99** (Clarke), **6-157** (Katich), **7-157** (Warne), **8-163** (Gilchrist), **9-175** (Kasprowicz), **10-218** (Lee).

Bowling	O	M	R	W	
Harmison	9	1	48	1	(3nb)
Hoggard	15	3	70	3	(4nb)
SP Jones	14.1	4	44	5	(1nb)
Flintoff	11	1	54	1	(8nb, 1w)

Australia 2nd innings (following on)			R	M	B	4	6
JL Langer	c Bell	b Giles	61	149	112	8	0
ML Hayden	c Giles	b Flintoff	26	57	41	4	0
*RT Ponting	run out (sub GJ Pratt)		48	137	89	3	1
DR Martyn	c GO Jones	b Flintoff	13	56	30	1	0
MJ Clarke	c GO Jones	b Hoggard	56	209	170	6	0
SM Katich	lbw	b Harmison	59	262	183	4	0
+AC Gilchrist	lbw	b Hoggard	11	20	11	2	0
SK Warne	st GO Jones	b Giles	45	68	42	5	2
B Lee	not out		26	77	39	3	0
MS Kasprowicz	c GO Jones	b Harmison	19	30	26	1	0
SW Tait	b Harmison		4	20	16	1	0
Extras	**19**	(b 1, lb 4, nb 14)					
Total	**387**	(all out, 124 overs, 548 minutes)					

FoW: **1-50** (Hayden), **2-129** (Langer), **3-155** (Ponting), **4-161** (Martyn), **5-261** (Clarke), **6-277** (Gilchrist), **7-314** (Katich), **8-342** (Warne), **9-373** (Kasprowicz), **10-387** (Tait).

Bowling	O	M	R	W	
Hoggard	27	7	72	2	(1nb)
SP Jones	4	0	15	0	
Harmison	30	5	93	3	(1nb)
Flintoff	29	4	83	2	(9nb)
Giles	28	3	107	2	
Bell	6	2	12	0	(3nb)

RESULT: England won by 3 wickets MAN OF THE MATCH: **A Flintoff**

THE OVAL

5TH TEST
8 SEPTEMBER–12 SEPTEMBER

FACING PAGE Kevin Pietersen crashes the ball through the off side on his way to his maiden Test century in England's second innings. **RIGHT** The veteran and the tyro. Shane Warne congratulates Pietersen on his match-saving knock.

So far virtually everything had gone right for England, at least since the first morning of the Second Test at Edgbaston. They had passed every challenge thrown at them, but the prospect of holding off a wounded Australian side who knew that only a win would suffice would provide the biggest challenge of all.

Could England hold their nerve? Would Australia produce their most serious onslaught of the summer? Was it possible to stop the likes of Hayden, Martyn and Gilchrist from scoring serious runs all series? And would Shane Warne and Glenn McGrath have one final and desperate lesson to hand out to the young upstarts in

England shirts before bowing out of Test cricket in England? These were the questions that were about to be answered, and the signs, as the English public threw themselves into unprecedented support for cricket, were beginning to look ominous. McGrath, for one, was insisting that he would be fit to play. The Australian management adopted a more cautious approach to this, but McGrath was telling anyone who cared to know that he would be fit for The Oval. 'I'll be there, and I'll be ready,' promised the man who had already taken two five-fors in the two Tests he had played in.

It was clear, though, that Simon Jones was struggling. Jones, one of the key reasons why England

would be entering the final Test one up, had tried everything to repair his damaged ankle, including pressure chambers in Poland, but on the Tuesday morning, 48 hours before the start of the Fifth Test, he pulled up lame after just a few jogs in the nets. 'It's a sickening blow,' a distraught Jones remarked, a comment Trescothick could only agree with. 'Simon has been such a big performer for us,' he said. 'We are losing a major player when we do not want to be without him.' His captain, Michael Vaughan, echoed these sentiments. 'Simon is a loss, and there's no like-for-like replacement around the world, never mind in England,' he said.

The withdrawal of Jones meant that it would be a straight fight between seamer James Anderson, who had rediscovered some of his previous form in the summer, and Paul Collingwood, who was one of the form batsmen in the country, and who could provide some useful back-up bowling. Chris Tremlett, the tall Hampshire fast bowler who had been England's twelfth man throughout the Ashes series, was released.

With the clock ticking down on the start of the biggest game in the history of English cricket, everyone had a view. 'We see this game as an exciting time,' Warne explained. 'The biggest feeling now is just "bring it on". The numbers have been pretty good for me this summer. I guess if you are doing well it doesn't matter how old you are. However well I've been bowling and batting, though, it's all irrelevant now. Now everything comes down to one match. It's our final, a situation we're used to. For me these are the situations I thrive on.'

Vaughan was well aware of what was at stake. 'England have been carving out pieces of history in the last few years with their performances, the way they have beaten teams and the manner in which they have played against Australia. This week is a great opportunity to cement their position in cricket history.'

His Australian counterpart, Ricky Ponting, could predict an unhappy homecoming if he and his team-mates returned back down under without the Ashes. 'If we lose there is no doubt the hammering we will take at home,' he said. 'We'll cop it, and maybe we deserve to get it. We haven't been good enough but I wouldn't like to think my position will be under threat if we lose. There are things I could have done differently, but we're all responsible for where we are. I have never sat back and taken all the accolades when the team has gone well. If it came back on me I'll have to accept it.'

Vaughan made it clear that as England had been playing positive cricket all summer, they would not

suddenly be looking for the draw they required to win back the urn. 'We've been outstanding since Lord's, so I don't see any reason to change our way of thinking or our approach to the game,' he argued. 'I've been impressed in the way the players have responded to every challenge thrown at them. This match is an even bigger challenge and we need to go out and play in similar fashion now we are 2–1 up.'

Ponting, despite being aware of the reception awaiting him if Australia were to fail, was brimming with excitement at the prospect of the final Test. 'I think a little bit of pressure has been lifted off our shoulders here,' he explained. 'Everything is ahead of us and we have to play the brand and style of cricket that has made us successful over a long period of time, but which hasn't been produced by us yet this summer. It's a must-win game for us. There is no other option for us to take. It's an exciting time in an exciting series and if the team can't get up for this one, then they never will. If we win the last Test it will be the finest series I've ever been involved in and that makes us extra hungry to do everything in our power to win this final game.'

FACING PAGE Ian Bell, Paul Collingwood and Michael Vaughan have a net before the Fifth Test. RIGHT Errol Alcott and Glenn McGrath share a joke. Despite elbow trouble, the great Australian pace bowler was certain that he would be fit to play at The Oval.

On the morning of day one, the big news overnight was that Glenn McGrath had been passed fit to play for Australia after recovering from the damaged elbow that kept him out of the Fourth Test at Trent Bridge, while Paul Collingwood had been preferred to the unlucky James Anderson in the England starting XI.

For England, the first day began as well as it had in the previous Test matches. Michael Vaughan won what appeared to be a vital toss and had no hesitation in batting first. The plan was to win this game, and the Ashes 3–1. It would have been no less than England deserved after their complete domination of Australia in the previous three Tests but, failing that, a draw would suffice to keep the score at a winning 2–1 margin to England. That meant compiling a huge first innings total to not only bat Australia out of the game but also apply, once again, massive pressure on the tourists.

at a corner of the ground. With the wicket a typical Oval one – dry, brown and inviting runs – and the sun still baking-hot despite it being the second week of September, this would be the best of the batting conditions. It was crucial England made the most of it.

For a while they did, as well. After the first hour the Ashes seemed to be virtually in England's grasp. Pre-Test, there had been talk of the England team enjoying a Rugby World Cup-style open-top bus parade through the streets of London. Crowds in their hundreds of thousands were predicted to line the roads, and ticker tape would be showered from every building. At around 11.30 on the Thursday morning, such scenes appeared to be all but confirmed. Marcus Trescothick and Andrew Strauss were at it again, the former in particular swatting boundaries off the fit-again-but-out-of-practice Glenn McGrath, as well as Brett Lee and Shaun Tait. Within an

ABOVE Australian opener Matthew Hayden in meditation on the wicket at The Oval. FACING PAGE The Oval groundsman, Bill Gordon, checks the wicket before the start of the Fifth Test.

With 23,000 packed inside the ground the atmosphere on the first morning was red-hot. The tempo was raised even further by a stirring rendition of William Blake's 'Jerusalem', blasted out of the tannoy system, with lyrics supplied helpfully on the large screen placed

hour of play starting, England had rattled along to 70 and a score of 450-plus looked on, in keeping with Test matches at this famous old ground.

Two words changed the course of this innings, the Test and, for quite a while, the destiny of the Ashes. Shane Warne. At times during this enthralling series, the 35-year-old – written off before the summer as someone too old and too beaten down by the trials and tribulations of his personal life – had taken it almost

upon himself to thwart this hungry English team. By far and away the leading wicket-taker in the series, as well as providing invaluable runs with the bat, Warne not only seemed able to take on England single-handed, he clearly relished the prospect. He had more than done his bit already in this series. But he had not finished yet.

Both England and Australia believed in the importance of winning the first session of a Test match.

England had won this particular battle every time, even the first morning's play at a Lord's Test they would eventually lose. At 82–0 England were streets ahead. At 104–3, however, Australia – or rather Warne – had hit back hard. With the lunchtime score on 115–3, and on this batsman's paradise of a wicket, Australia now held the advantage.

The first sign of a turning tide was when Trescothick, after a rapid 43 that had included eight fours, played back to a drifting Warne delivery and edged to first slip. Matthew Hayden had put down more chances than he had held during this series, some of them proving to be incredibly damaging. This time, however, the Australian opening batsman pulled off a superb effort, falling back on his heels but still managing to shovel both hands forward to take the catch. In doing so Hayden showed tremendous agility and dismissed an English batsman whose average on this ground in Tests was over 80.

It appeared to be nothing more than a minor hiccup. Vaughan came to the crease, hit a couple of textbook cover-driven boundaries and looked to be in the mood for runs. The nature of his dismissal will, therefore, haunt him. Many have been beaten by incredible turn and spin from Warne, but Vaughan seized upon a delivery that pitched short and stood up. The ball should have been despatched directly to the boundary. Instead Vaughan only managed to pull it straight into the welcoming hands of Michael Clarke at mid-wicket. Vaughan's form had been inconsistent during this series, but a man who can score 166 at Old Trafford is always a crucial wicket to take.

Worse was to befall England and Ian Bell. The Warwickshire batsman should have entered the fray with confidence from his two half-centuries at Old Trafford, even if he did follow them up with two failures at Trent Bridge, but after just seven balls he was undone by a Warne delivery that straightened to leave him leg before. He had fallen foul of the Warne slider before, but this time the ball appeared to be heading down the leg side. Bell had registered another duck, poking forward inside the line, and England were now on 104–3. The belief in Bell's long-term international career remains intact, but on this occasion, with so much riding on the outcome, the obstinacy of Graham Thorpe was sorely missed.

Shortly after lunch England's lot worsened. Kevin Pietersen, who had begun the series so well, and who was still second in the England batting averages, let his natural attacking instincts get the better of him. The shot that undid him was neither a full-blown drive, nor a defensive push, but rather an in-between swish across his pads to a Warne ball that turned. He had gone for a brisk

14 and England were struggling, on a pitch such as this, on 131–4. The plan had been to amass a massive total. McGrath was performing tidily but without any menace. Lee and Tait were relatively easy to face here. But Warne had picked up four wickets from nowhere. The vast majority of the capacity crowd packed inside The Oval lowered their heads. Were they in the process of witnessing England stumble so close to the finish line?

Andrew Strauss did not think so. And in Andrew Flintoff he found an unlikely ally. Unlikely, not because Flintoff could not bat – the two half-centuries at Edgbaston and the century at Old Trafford had played a massive part in the current state of this series. Unlikely because, amazingly, these two batsmen had never batted together before, an indication that for all the merits of Strauss's wonderful start to Test match cricket, he had failed to convert any of his centuries into big hundreds.

Ironically, it was Strauss whom Australia had anointed before the start of the Ashes series as their 'bunny' – in other words the England batsman whom they targeted more than anyone else. He had made a good, indeed a brilliant, start to his international career, often proving to be the scourge of the South Africans during the winter, but he had never before faced the kind of pressure Messrs McGrath and Warne had in mind for him. In many ways it was a compliment to Strauss that they should pick him out. If Strauss hit good form, then the chances were so would England. Up until Old Trafford Strauss had promised much without really delivering at the crease. Yet when he reached three figures at The Oval, he became the first player on either side to have scored two centuries in this series. After Strauss had completed his customary celebration, a few throws of his bat in the direction of the England dressing room and a few flicks to the crowd, he was subjected to the biggest bear hug of his life from a delighted Flintoff, who all but squeezed every last breath out of the centurion.

Strauss's only slice of luck came on 114, when umpire Rudi Koertzen somehow missed a thin edge caught behind off Lee. By the time he was out, Strauss was looking shattered. Seven minutes short of six hours at the crease, he went half forward to the relentless Warne and offered a bat-pad chance to Simon Katich, who threw himself forward from silly mid-on to take the chance inches off the ground. As Strauss trooped off the pitch, the standing ovation was not only for the English opening batsman but also for Warne, who, on his last Test match appearance at The Oval, had taken the first five wickets to fall. The 129 runs Strauss produced were 18 short of his best total – 147 in Johannesburg the previous January against South Africa – but in the context of this game and the series, it was his best and most important innings.

'In terms of importance it's probably the best innings I've ever played,' Strauss confirmed later. 'Today was crucial in the context of the series and it was vitally important that one of us stayed in and put together a big score.'

In compiling his seventh Test century Strauss added a further note to his name. Only three batsmen in Test history had scored more tons in the 19 Tests it had taken Strauss – Don Bradman with 12, George Headley with 10, and Arthur Morris with 9. Strauss was equal fourth now in the list, together with England's Herbert Sutcliffe and West Indian Viv Richards.

Strauss and Flintoff had put on 143 runs in their first ever partnership, with both revealing patience and restraint. One might expect that of Strauss. But Flintoff, one of the most destructive batsmen in the world, had

BELOW Shane Warne bowls Kevin Pietersen for 14. FACING PAGE A chastened Pietersen returns to the pavilion after his dismissal.

added this new weapon to his impressive armoury. He had proved this during his ton at Trent Bridge and he showed off his new-found skill again in south London. Even last summer Flintoff knew of only one way to bat. To ask him to shore up one end was like asking the Australians to concede defeat. Yet now Flintoff was becoming increasingly dependable.

Flintoff recovered well, too, to play a measured innings after a 93 mph bouncer from Lee hit him on the head early in his innings. It would have been asking too much for Flintoff to be morphed into a defensive batsman, as his 12 fours and one, towering six proved, but at least he played with the responsibility lacking in those English batsmen who had preceded him. He afforded Warne the respect that others had failed, to their peril, to give him, only laying in to the leg-spinner after tea when three fours in successive balls brought up his fifty. Later he would also strike that six into the heart of the new stand.

When he and Strauss joined forces England were 131–4. When Flintoff departed England had forged ahead to a more pleasing 274–5. It was the second highest English partnership of the summer. If the morning session had gone to Australia, the afternoon had belonged to England. Yet there would be another twist in the day, totally in keeping with the nature of this Ashes series.

By the close of play Australia had taken two further wickets to reduce England to 319–7. After McGrath had put paid to Flintoff, inducing an edge to Warne at slip on 72 just when the big Lancastrian was homing in on

FACING PAGE It's another Ashes hundred for Andrew Strauss.
ABOVE Gone for 129. A spectacular catch by Simon Katich accounts for Strauss off the bowling of Warne.

another century, and Warne had finally seen off Strauss, Shaun Tait then dismissed Paul Collingwood for seven, although the Durham man can consider himself unlucky to be given out leg before to a slinging delivery that struck him outside the line of off stump. Geraint Jones and Ashley Giles, the latter playing in his fiftieth and most important Test match, saw off the remaining few overs of another absorbing day's cricket, and a day that Australia, just, had edged. The Ashes, and the champagne, were definitely still on ice.

'I feel we created a bit of pressure with partnerships which is something we have not done throughout this series,' Warne said, after claiming 5–118. 'We were able to build up a bit of pressure and I was able to try a few things to get wickets. I had to try and create a bit of doubt in Andrew Strauss's mind and force him into an error.' His latest five-for had hauled his wickets tally for the series up to 33, just one short of his best ever Ashes total with still one English innings to go. 'I'm pretty proud of my efforts and to bowl 20-odd overs in one spell shows what a young athlete can do,' he joked. 'We have probably got our noses in front but I'm not sure we've got England by the throat.' Warne did reserve some praise for Strauss, however. 'He hung in there and toughed it out, which is one of the hallmarks of the series. Although I think he would be the first to say he had a bit of luck.'

Strauss explained that at last he was beginning to get on top of Warne. 'Merlyn [the England bowling machine] has helped a bit with Warney but I think I've improved against him because I've been able to get in his mind. Only by playing against him can you work out how he tries to get you out. I certainly didn't at any stage enjoy the innings because of the game situation. The high level of expectation has been very hard to get away from over the last week or so. It was frustrating that I got out in the end but I will wake up tomorrow morning feeling pretty happy with life. If we can get to 370-plus

then we are in the game. I certainly hope this game isn't another nail-biter but the way it has gone today shows it might well be another very close match. I think there will definitely be a result.'

Weather permitting. It was always going to be a big ask to expect a five-day Test in the middle of an English September to be played uninterrupted. Now Australia were praying that the weather, as it had been for much

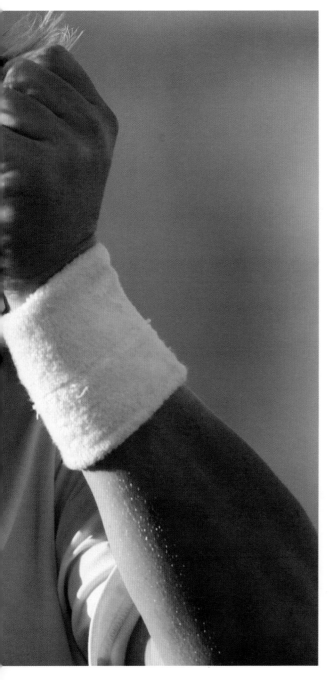

of the summer, would remain kind to them. The only time it rained it served them a massive favour in Manchester, where England just ran out of time to bowl Australia out and win. Now they looked for no rain to fall at all if they were to win this match and retain the Ashes.

England would have been happy with rain but even happier to have kicked on in the morning and amassed the kind of first innings total that would bat Australia out of the game. The best scenario would be to win this match. The second best would be to draw after five days, with England more than holding their own. To draw due to inclement weather would only be third best, but it would still be preferable to losing.

The onus was on Geraint Jones. He began well enough, driving Lee off the back foot for a textbook boundary, but then lost his off stump to the ninth, and next, ball of the day, playing seemingly down the wrong line to a Lee delivery of ideal length and high pace that sent the stump flying out of the ground. With England 325–8, Australia were now, quite clearly, on top.

Given the situation, England were more than happy to eke out a further 48 runs before being bowled out. Ashley Giles was mostly responsible for this, although Hoggard hung around for 36 balls for his two runs, before being undone by a slower ball from McGrath that saw him spoon up a simple catch to Damien Martyn at mid-off. This was only what Australia had deserved. Earlier Ponting had dropped a Hoggard edge off McGrath, and then umpire Koertzen failed to hear a clear nick from Giles off the same bowler that flew straight to Gilchrist, who started his appeal even before the ball had stuck in his gloves. McGrath was so annoyed that he sent Michael Clarke to retrieve his cap from the umpire. Ponting, meanwhile, demanded an explanation and on hearing Koertzen's version continued to argue.

Harmison took the alternative route to Hoggard's approach, smashing 20 off just 20 deliveries. This included an entertaining mini-innings of 12 off just three balls in the middle of an over from Lee. The first four was a beauty, struck firmly back between Lee and mid-off at a fantastic rate of knots. The second came from the predictable bouncer, an attempted hook shot that flew upwards and over wicket-keeper Gilchrist from a top edge. Ball three was another short delivery, which Harmison connected with properly this time to pull the ball to the square-leg boundary. So well was Harmison batting that he must have been miffed when Giles turned down an easy single for himself to protect Harmison from Warne. If the pair had run well they could probably have managed two at a time when England needed every run on offer. Giles's decision to stay put was made to look

LEFT **An apparently exasperated Shane Warne seems to be pulling his hair out during England's first innings.**

even worse when, next ball, umpire Billy Bowden rose his arthritic finger skywards to adjudge Giles out, leg before to Warne. In defence of Giles it was a poor decision. Replays proved that Warne's delivery was spinning past the off stump by some distance. It gave

Warne final figures of 6–122, and his 34th wicket of the series, equalling the 34 from the 1993 Ashes that included his 'wonder ball' to dismiss Mike Gatting.

England's final first innings total was 373. It was not exactly a poor score, nor one that would necessarily lose a match, but it was below par on the kind of batting pitch offered up by The Oval. Australia saw their chance, only to then make a decision that baffled every observer.

For the whole summer the Australian opening partnership of Justin Langer and Matthew Hayden had been misfiring. Langer had been the better of the two, scoring a couple of stubborn half-centuries, without ever finding his true form. Hayden, by his lofty standards, had endured a miserable time. The fact that their best opening partnership up to this point in the series had been 58 told its own story.

This was about to change. At the close of play Australia had reached 112 without loss, with Langer scoring the lion's share of the runs with 75. This was

FACING PAGE On your way! Brett Lee bowls Geraint Jones for 25. BELOW Glenn McGrath cannot believe that Rudi Koertzen has given Ashley Giles not out after he seemingly edged to Gilchrist. RIGHT Skipper Ponting asks umpire Koertzen for an explanation.

their fourteenth hundred partnership. Hayden, having been dismissed so often in the series playing aggressive strokes when seemingly settled, set about producing a very un-Hayden style of innings. At stumps he remained undefeated on 32, gained from 96 balls, and a sure sign that he had turned up the chance of hitting himself back into form in favour of spending time at the crease.

The pair performed a role reversal. Langer's innings was more of a hot-potch of strokes. Always able to dig in, Langer had added to his repertoire of shots in recent years and mixed it up as the light began to fade. He also took his fair share of knocks and hits, as is Langer's wont. The last time he played in an Ashes Test at The Oval he suffered concussion after being struck by Andrew Caddick. He went on to make a hundred.

It was easier for him this time. Harmison appeared strangely subdued, and the umpires were keen to ensure

ABOVE An Australian fan watches Hayden and Langer pile up the runs from a perch on a pub roof overlooking The Oval.

that any ruses England tried in order to induce early reverse swing were nullified. When Flintoff threw the ball in from long on, for example, so that it bounced on to the pitch well short of Geraint Jones behind the stumps, he received an unofficial warning from umpire Bowden.

Langer also had a preconceived plan to go for Giles. England had taken the gamble of playing an extra batsman in Collingwood at the expense of a fourth seamer in James Anderson, although Collingwood could be a useful bowler in his own right. Now it was looking as if the wrong selection had been made. Langer knew this. He also knew that if he could hit Giles out of the attack

early on, then England's three main seamers would be required to toil away. In Giles's first over Langer hit him for two sixes. Vaughan removed Giles, then put him on again at the other end where the boundary was a little further to clear.

Two difficult chances were offered by Langer as he attempted to push on. The first flew head high past Strauss in the gully, barely a chance at all. The second was parried by Trescothick going high to his right at a wide first slip. Langer was on 53 at the time, but this chance, too, would have been extremely difficult to hold.

Then came the inexplicable. Offered the light immediately after the tea interval, the opening pair took it and strode purposefully off the pitch in the belief that some brighter conditions would come before the day was

people are jumping up and down about it but we have no control over that. Before tea it seemed OK, but the moment we walked out we saw how lit up the scoreboard was. We were not expecting to lose as much time but the way the series has played out, most of the Tests have been decided inside four days. It was a magnificent batting wicket with a very fast outfield, and we have got the opportunity to score heavily tomorrow or the next day, whenever the weather allows.'

England had a different point of view. 'We were surprised Australia took the light,' Ashley Giles admitted. 'It was a bit dark and I don't know what we would have done in the same situation. They could have batted on and lost a few quick wickets. Of course, I hope they live to regret it but there are three days left in this Test match.'

On the face of it this still seemed like an extraordinarily cautious decision when caution was the last thing Australia needed. Would Ponting's call to bring in his men be as poor as his decision to put England in to bat first at Edgbaston? Time would tell. But the partisan crowd, for once, were not complaining. They may have missed out on 85 minutes' cricket, but they also knew England were 85 minutes closer to winning back the Ashes. Australia should have quite clearly carried on, though. At 112–0 the onus was on them to keep going in search of a score of around 500-plus. England's depleted bowling attack had barely threatened, Simon Jones was not in the match, and the wicket remained true. Having worked so very hard to gain it, it now seemed as if Australia had surrendered the initiative. They saw it differently. The plan would be for Langer and Hayden to carry on, accumulating runs at first on Saturday morning then setting up a feeding frenzy for their middle-order batsmen, with so many wickets in hand, to establish a huge first innings lead. But the weather intervened.

At first it hardly seemed to matter. Play began half an hour later and by lunch Australia had moved on without losing a wicket, although they were fortunate to do so. Langer somehow survived a leg-before appeal from the first ball of the day, bowled by Hoggard. Umpire Bowden remained motionless behind the non-striker's stumps. During the first passage of play, lasting 35 minutes, England seemed capable of taking a wicket at any time. There were plenty of other close calls for leg before, while Hayden would have been run out in the third over had a Collingwood shy from mid-wicket found its target. The afternoon session, though, was limited to just 25 minutes and in that time England finally made a breakthrough. By then Langer had reached his twenty-second Test century, having slowed down a little in the nervous nineties. With his next shot he also reached 7000 runs in Test cricket. Shortly afterwards, though, when on 105, Langer dragged a ball delivered by an

through. They did not, and when rain eventually ended play early with just over half of the scheduled overs bowled, Australia must have wondered whether their gamble would pay off. Before the early evening rain came they had passed up 85 minutes' play in a game they needed to win. Put another way, some 20 overs and a possible 60 to 80 runs. England's bowling had looked anything but probing, and the opening partnership appeared at ease. The Saturday forecast was far from promising, either.

'We spoke about it briefly at tea,' Langer explained. 'Ricky and Adam Gilchrist agreed it was the same as any other Test match. It was very dark, and Andrew Flintoff was reverse-swinging the ball before tea. It was important we played him in the best conditions possible. I know

appreciably faster Harmison on to his stumps. Australia were 185–1, and Langer and Hayden had just put on the largest stand for any wicket in the whole Ashes series.

Ponting joined Hayden, the latter finally beginning to play some shots. Watery sunshine permitted some more play after tea. Giles was unlucky, twice. First he saw a thick edge fly off Hayden's bat, when the batsman was on 84, and past the wicket-keeper. Then he had a bat-pad chance caught by Bell refused by umpire Bowden.

FACING PAGE Andrew Flintoff appeals unsuccessfully for lbw against Matthew Hayden. ABOVE Justin Langer goes after Ashley Giles.

After another stoppage – there were five in total, which not only truncated the day's play but also gave England's reduced bowling attack time to recover each time – Hayden completed the most patient century of his career. In the process of notching up a twenty-first Test hundred, he also passed 6000 Test runs. Ponting was out shortly afterwards, fending off a lifter from Flintoff that carried, just, to gully, where Strauss dived forward and to his right to take the catch. Hayden, joined by Damien Martyn, added a further 13 runs before stumps to leave Australia on a commanding 277–2, now 96 runs behind England's first innings total. There were still two days remaining of this final Test match, and Australia really needed to accelerate on the Sunday. But if they could carve out a lead of around 200 and have time to bowl a tricky ten overs at England before the close of play, and then have the best part of three sessions to bowl them

BELOW Matthew Hayden pulls for four during his innings of 138. RIGHT Glenn McGrath and Justin Langer in the pavilion after the Australian batsmen came off for bad light on Friday afternoon.

out on the Monday, then Australia would have every chance of retaining the Ashes.

England's task was very different. First they had to start making inroads the next day into the Australian batting line-up to prevent them securing a major first innings advantage. They would be given the new ball after just 1.2 overs in the morning to help their cause. Then England would need to produce a rearguard action in their second innings, something they had not grown accustomed to in recent years, and something

they would need to do against Shane Warne. Time may have been against Australia, but they stood as good a chance of winning this Test match as drawing it.

Certainly Langer felt the win was well within Australia's grasp. 'We're in a good position because we've laid a pretty good foundation,' he argued. 'Damien Martyn is a champion who is due a big score and Michael Clarke is one of the world's best one-day players. Some of England's batsmen are under pressure and we have the great Glenn McGrath and Shane Warne. Brett Lee is

bowling beautifully and Shaun Tait is ready to rip a few toes up.' Langer was also pleased to see his friend Hayden finally back in the runs. 'He never talked about saving his career,' Langer explained. 'This game is not about individual glory. This is about the Australian cricket team beating England. Over the last few years there's been moments of personal glory, but this match is different. This is such a big game.'

Strauss made no secret of his happiness to come off the pitch on a weather-affected day. 'Obviously any rain

ABOVE Justin Langer plays on to Steve Harmison after scoring a 146-ball 105. FACING PAGE Freddie Flintoff chats with a gathering of Ian Bothams, Batmen and Robins.

is probably in our favour so I wasn't too disappointed to lose a lot of play today,' he admitted. 'But tomorrow, we can safely say, is going to be very important in the context of this series.'

Flintoff, who made a point of congratulating Hayden when the Australian reached three figures, produced some fighting talk on the Saturday night. He had been magnificent throughout the punctured day, beginning it with three maidens, and ending it by giving Ponting such a torrid time that, eventually, he claimed his wicket. In doing so he became only the second Englishman in history, after Ian Botham, to claim 20 wickets and score 300 runs in an Ashes series. 'We've scrapped and fought for a long time now,' he said. 'This side have put in some special performances and now we need to put in another one. My gut feeling is that Australia have their noses in front, but we have to come out strongly and take a few early wickets. By no means are we out of this game. Every

ounce we have in our tanks has to be left out in the middle. There's so much at stake, and not many people are complaining about it being a long summer, but it's a massive two days now, and we'll be out there fighting. Anything less and the Australians will find us out.'

Indeed England, and Flintoff in particular, would be out there fighting. Much of the crowd may have started the Sunday morning hoping that rain would prevent Australia from taking a large first innings lead. But who needs rain if you have Flintoff, and Hoggard, for that matter, in your side?

Day four began with The Oval once more packed to its rafters. People, as they had been for the previous three days, were sitting on rooftops close by or hanging out of windows five floors up in neighbouring apartment blocks. If English cricket was on the verge of its greatest success in 18 years, then as many people as possible wanted to say that they had been there.

Maybe they knew something that we did not. For all the world it seemed that Australia were in the dominant position. England, their confidence and determination intact, thought otherwise. Captain Vaughan assembled his ten other men for a pre-start team talk, delivered in a circular huddle. By the time he had finished, his troops were sprinting off into the outfield. By tea England had not only bowled Australia out but had even accomplished it with a six-run first innings advantage.

From 277–2, Australia capitulated to 367 all out amid murky conditions that favoured the swing of Matthew Hoggard and the movement off the seam of Andrew Flintoff. By mid-afternoon Hoggard had returned to the often unplayable form that had terrorised the South Africans the winter before, and Flintoff had collected the second five-wicket haul of his Test career.

In truth the England fightback had begun the night before when the indefatigable Flintoff, with little reward, kept piling into the Australian batsmen. The wicket of Ponting was richly deserved on the Saturday evening, and it proved to be the catalyst for what was to take place come Sunday. That, and the rousing battle cry that Flintoff delivered to the rest of the side.

By then Australia had no choice but to bat in poor light. Both Hayden and Damien Martyn were offered the light by umpires Koertzen and Bowden, and both turned it down flat. The irony of this was that now Australia wished Hayden and Langer had continued batting on the Friday evening instead of taking up the umpires' offer. With time fast running out for them to force a win, by Sunday morning Australia had no choice but to face Flintoff and company in a light that had the bulbs on the scoreboard shining brightly.

This was the chance England were looking for. Australia would still be wanting to pile on a big enough first innings total to then bowl England out again without needing to bat a second time. They could not afford to declare, certainly not before tea, because the England batsmen would take the first opportunity to return to the pavilion when offered the light themselves.

The fightback began in the third over of Sunday morning, when Martyn received a brute of a short ball from Flintoff that reared up into his face. The number four batsman, bereft of serious runs this tour, played a half pull that looped up and into the hands of the advancing Collingwood. As Martyn departed so Australia's twelfth man, Stuart MacGill, emerged to deliver an order from the dressing room. Within a few balls the message was clear. Start hitting out!

ABOVE Andrew Flintoff watches Matthew Hayden and Damien Martyn leave for the pavilion, having accepted an offer of bad light to bring play to a close on Saturday evening. FACING PAGE TOP Paul Collingwood has just caught Martyn off Flintoff on Sunday morning. FACING PAGE BOTTOM Geraint Jones drops Michael Clarke off Matthew Hoggard.

It was a strange decision to make in the circumstances. Australia needed the runs, but they did not need to be losing too many wickets in the process. Much better to stay at the crease, gain a reasonable advantage, and then have the best part of four sessions over the Sunday evening and Monday to bowl England out. Instead they went for all-out aggression and, with the aid of Flintoff and Hoggard, fell on their swords.

For a while, though, it was still looking dangerous for England. They had to wait for over an hour to capture the key wicket with the second new ball. Hayden had moved on to 138 when he received the ball of the match. Looking to push on, he was beginning to look like the bullying, bludgeoning batsman of old when Flintoff produced a delivery that moved in on the left-hander like a leg break at over 90 mph. Hayden knew as soon as the ball slammed into his pads that he was out, leg before. Simon Katich fell in similar fashion in Flintoff's next over, and suddenly Australia were 329–5.

In came Adam Gilchrist. All summer the wicket-keeper had suggested he was on the verge of producing something big. All summer England had snuffed him out. Could they do this one more time? Flintoff had had the measure of the man for much of this time, but Flintoff was not going to completely dominate the proceedings. Up stepped Hoggard. With Gilchrist joining forces with Clarke, this was Australia's potentially most destructive pairing. Natural one-day players both, this was their chance to become heroes.

In reality, neither had a prayer. Clarke survived two lucky reprieves, both off Hoggard. First Flintoff, of all people, missed a simple chance at slip, proving to those who wondered that he was, indeed, a mere mortal. Then Geraint Jones – again – put down a snick behind when he dived in vain to his right. Trescothick, standing at first slip, would have had a better chance if allowed.

Gilchrist, meanwhile, had looked threatening once again. He had already smashed 23 off just 20 balls when he fell, leg before, to a Hoggard inswinger for the second time in the game. The wicket heralded a slightly early lunch, and rapturous applause from a disbelieving Oval crowd. England had been under the cosh. Suddenly they were on top.

If the morning had belonged to Flintoff, the afternoon was Hoggard's. Vaughan had decided to call upon Hoggard, and not the out-of-sorts Harmison, to back up Flintoff in swing-friendly conditions. It was another inspired decision. Unperturbed by the two missed chances off his bowling before lunch, Hoggard finally got his man, pinning Clarke in front of his stumps with a delivery that straightened. Hoggard implored umpire Koertzen to raise his finger. The South African takes an interminably long time to do this, but eventually he did. For Clarke, it was like a slow death.

Now England were into the Australian tail, a tail that had wagged all summer. Warne and Lee had been especially hard to pin down, and even McGrath had proven dogged, but not on this day. Flintoff knew that Warne would be aggressive and so returned the favour. In one exceptional over he beat Warne time and time again with moving balls that had the Australian leg-spinner smiling wryly. 'You can't expect me to hit those,'

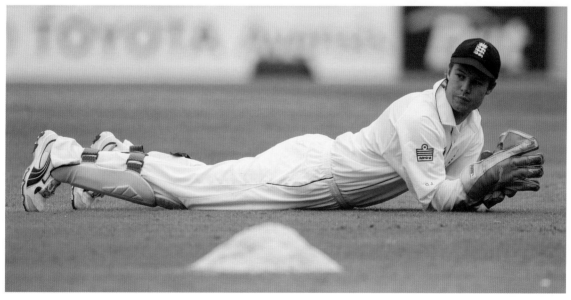

he said to the English fielders, acknowledging his own batting frailties and the brilliance of Flintoff. When Flintoff finally dug one in short, Warne attempted to pull but, beaten by the pace, only lofted the ball back towards Vaughan at mid-on. The England captain juggled with the ball for a heart-stopping moment, then grinned from ear to ear as both hands smothered it. Flintoff was pretty happy, too. He had just collected his fifth wicket of the innings.

It was left to Hoggard to wrap the innings up. McGrath had wasted little time in informing people how much his batting had improved over the course of the summer. Australia believed this to be the case, too, hence McGrath's promotion to number ten. Yet he would last only six balls, thick-edging an outswinger to Strauss at second slip. With just Shaun Tait remaining, Brett Lee decided to hit out. It was a policy that had brought him plenty of runs in the previous Tests, but on this occasion it proved to be his undoing. Lee swung to deep mid-wicket, Giles ran smartly round and took a hard catch above his head close to the boundary.

Australia were all out for 367, six runs short of England. Their last seven wickets had fallen for just 44 runs in 90 balls, Australia having taken 434 balls to lose their first two. Flintoff had bowled unchanged from one end, revealing extraordinary fortitude and the merits of a get-fit campaign a couple of years back that improved his stamina no end. His figures of 5–78 produced only his second five-for in his Test career, following one against the West Indies 18 months previously. Hoggard ended up with 4–97 and, like Strauss, had grown better and better the longer this series had gone on. In one devastating spell, the Yorkshireman had recorded figures of 4–4 in 19 balls. He and Flintoff walked off the field arm in arm, having snared nine of the ten Australian first innings wickets.

The only concern now for England was that, having seen Australia struggle so much in seamer-friendly conditions, they now had to venture out and face the Australian bowling. Although England were happy to bowl Australia out, it gave the tourists much longer to bowl England out now and then knock off however many runs they were in deficit. A tremendous half-day for England it may have been, but this Test match, and the Ashes, were still hanging by a thread.

Once again the fading light became the telling factor. Even when England were bowling they were keen to remind the umpires of the darkening skies above. 'Can you put some lights on the bails?' Flintoff asked umpire Koertzen. 'I can't see them. I don't know where I'm bowling.' A ball flashed past Giles at gully, an incident that prompted the spinner to call for a helmet. Ian Bell blinked repeatedly after a possible catch bounced just in front of him, the ball ending up striking the player on the knee. Michael Vaughan kept drying the ball with a rag, each wipe delivered with exaggeration.

The Australian team emerged from their dressing room resplendent in sunglasses and smiles. The smattering of Australian supporters amid a predominantly partisan crowd of English cricket fans peeled off their shirts and pretended to tan themselves in the full glare of a non-existent sun. Much of the rest of The Oval responded by lifting their umbrellas to the sky to perform a rain dance. Every summer a Test series is affected at some point by inclement weather. Every English summer a match at some point is disrupted by bad light and falling rain. And every summer such scenes are met with groans. Not on the penultimate day of the Ashes, however. Over 20,000 people inside the ground and a further ten million viewers watching on television in England were hoping for bad weather.

England went into bat just before 2.00 pm, the opening pair of Trescothick and Strauss making sure that their long, squinting stares up into the murky sky could be seen by both umpires. It seemed to do the trick. After just one over from Lee, captain Ricky Ponting was forced to bring on Shane Warne. Improbably, Australia were using a leg-spinner with the new ball. Nevertheless, with just his fourth ball Warne accounted for Andrew Strauss, who prodded half-forward and offered a bat-pad catch to Katich at short leg. Strauss had gone for just one run, and England were 2–1.

The next over McGrath, for once not using his brain, sent down a bouncer to Vaughan. Perhaps it was the realisation that he was deemed slow enough these days to be regarded as safe to face in poor light. Whatever the reason, McGrath's bouncer prompted action. Umpire Billy Bowden first lectured McGrath, then listened to Vaughan's pleas after a single to the England captain had brought him down to the non-striker's end. Bowden looked across at his fellow umpire, Rudi Koertzen, and ran his fingers across his throat as if slitting it. After the briefest of conferences between the umpires, the light was offered to the England captain and vice-captain. Trescothick and Vaughan were almost running back to their dressing room before the offer had even been completed. It was 7–1.

There then followed some of the most amazing scenes ever witnessed inside a cricket ground. People had paid between £40 and £60 for a seat at The Oval to watch riveting action in this compelling series, and now they were chanting 'Off, off, off'. As the players scampered from the field, the majority of the crowd were

cheering, and champagne bottles were demonstratively uncorked in the corporate boxes.

Australia were far from happy. How, they argued, could play be deemed dangerous when they were now using a twin spin attack of Warne and Michael Clarke? 'If it is dangerous with the quicks on, that is when we give the fielding side the option to put the spinners on,' umpire Koertzen said, explaining Law 3.9 of the laws of cricket. 'If that becomes unfair then we will take them off the field. In the case of spin bowlers we give them a lot more leeway, but when it gets to the stage when it is unfair then we offer the light to the batsmen. You can lose the ball, even when it is bowled slowly.'

LEFT Moment of truth. Warne drops Pietersen off Lee with the England number five on 15. He went on to make 158. BELOW Even when the Australian cause became hopeless, Brett Lee still thundered in and gave everything. FACING PAGE Kevin Pietersen at the business end of a Lee bouncer.

up facing Shane Warne and Glenn McGrath for the very last time in England.

Hoggard had lived through enough of this series to know that only a fool would assume the urn was in England's grasp. 'It's by no means over,' he said. 'We're playing the best in the world, and there's the small matter of Mr Warne to contend with. We know we're up for a big fight. We know they're going to come out at us hard. We know they've got one last chance to keep the Ashes. We'll be looking to bat a long time, put some runs on the board and, hopefully, not have to bowl again.'

He preferred to praise Flintoff's display to talking about his own. 'To lose Simon Jones and see Fred bowl 15 overs. Well, who would have thought Fred would bowl all those overs on the trot? It's unbelievable, a Herculean effort. Everyone's put their hands up. We all want to win the Ashes. If we can it's going to be fantastic, not just for cricket, but for every sport in England. Cricket has been in the headlines, on the front page and on the back. Even David Beckham has been talking about it. Can you believe it, football talking about cricket?'

Play later resumed for a while. England moved on to 34–1 without any further scares before bad light ended the proceedings for the day once and for all. With play officially abandoned at 6.15 pm the whole of England started to make calculations. The forecast for the last day's play of this final Ashes Test was good. A full day's play was more than likely. With England 40 runs ahead, at what point on the Monday would they feel safe and confident that the Ashes had been won?

At the least they would need to bat until tea, by which time they should have an advantage of around 230 to 240 runs. That would leave Australia the tall order of chasing such a total in one session. It was not impossible, especially with Hayden and Langer back in form, and Ponting, Clarke and Gilchrist, even Warne and Lee, capable of running amok, but it would be a big, big ask of them. That said, batting through until tea, and taking up 60 of the 98 overs scheduled for the day, might also be a major challenge for a nervous English batting line-

Australia's coach, John Buchanan, issued a promise that this Test, like all those before, would be a fight to the finish. 'I know how our players will approach the final day's play,' he said. 'They are keen and they are ready to go. We will be trying to take what wickets we can. We need to take them early, and keep the runs down. If we can do that, who knows? As we have all seen through the series, there have been plenty of twists and turns and I'm sure there will be more.' After everything else that had taken place in the past two months, who would disagree?

And so we had come down to day five of the Fifth Test. Who would have predicted that the whole series would still be dangling on a serrated knife's edge on the twenty-fifth and final day of the best Ashes series in history? The last time an Ashes contest genuinely went down to the wire was almost 35 years ago, in the 1970–71 series, when England were led by Ray Illingworth. England, for those looking for omens, went on to win.

Now came the most important day, arguably, in English cricket history and in English sport for almost 40 years. Only the day of the 2003 Rugby World Cup final between England and Australia came close, and that was a sporting occasion witnessed on the other side of the world, in Sydney. On 12 September 2005 London came to a virtual standstill. The number of workers strangely absent through sickness shot up as rapidly as the number of cars in the rush hour went down. Sales in shops shrank dramatically, and even in the schools television and radio sets were switched on and lessons went to pot. Only the pubs and bars remained full, and all eyes were fixed on the screens showing the final day's action.

Once again the strains of Blake's 'Jerusalem' shrilled out of the tannoy system around The Oval to start the day's proceedings. Australia appeared from their dressing room and bounded down the long flight of

FACING PAGE That's it! Kevin Pietersen completes his maiden Test century, steering England to safety at The Oval. BELOW Once in a lifetime players. Two of cricket's all-time greats, Glenn McGrath and Shane Warne, bid farewell to Test cricket in England.

steps with genuine purpose. Trescothick and Vaughan followed, their arrival on to the field of play met with a tumultuous reception from a fiercely patriotic and apprehensive crowd.

For a while they had little to worry about. Vaughan and Trescothick started well, the former adopting an aggressive approach as he raced towards a half-century. Five runs short, he fell to a beauty from McGrath, the ball leaving the England captain, finding the edge of his bat and producing a diving, one-handed catch from Gilchrist behind.

In walked Ian Bell. It was one thing smacking big hundreds against Bangladesh. It was entirely another thing entering the cauldron, with the small matter of the Ashes at stake. McGrath produced a replica of the ball that had dismissed Vaughan. Bell nudged forward, edged to first slip, and Warne did the rest. Bell was out first ball, which made it a pair in the match, and England were suddenly 63–3.

Kevin Pietersen, sporting a white stripe in his hair that made him look like a skunk, came to the crease. His contribution to the England cause with the bat had been

large but, by his standards, his form had slightly tailed off since Birmingham. If ever a big innings was required from him, this was the moment. McGrath had other ideas. He steamed in on a hat-trick, sent a brute of a bouncer down towards Pietersen, and then appealed with the rest of his team-mates, convinced that the batsman had gloved the ball to the slips. Umpire Bowden remained impassive. Television replays proved that the ball had missed a glove by a whisker and struck Pietersen's shoulder.

Moments later Warne induced a faint edge from his Hampshire colleague. Pietersen got lucky this time. The edge deflected off Gilchrist's glove enough to deviate away from Hayden's hands at first slip and on to his leg instead. Pietersen had not yet scored. Then, when on 15, Lee persuaded him to drive at a full-length ball. This had been his undoing before, and it should have been again. The edge flew to Warne at first slip for a regulation catch. Or at least it should have been. Instead it popped out of Warne's cupped hands on to the turf. Flintoff had dropped a similar sitter the day before. Now Warne, a world-class slip fielder, had done the same. The

leg-spinner had been outstanding throughout the Ashes series, primarily with his unprecedented haul of wickets but also with the bat. At times he had taken on England single-handedly. Yet now he had dropped Pietersen and, as the day went on, it became clear how big a blunder this was. Warne had just dropped the Ashes.

He made some amends for this by pinning Trescothick leg before for 33 with a ball that turned viciously out of the rough and into the left-hander. Flintoff emerged from the England dressing room amid deafening cheers but, after cutting one, sweet four off Warne, clipped a lofted shot straight back to the spinner who gobbled up the catch. The silence that greeted this dismissal was in some contrast to Flintoff's welcome.

England were now 125-5 – 131 runs ahead with a couple of overs to go before lunch. At this point Australia were marginal favourites to win the Test and retain the Ashes. The tension was becoming unbearable as the realisation dawned on a packed Oval that the series appeared to be going the whole way, with the wrong result becoming increasingly likely.

Paul Collingwood would score only ten runs – but these were ten of the most important runs in his career – off 51 balls and in a crucial 71 minutes that witnessed a 60-run partnership. While he dug in at one end, Pietersen decided to let fly at the other. He had been dropped twice and reckoned that Australia now needed to pay. Attack, for this new star of world cricket, was the best form of defence. Warne went for an incredible six over mid-wicket and, later, another one over his head, but Lee would be the bowler Pietersen laid into most. In one unforgettable over he top-edged a hook for six, hooked the next ball for four, via the outstretched hand of the diving Shaun Tait at long leg, and then clipped another four even finer. He took 16 runs in all off the over as England's advantage began to rocket.

The game was far from won, however, when Collingwood fell to Warne, taken smartly by the predatory Ponting off a bat-pad chance. Then when Geraint Jones lost his off stump to a ball that kept low from Tait, Australia were back in business. England were 195-7 and if their tail failed to perform Australia still had every chance of winning.

Striking the winning runs off Warne at Trent Bridge would have been hard to beat, but Ashley Giles now produced an innings that matched that experience. With an increasingly rampant Pietersen, he put on a devastating partnership of 136, the highest eighth-wicket partnership by England against Australia at The

FACING PAGE Bad light forces the players from the field after only four deliveries of Australia's second innings. RIGHT Ashley Giles, one of the heroes with the bat for England, waits patiently in the pavilion for the officials to decide what happens next.

ABOVE Simon Jones and Andrew Strauss – two key members of the Class of '05. RIGHT Kevin Pietersen is interviewed by Paul Allott as dusk gathers at The Oval.

Oval. Pietersen reached his maiden Test century with a sumptuous drive off McGrath, a boundary that prompted wild celebrations from the South African-born batsman as he waved to his brother in the crowd and shook his bat to all points of the boundary. The shackles were virtually off England now. The crowd began to sing their victory songs. 'Sweet Chariot', borrowed from English rugby, soon bellowed from the stands.

Pietersen's innings was, quite simply, astonishing. He had proven himself capable of scoring violent half-centuries in Test match cricket already, but to go on to make a big century, and one littered with aggression, was beyond belief. McGrath finally got rid of him, moving the ball off the seam to remove his off stump, but by then Pietersen and McGrath both knew the game was up. Pietersen's incredible 158 came from just 187 balls and included 15 fours and seven sixes, the number of sixes beating the innings record against Australia set by Ian

Botham in 1981. Who cared about those six dropped catches during the Ashes series? Pietersen had just ensured that the urn would be won by an England team now on 308–8 and home and dry.

Giles deserved the plaudits, too, for his role on the last day. When he came to the crease England were still stuttering on 199–7. When he left, bowled behind his legs by Warne, his country had raced on to 335–9. The 59 Giles hit was immensely valuable. All his early series doubts were now long forgotten. Warne ended the England innings two balls later by inducing Harmison to edge to Hayden at first slip, the veteran leg-spinner still able to turn the ball after bowling 39 overs in the innings. England had been dismissed for 335. Warne's final innings figures in his last Test appearance in England read 6–124, making 12 wickets in the Test. He ended the series with 40 English wickets to his name. In doing so he became the leading wicket-taker in the history of the Ashes, his 172 English victims five more than Dennis Lillee's haul. Warne and McGrath left the field arm in arm, waving their caps and rightly accepting applause from a standing ovation at The Oval.

That should have been that. The England dressing room was now awash with smiles. Pietersen and Giles, in particular, received huge bear hugs from just about everyone. Technically, though, there was still time for some play. Australia required 342 runs to win, with just 18 overs remaining. They could still win the Test – if they could score at 19 runs an over. The England team ran back on to the pitch to field, smiling and waving at the crowd. Justin Langer and Matthew Hayden came out to join them, survived four balls from Harmison, including one that bounced over both Langer and Geraint Jones on its way to the boundary, and then took the light offered to them by the umpires.

Still the game was not officially over. Then at 6.18 on the evening of Monday 12 September, umpires Billy Bowden and Rudi Koertzen walked theatrically out to the middle, removed the bails, and threw the stumps on to the ground. Now it was official. The Fifth Test had finished, England and Australia had drawn, and England, as a result, had won back the Ashes after winning the series 2–1.

Amid cheers that could be heard all over London, the teams embraced. One of the most striking elements of this Ashes series had been, in between the fire and brimstone served up by both teams, the sportsmanship on show. Here, at the end of a long summer, both sets of players shook hands and hugged each other. They knew there had been little between them, and they knew they had played their part in producing the most incredible series of Ashes Test matches ever.

At the presentation ceremony Shane Warne was voted Australia's Man of the Series, Kevin Pietersen the Man of the Match, and Andrew Flintoff picked up both the England Man of the Series award and the Compton-Miller Man of the Series award. It was left to England captain Michael Vaughan to pick up the most important prize of all. At 6.32 pm he lifted a replica of the urn that holds the Ashes above his head. Fireworks exploded into life, a shower of multi-coloured ticker tape poured down from the sky, the players began the most memorable lap of honour of their lives, and the whole of England began celebrations that would go on long into the night.

ABOVE 'Here, at the end of a long summer, both sets of players ... knew there had been little between them, and they knew they had played their part in producing the most incredible series of Ashes Test matches ever.' FACING PAGE Freddie and KP. 'We didn't do too bad a job did we?'

'It's just an amazing feeling,' Vaughan admitted. 'And it's been a real roller-coaster of a summer. Today we were set one hell of a challenge against Warne and McGrath. At the start of the summer winning the Ashes may have seemed like a distant dream, but I always believed we had ability and in this series we've expressed ourselves. It's been an incredible day, and an incredible series. Full credit to Australia. Ricky's team made us fight all the way. We've all aged years but the way the England team has responded to the challenge thrown down to them has been incredible.'

The Australians were gracious to the end. 'England outplayed us and did a fantastic job,' Ponting concluded. 'You'd expect an Australian team to keep on fighting to the end but England were too good. It's the best Test series I've ever been a part of.' Warne agreed. 'All credit must go to England,' he said. 'It was my best ever series, and the greatest series of Test matches I've ever played in, but England were just too good for us. We tried everything we could, but it wasn't enough against this England team.'

Everyone was talking about the Pietersen innings, too. 'KP was outstanding,' said Vaughan. Ponting agreed. 'It was a sensational knock. He has got a little bit of genius in him because he can play an extraordinary innings. Today he did just that.' Flintoff doffed his cap in honour of a superhuman display he approved of. 'Unbelievable,' he announced. 'That was one of the great Test innings.' Strauss concurred. 'It was the best innings I've ever seen.'

The man himself admitted to being virtually speechless. 'I'm pinching myself,' Pietersen said. 'I can't believe this day has happened. It's been a fantastic day. To score my first Test hundred in front of my Mum and brother is very special, but I have to say all the boys in the squad have been incredible for the whole two months. I'm so very grateful and this is absolutely fantastic. That's probably the best innings I'll ever play. It will be difficult to beat it.' Back in South Africa certain selectors must have been burrowing into the ground. In London, by contrast, they were thanking the Lord that Pietersen's mother, Penny, was born an Englishwoman.

The whole of the England team wanted to have their say. Strauss was one of the more eloquent. 'It's been seven weeks of emotional turmoil and we're absolutely knackered,' he admitted. 'But I'm a very proud man tonight.' Giles revealed that his morning net did not suggest the half-century to come. 'I had a terrible net and was out three times,' he said. 'Maybe I got rid of all the bad shots then. I'm so relieved we've come through.'

Coach Duncan Fletcher usually keeps his own counsel, but even he was caught up in the euphoria smothering The Oval. 'The players should be very proud of themselves, and England should be very proud of them,' he said. Paul Collingwood explained how it was better to play than to watch. 'I've been watching all summer and most of that time I've been in a terribly nervous state,' he said. 'It's worse watching it than playing. To come in for the last Test and to be here now when we've won the Ashes. Well, it's difficult to take in.'

Flintoff, naturally, spoke from the heart. 'As a kid I dreamt of moments like this,' he said. 'I used to watch the Ashes on TV, and that meant watching Australia win them. To play a major part in bringing the Ashes back home to England is unbelievable. It's pinch yourself time, isn't it? Today epitomised what this England team is all about. When something needs to be done there is always someone who sticks his hand up. Today was no different.'

No different in that sense, but very different in every other sense. That evening, as congratulations rained in on The Oval from the Queen and the Prime Minister, the streets of Kennington filled with partying cricket fans and the England team began their preparations for their open-top bus parade around Trafalgar Square the following day, the old urn was safely back in the keeping of English cricket. The Ashes had been won after the most thrilling, dramatic and quite brilliant series. The old guard that was Australia had finally fallen and world cricket was ready to embrace new champions. England had become the best cricket team in the world.

'We didn't do too bad a job, did we?' said Andrew 'Freddie' Flintoff, as he delivered the biggest smile of an English summer that had ended in the most glorious way. The man who more than anyone else had helped deliver the greatest prize in cricket was right. Not too bad a job? Not too bad at all.

PAGE 212 England salutes the Ashes winners – Trafalgar Square, 13 September 2005.

ENGLAND V AUSTRALIA, 5th Test, The Oval
8, 9, 10, 11, 12 SEPTEMBER 2005

TOSS: England
UMPIRES: BF Bowden (NZ) and RE Koertzen (SA)
TV UMPIRE: JW Lloyds **FOURTH UMPIRE:** JF Steele
MATCH REFEREE: RS Madugalle (SL)

Close of Play:
- **Day 1:** England 319-7 (Jones 21*, Giles 5*)
- **Day 2:** England 373, Australia 112-0 (Langer 75*, Hayden 32*)
- **Day 3:** Australia 277-2 (Hayden 110*, Martyn 9*)
- **Day 4:** Australia 367, England 34-1 (Trescothick 14*, Vaughan 19*)

England 1st innings			R	M	B	4	6
ME Trescothick	c Hayden	b Warne	43	77	65	8	0
AJ Strauss	c Katich	b Warne	129	351	210	17	0
*MP Vaughan	c Clarke	b Warne	11	26	25	2	0
IR Bell	lbw	b Warne	0	9	7	0	0
KP Pietersen	b Warne		14	30	25	2	0
A Flintoff	c Warne	b McGrath	72	162	115	12	1
PD Collingwood	lbw	b Tait	7	26	26	1	0
+GO Jones	b Lee		25	60	41	5	0
AF Giles	lbw	b Warne	32	120	70	1	0
MJ Hoggard	c Martyn	b McGrath	2	47	36	0	0
SJ Harmison	not out		20	25	20	4	0
Extras	**18**	(b 4, lb 6, w 1, nb 7)					
Total	**373**	(all out, 105.3 overs, 471 minutes)					

FoW: 1-82 (Trescothick), 2-102 (Vaughan), 3-104 (Bell), 4-131 (Pietersen), 5-274 (Flintoff), 6-289 (Collingwood), 7-297 (Strauss), 8-325 (Jones), 9-345 (Hoggard), 10-373 (Giles).

Bowling	O	M	R	W	
McGrath	27	5	72	2	(1w)
Lee	23	3	94	1	(3nb)
Tait	15	1	61	1	(3nb)
Warne	37.3	5	122	6	
Katich	3	0	14	0	

England 2nd innings			R	M	B	4	6
ME Trescothick	lbw	b Warne	33	150	84	1	0
AJ Strauss	c Katich	b Warne	1	16	7	0	0
*MP Vaughan	c Gilchrist	b McGrath	45	80	65	6	0
IR Bell	c Warne	b McGrath	0	2	1	0	0
KP Pietersen	b McGrath		158	285	187	15	7
A Flintoff	c & b Warne		8	20	13	1	0
PD Collingwood	c Ponting	b Warne	10	72	51	1	0
+GO Jones	b Tait		1	24	12	0	0
AF Giles	b Warne		59	159	97	7	0
MJ Hoggard	not out		4	45	35	0	0
SJ Harmison	c Hayden	b Warne	0	2	2	0	0
Extras	**16**	(b 4, w 7, nb 5)					
Total	**335**	(all out, 91.3 overs, 432 minutes)					

FoW: 1-2 (Strauss), 2-67 (Vaughan), 3-67 (Bell), 4-109 (Trescothick), 5-126 (Flintoff), 6-186 (Collingwood), 7-199 (Jones), 8-308 (Pietersen), 9-335 (Giles), 10-335 (Harmison).

Bowling	O	M	R	W	
McGrath	26	3	85	3	(1nb)
Lee	20	4	88	0	(4nb, 1w)
Warne	38.3	3	124	6	(1w)
Clarke	2	0	6	0	
Tait	5	0	28	1	(1w)

Australia 1st innings			R	M	B	4	6
JL Langer	b Harmison		105	233	146	11	2
ML Hayden	lbw	b Flintoff	138	416	303	18	0
*RT Ponting	c Strauss	b Flintoff	35	81	56	3	0
DR Martyn	c Collingwood	b Flintoff	10	36	29	1	0
MJ Clarke	lbw	b Hoggard	25	119	59	2	0
SM Katich	lbw	b Flintoff	1	12	11	0	0
+AC Gilchrist	lbw	b Hoggard	23	32	20	4	0
SK Warne	c Vaughan	b Flintoff	0	18	10	0	0
B Lee	c Giles	b Hoggard	6	22	10	0	0
GD McGrath	c Strauss	b Hoggard	0	6	6	0	0
SW Tait	not out		1	7	2	0	0
Extras	**23**	(b 4, lb 8, w 2, nb 9)					
Total	**367**	(all out, 107.1 overs, 494 minutes)					

FoW: 1-185 (Langer), 2-264 (Ponting), 3-281 (Martyn), 4-323 (Hayden), 5-329 (Katich), 6-356 (Gilchrist), 7-359 (Clarke), 8-363 (Warne), 9-363 (McGrath), 10-367 (Lee).

Bowling	O	M	R	W	
Harmison	22	2	87	1	(2nb, 2w)
Hoggard	24.1	2	97	4	(1nb)
Flintoff	34	10	78	5	(6nb)
Giles	23	1	76	0	
Collingwood	4	0	17	0	

Australia 2nd innings			R	M	B	4	6
JL Langer	not out		0	3	4	0	0
ML Hayden	not out		0	3	0	0	0
Extras	**4**	(lb 4)					
Total	**4**	(0 wickets, 0.4 overs, 3 minutes)					

DNB: *RT Ponting, DR Martyn, MJ Clarke, SM Katich, +AC Gilchrist, SK Warne, B Lee, GD McGrath, SW Tait.

Bowling	O	M	R	W
Harmison	0.4	0	0	0

RESULT: Match drawn
MAN OF THE MATCH: KP Pietersen
SERIES RESULT: England win the series 2–1 and regain the Ashes
PLAYERS OF THE SERIES: A Flintoff, SK Warne
COMPTON–MILLER MEDAL: A Flintoff

APPENDIX

TOUR SCORECARDS & AVERAGES

Twenty20 International Match 2005
England v Australia
THE ROSE BOWL, Southampton, 13 June 2005 (20-over match)

TOSS: England **UMPIRES:** NJ Llong and JW Lloyds **TV UMPIRE:** MR Benson **MATCH REFEREE:** JJ Crowe (NZ) **TWENTY20 INTERNATIONAL DEBUTS:** PD Collingwood, D Gough, A Flintoff, SJ Harmison, GO Jones, J Lewis, KP Pietersen, VS Solanki, AJ Strauss, ME Trescothick, MP Vaughan (Eng); JN Gillespie, ML Hayden (Aus).

England innings			R	M	B	4	6
ME Trescothick	c Hussey	b Symonds	41	55	37	5	0
+GO Jones	c Kasprowicz	b McGrath	19	17	14	4	0
A Flintoff	c Symonds	b Kasprowicz	6	9	5	0	0
KP Pietersen	c Hayden	b Clarke	34	19	18	3	1
*MP Vaughan	c Ponting	b Symonds	0	2	1	0	0
PD Collingwood	c Ponting	b McGrath	46	28	26	5	2
AJ Strauss	b Gillespie		18	15	16	1	0
VS Solanki	c Hussey	b McGrath	9	5	5	1	0
J Lewis	not out		0	1	0	0	0
Extras 6	(lb 1, w 3, nb 2)						
Total 179	(8 wickets, 20 overs, 79 mins)						

DNB: D Gough, SJ Harmison.

FoW: 1-28 (Jones), **2-49** (Flintoff), **3-100** (Pietersen), **4-102** (Vaughan), **5-109** (Trescothick), **6-158** (Strauss), **7-175** (Solanki), **8-179** (Collingwood).

Bowling	O	M	R	W	
Lee	3	0	31	0	(2nb, 1w)
McGrath	4	0	31	3	(1w)
Kasprowicz	3	0	28	1	
Gillespie	4	0	49	1	(1w)
Clarke	3	0	25	1	
Symonds	3	0	14	2	

Australia innings			R	M	B	4	6
+AC Gilchrist	c Pietersen	b Gough	15	11	14	3	0
ML Hayden	c Pietersen	b Gough	6	12	4	1	0
A Symonds	c Pietersen	b Lewis	0	5	2	0	0
MJ Clarke	c Jones	b Lewis	0	1	1	0	0
MEK Hussey	c Flintoff	b Gough	1	6	6	0	0
*RT Ponting	c Solanki	b Lewis	0	6	3	0	0
DR Martyn	c Trescothick	b Lewis	4	6	4	1	0
B Lee	c Harmison	b C'wood	15	29	20	1	0
JN Gillespie	c Trescothick	b C'wood	24	18	18	4	0
MS Kasprowicz	not out		3	16	5	0	0
GD McGrath	b Harmison		5	9	12	0	0
Extras 6	(b 1, lb 2, w 1, nb 2)						
Total 79	(all out, 14.3 overs, 64 mins)						

FoW: 1-23 (Gilchrist), **2-23** (Hayden), **3-23** (Clarke), **4-24** (Symonds), **5-24** (Hussey), **6-28** (Ponting), **7-31** (Martyn), **8-67** (Gillespie), **9-72** (Lee), **10-79** (McGrath).

Bowling	O	M	R	W	
Gough	3	0	16	3	(1nb)
Lewis	4	0	24	4	
Harmison	2.3	0	13	1	(1nb)
Flintoff	3	0	15	0	(1w)
Collingwood	2	0	8	2	

RESULT: England won by 100 runs
MAN OF THE MATCH: KP Pietersen

NatWest Series 2005
1st Match England v Bangladesh
THE OVAL, London, 16 June 2005 (50-over match)

TOSS: England **UMPIRES:** Aleem Dar (Pak) and MR Benson **TV UMPIRE:** NJ Llong **MATCH REFEREE:** JJ Crowe (NZ) **ODI DEBUT:** J Lewis (Eng).

Bangladesh innings			R	M	B	4	6
Javed Omar	lbw	b Lewis	13	21	19	2	0
Nafees Iqbal	c Jones	b Lewis	19	43	28	1	0
Mohammad Ashraful	c Flintoff	b Lewis	0	1	1	0	0
Tushar Imran	b Harmison		10	42	27	0	0
*Habibul Bashar	c Jones	b Harmison	19	34	28	2	0
Aftab Ahmed	run out (Pietersen/Jones)		51	97	58	4	2
+Khaled Mashud	c Jones	b Harmison	1	11	10	0	0
Mohammad Rafique	c Harmison	b Gough	30	62	57	2	1
Mashrafe Mortaza	not out		29	38	24	4	0
Khaled Mahmud	c Pietersen	b Harmison	0	1	1	0	0
Nazmul Hossain	c Jones	b Gough	6	29	23	0	0
Extras 12	(lb 4, w 4, nb 4)						
Total 190	(all out, 45.2 overs, 189 mins)						

FoW: 1-19 (Javed Omar), **2-19** (Mohammad Ashraful), **3-39** (Nafees Iqbal), **4-57** (Tushar Imran), **5-72** (Habibul Bashar), **6-76** (Khaled Mashud), **7-152** (Mohammad Rafique), **8-159** (Aftab Ahmed), **9-159** (Khaled Mahmud), **10-190** (Nazmul Hossain).

Bowling	O	M	R	W	
Gough	8.2	0	33	2	(3nb)
Lewis	10	0	32	3	(1w)
Harmison	10	0	39	4	(1nb, 2w)
Collingwood	8	0	36	0	
Flintoff	9	2	46	0	(1w)

England innings		R	M	B	4	6
ME Trescothick	not out	100	103	76	16	0
AJ Strauss	not out	82	103	77	10	1
Extras 10	(lb 5, w 1, nb 4)					
Total 192	(0 wickets, 24.5 overs, 103 mins)					

DNB: *MP Vaughan, PD Collingwood, A Flintoff, KP Pietersen, +GO Jones, VS Solanki, J Lewis, D Gough, SJ Harmison.

Bowling	O	M	R	W	
Mashrafe Mortaza	6	1	33	0	
Nazmul Hossain	7	0	61	0	(1nb, 1w)
Khaled Mahmud	3	0	39	0	(3nb)
Mohammad Rafique	6	0	40	0	
Aftab Ahmed	2.5	0	14	0	

RESULT: England won by 10 wickets
POINTS: England 6, Bangladesh 0
MAN OF THE MATCH: ME Trescothick

NatWest Series 2005
2nd Match Australia v Bangladesh
SOPHIA GARDENS, Cardiff, 18 June 2005 (50-over match)

TOSS: Australia **UMPIRES:** BF Bowden (NZ) and DR Shepherd **TV UMPIRE:** MR Benson **MATCH REFEREE:** JJ Crowe (NZ)

Australia innings			R	M	B	4	6
+AC Gilchrist	lbw	b M Mortaza	0	1	2	0	0
ML Hayden	b Nazmul Hossain		37	71	50	4	1
*RT Ponting	lbw	b T Baisya	1	21	16	0	0
DR Martyn	c Nafees Iqbal	b T Baisya	77	138	112	2	0
MJ Clarke	c M Mortaza	b T Baisya	54	100	84	4	0
MEK Hussey	not out		31	38	25	5	0
SM Katich	not out		36	27	23	4	0
Extras 13	(lb 3, w 2, nb 8)						
Total 249	(5 wickets, 50 overs, 205 mins)						

DNB: GB Hogg, JN Gillespie, MS Kasprowicz, GD McGrath.

FoW: 1-0 (Gilchrist), **2-9** (Ponting), **3-57** (Hayden), **4-165** (Martyn), **5-183** (Clarke).

Bowling	O	M	R	W	
Mashrafe Mortaza	10	2	33	1	(1w)
Tapash Baisya	10	1	69	3	(8nb)
Nazmul Hossain	10	2	65	1	
Mohammad Rafique	10	0	31	0	(1w)
Aftab Ahmed	10	0	48	0	

Bangladesh innings			R	M	B	4	6
Javed Omar	c Hayden	b Kasprowicz	19	84	51	3	0
Nafees Iqbal	c Gilchrist	b Gillespie	8	27	21	1	0
Tushar Imran	c Katich	b Hogg	24	35	35	4	0
Mohammad Ashraful	c Hogg	b Gillespie	100	118	101	11	0
*Habibul Bashar	run out (Gillespie)		47	82	72	3	0
Aftab Ahmed	not out		21	28	13	2	1
Mohammad Rafique	not out		9	11	7	2	0
Extras 22	(b 1, lb 11, w 6, nb 4)						
Total 250	(5 wickets, 49.2 overs, 199 mins)						

DNB: +Khaled Mashud, Mashrafe Mortaza, Tapash Baisya, Nazmul Hossain.

FoW: 1-17 (Nafees Iqbal), **2-51** (Tushar Imran), **3-72** (Javed Omar), **4-202** (Habibul Bashar), **5-227** (Mohammad Ashraful).

Bowling	O	M	R	W	
McGrath	10	1	43	0	(2nb)
Gillespie	9.2	1	41	2	(2w)
Kasprowicz	10	0	40	1	(2nb)
Hogg	9	0	52	1	(1w)
Clarke	6	0	38	0	(1w)
Hussey	5	0	24	0	

RESULT: Bangladesh won by 5 wickets
POINTS: Bangladesh 5, Australia 1
MAN OF THE MATCH: Mohammad Ashraful

NatWest Series 2005
3rd Match England v Australia
COUNTY GROUND, Bristol, 19 June 2005 (50-over match)

TOSS: Australia **UMPIRES:** Aleem Dar (Pak) and JW Lloyds **TV UMPIRE:** NJ Llong **MATCH REFEREE:** JJ Crowe (NZ)

Australia innings			R	M	B	4	6
+AC Gilchrist	c Jones	b Harmison	26	48	32	0	1
ML Hayden	c C'wood	b Harmison	31	71	44	2	1
*RT Ponting	lbw	b Harmison	0	1	1	0	0
DR Martyn	c Pietersen	b Harmison	0	1	2	0	0
MJ Clarke	b Lewis		45	92	71	2	1
MEK Hussey	b Harmison		84	109	83	11	0
SR Watson	b Flintoff		25	37	36	1	1
GB Hogg	not out		10	28	13	0	0
JN Gillespie	c Jones	b Flintoff	14	19	18	1	1
MS Kasprowicz	b Gough		1	3	3	0	0
GD McGrath	not out		0	1	1	0	0
Extras 16	(lb 6, w 6, nb 4)						
Total 252	(9 wickets, 50 overs, 216 mins)						

FoW: 1-57 (Gilchrist), **2-57** (Ponting), **3-57** (Martyn), **4-63** (Hayden), **5-168** (Clarke), **6-220** (Hussey), **7-220** (Watson), **8-244** (Gillespie), **9-248** (Kasprowicz).

Bowling	O	M	R	W	
Gough	10	0	47	1	(3nb)
Lewis	10	0	69	1	(1nb)
Harmison	10	0	33	5	(2w)
Flintoff	10	1	39	2	(4w)
Collingwood	2	0	11	0	
Vaughan	6	0	33	0	
Solanki	2	0	14	0	

England innings			R	M	B	4	6
ME Trescothick	b McGrath		16	31	32	3	0
AJ Strauss	b McGrath		16	40	23	3	0
*MP Vaughan	lbw	b Hogg	57	121	92	6	0
PD Collingwood	b Kasprowicz		14	41	28	1	0
A Flintoff	c Kasprowicz	b Hogg	19	37	22	1	1
KP Pietersen	not out		91	94	65	8	4
+GO Jones	c Martyn	b Hogg	2	8	5	0	0
VS Solanki	run out (Gilchrist)		13	24	14	0	1
J Lewis	not out		7	25	15	0	0
Extras 18	(lb 1, w 7, nb 10)						
Total 253	(7 wickets, 47.3 overs, 217 mins)						

DNB: D Gough, SJ Harmison.

FoW: 1-39 (Trescothick), **2-42** (Strauss), **3-82** (Collingwood), **4-119** (Flintoff), **5-150** (Vaughan), **6-160** (Jones), **7-214** (Solanki).

Bowling	O	M	R	W	
McGrath	9	1	34	2	(3nb, 1w)
Gillespie	10	1	66	0	(1nb, 5w)
Kasprowicz	9	0	68	1	(6nb)
Watson	9.3	0	42	0	
Hogg	10	1	42	3	(1w)

RESULT: England won by 3 wickets
POINTS: England 5, Australia 1
MAN OF THE MATCH: KP Pietersen

NatWest Series 2005
4th Match England v Bangladesh
TRENT BRIDGE, Nottingham (d/n), 21 June 2005 (50-over match)

TOSS: England UMPIRES: BF Bowden (NZ) and DR Shepherd TV UMPIRE: MR Benson MATCH REFEREE: JJ Crowe (NZ) ODI DEBUT: CT Tremlett (Eng); Shahriar Nafees (Ban).

England innings			R	M	B	4	6
ME Trescothick	c S Nafees	b N Hossain	85	81	65	14	2
AJ Strauss	lbw	b N Hossain	152	207	128	19	0
*MP Vaughan	b Nazmul Hossain		0	8	8	0	0
A Flintoff	c H Bashar	b A Ahmed	17	19	21	1	1
PD Collingwood	not out		112	96	86	10	5
+GO Jones	not out		2	1	1	0	0
Extras 23	(b 1, lb 4, w 9, nb 9)						
Total 391	(4 wickets, 50 overs, 211 mins)						

DNB: KP Pietersen, AF Giles, J Lewis, CT Tremlett, SJ Harmison.

FoW: 1-141 (Trescothick), 2-148 (Vaughan), 3-179 (Flintoff), 4-389 (Strauss).

Bowling	O	M	R	W	
Mashrafe Mortaza	10	0	71	0	(2nb, 2w)
Tapash Baisya	7	0	87	0	(7nb, 2w)
Nazmul Hossain	10	0	83	3	(2w)
Mohammad Rafique	10	0	54	0	(1w)
Aftab Ahmed	10	0	65	1	(1w)
Tushar Imran	3	0	26	0	

Bangladesh innings			R	M	B	4	6
Javed Omar	b Collingwood		59	145	106	7	0
Shahriar Nafees	b Tremlett		10	37	28	1	0
Tushar Imran	c Jones	b Tremlett	0	1	1	0	0
Mohammad Ashraful	b Collingwood		94	64	52	11	3
*Habibul Bashar	c Strauss	b C'wood	16	22	23	1	0
Aftab Ahmed	c & b Collingwood		0	1	1	0	0
+Khaled Mashud	c Jones	b C'wood	8	18	12	0	0
Mohammad Rafique	b Tremlett		19	40	33	2	0
Mashrafe Mortaza	b Collingwood		0	7	8	0	0
Tapash Baisya	b Tremlett		3	6	6	0	0
Nazmul Hossain	not out		2	13	6	0	0
Extras 12	(w 6, nb 6)						
Total 223	(all out, 45.2 overs, 187 mins)						

FoW: 1-30 (Shahriar Nafees), 2-30 (Tushar Imran), 3-155 (Mohammad Ashraful), 4-181 (Habibul Bashar), 5-181 (Aftab Ahmed), 6-196 (Javed Omar), 7-201 (Khaled Mashud), 8-201 (Mashrafe Mortaza), 9-205 (Tapash Baisya), 10-223 (Mohammad Rafique).

Bowling	O	M	R	W	
Lewis	5	1	23	0	(2nb, 3w)
Tremlett	8.2	1	32	4	(1nb, 2w)
Harmison	8	1	55	0	(3nb, 1w)
Flintoff	4	0	30	0	
Giles	10	0	52	0	
Collingwood	10	1	31	6	

RESULT: England won by 168 runs
POINTS: England 6, Bangladesh 0
MAN OF THE MATCH: PD Collingwood

NatWest Series 2005
5th Match England v Australia
RIVERSIDE GROUND, Chester-le-Street (d/n), 23 June 2005 (50-over match)

TOSS: England UMPIRES: Aleem Dar (Pak) and MR Benson TV UMPIRE: JW Lloyds MATCH REFEREE: JJ Crowe (NZ)

Australia innings			R	M	B	4	6
+AC Gilchrist	c Jones	b Tremlett	18	38	31	2	0
ML Hayden	c Jones	b Flintoff	39	94	56	5	0
*RT Ponting	c Giles	b Harmison	27	51	40	4	0
DR Martyn	not out		68	118	81	3	0
A Symonds	run out (Trescothick)		73	94	81	4	2
MEK Hussey	c C'wood	b Flintoff	5	9	10	0	0
SR Watson	not out		11	7	7	1	0
Extras 25	(lb 12, w 7, nb 6)						
Total 266	(5 wickets, 50 overs, 211 mins)						

DNB: GB Hogg, JN Gillespie, B Lee, GD McGrath.

FoW: 1-44 (Gilchrist), 2-95 (Ponting), 3-96 (Hayden), 4-238 (Symonds), 5-247 (Hussey).

Bowling	O	M	R	W	
Gough	10	0	41	0	(3nb)
Tremlett	9	0	53	1	(1nb, 1w)
Harmison	9	2	44	1	(2nb, 2w)
Flintoff	10	0	55	2	(3w)
Giles	9	1	44	0	(1w)
Collingwood	3	0	17	0	

England innings			R	M	B	4	6
*ME Trescothick	c Gilchrist	b McGrath	0	23	15	0	0
AJ Strauss	b Lee		3	17	13	0	0
VS Solanki	c Ponting	b Hogg	34	87	69	2	0
PD Collingwood	b McGrath		0	1	2	0	0
A Flintoff	c Gillespie	b Hogg	44	90	61	6	0
KP Pietersen	c Hussey	b Symonds	19	37	28	2	0
+GO Jones	c Hayden	b Watson	23	45	31	2	0
AF Giles	c Symonds	b Lee	4	4	3	1	0
CT Tremlett	c Hussey	b Gillespie	8	25	18	0	0
D Gough	not out		46	50	47	7	0
SJ Harmison	not out		11	37	17	0	0
Extras 17	(lb 8, w 5, nb 4)						
Total 209	(9 wickets, 50 overs, 217 mins)						

FoW: 1-4 (Strauss), 2-6 (Trescothick), 3-6 (Collingwood), 4-85 (Solanki), 5-94 (Flintoff), 6-123 (Pietersen), 7-133 (Giles), 8-145 (Jones), 9-159 (Tremlett).

Bowling	O	M	R	W	
Lee	10	2	27	2	(2nb, 3w)
McGrath	10	1	31	2	(1nb)
Gillespie	9	0	36	1	(1w)
Watson	8	0	51	1	(1nb, 1w)
Hogg	6	0	19	2	
Symonds	7	0	37	1	

RESULT: Australia won by 57 runs
POINTS: Australia 6, England 0
MAN OF THE MATCH: A Symonds

NatWest Series 2005
6th Match Australia v Bangladesh
OLD TRAFFORD, Manchester, 25 June 2005 (50-over match)

TOSS: Australia **UMPIRES:** BF Bowden (NZ) and JW Lloyds
TV UMPIRE: NJ Llong **MATCH REFEREE:** JJ Crowe (NZ)

Bangladesh innings			R	M	B	4	6
Javed Omar	lbw	b Lee	3	25	20	0	0
Shahriar Nafees	b Symonds		47	108	57	6	0
Tushar Imran	c Gilchrist	b Lee	4	12	12	1	0
Mohammad Ashraful	c & b Symonds		58	102	86	2	2
*Habibul Bashar	c Gilchrist	b Symonds	0	1	1	0	0
Aftab Ahmed	b Symonds		5	10	13	0	0
+Khaled Mashud	b Hogg		4	12	12	0	0
Manjural Islam Rana	st Gilchrist	b Hogg	2	7	5	0	0
Mohammad Rafique	b Symonds		0	8	6	0	0
Mashrafe Mortaza	c Martyn	b Hogg	0	1	3	0	0
Nazmul Hossain	not out		0	1	1	0	0
Extras 16	(lb 6, w 6, nb 4)						
Total 139	(all out, 35.2 overs, 154 mins)						

FoW: 1-13 (Javed Omar), **2-23** (Tushar Imran), **3-113** (Shahriar Nafees), **4-113** (Habibul Bashar), **5-124** (Aftab Ahmed), **6-137** (Khaled Mashud), **7-139** (Mohammad Ashraful), **8-139** (Manjural Islam Rana), **9-139** (Mashrafe Mortaza), **10-139** (Mohammad Rafique).

Bowling	O	M	R	W	
Lee	6	1	36	2	(4nb, 3w)
McGrath	6	1	19	0	
Gillespie	3	0	17	0	
Watson	4	0	14	0	(1w)
Hogg	9	1	29	3	(1w)
Symonds	7.2	1	18	5	(1w)

Australia innings		R	M	B	4	6
+AC Gilchrist	not out	66	73	60	7	1
ML Hayden	not out	66	73	54	9	2
Extras 8	(w 7, nb 1)					
Total 140	(0 wickets, 19 overs, 73 mins)					

DNB: *RT Ponting, DR Martyn, A Symonds, MEK Hussey, SR Watson, GB Hogg, JN Gillespie, B Lee, GD McGrath.

Bowling	O	M	R	W	
Mashrafe Mortaza	6	0	32	0	
Nazmul Hossain	3	0	29	0	(1nb, 1w)
Mohammad Rafique	6	0	53	0	
Manjural Islam Rana	4	0	26	0	(2w)

RESULT: Australia won by 10 wickets
POINTS: Australia 6, Bangladesh 0
MAN OF THE MATCH: A Symonds

NatWest Series 2005
7th Match England v Bangladesh
HEADINGLEY, Leeds, 26 June 2005 (50-over match)

TOSS: Bangladesh **UMPIRES:** Aleem Dar (Pak) and MR Benson **TV UMPIRE:** NJ Llong **MATCH REFEREE:** JJ Crowe (NZ)

Bangladesh innings		R	M	B	4	6
Javed Omar	b Flintoff	81	186	150	5	0
Shahriar Nafees	c Trescothick b SP Jones	11	24	15	2	0
Tushar Imran	b Flintoff	32	67	34	4	0
Mohammad Ashraful	c Trescothick b Flintoff	0	1	1	0	0
*Habibul Bashar	run out (Collingwood)	10	27	24	0	0
Aftab Ahmed	b Giles	15	26	27	1	0
+Khaled Mashud	not out	42	48	43	4	0
Mashrafe Mortaza	b Flintoff	1	6	3	0	0
Mohammad Rafique	not out	2	9	5	0	0
Extras 14	(lb 1, w 11, nb 2)					
Total 208	(7 wickets, 50 overs, 205 mins)					

DNB: Manjural Islam Rana, Nazmul Hossain.

FoW: 1-22 (Shahriar Nafees), **2-92** (Tushar Imran), **3-92** (Mohammad Ashraful), **4-112** (Habibul Bashar), **5-138** (Aftab Ahmed), **6-183** (Javed Omar), **7-189** (Mashrafe Mortaza).

Bowling	O	M	R	W	
Gough	9	0	59	0	(1nb, 1w)
SP Jones	9	0	44	1	(8w)
Tremlett	7	0	26	0	
Flintoff	9	1	29	4	(1nb)
Collingwood	6	0	21	0	
Giles	10	0	28	1	(1w)

England innings			R	M	B	4	6
*ME Trescothick	c K Mashud	b MI Rana	43	66	38	3	2
AJ Strauss	b Manjural Islam Rana		98	149	104	7	1
A Flintoff	lbw	b M Rafique	22	22	29	3	0
VS Solanki	lbw	b M Rafique	8	16	25	0	0
KP Pietersen	c M Rafique	b MI Rana	23	22	26	2	1
PD Collingwood	not out		8	16	8	1	0
+GO Jones	not out		0	1	3	0	0
Extras 7	(lb 4, w 3)						
Total 209	(5 wickets, 38.5 overs, 153 mins)						

DNB: AF Giles, D Gough, CT Tremlett, SP Jones.

FoW: 1-99 (Trescothick), **2-134** (Flintoff), **3-151** (Solanki), **4-182** (Pietersen), **5-208** (Strauss).

Bowling	O	M	R	W	
Nazmul Hossain	7	1	43	0	
Mashrafe Mortaza	9	0	48	0	(1w)
Manjural Islam Rana	9.5	0	57	3	(1w)
Mohammad Rafique	10	1	44	2	(1w)
Aftab Ahmed	3	0	13	0	

RESULT: England won by 5 wickets
POINTS: England 6, Bangladesh 0
MAN OF THE MATCH: AJ Strauss

NatWest Series 2005
8th Match England v Australia
EDGBASTON, Birmingham (d/n), 28 June 2005 (50-over match)

TOSS: Australia **UMPIRES:** BF Bowden (NZ) and DR Shepherd **TV UMPIRE:** JW Lloyds **MATCH REFEREE:** JJ Crowe (NZ)

Australia innings			R	M	B	4	6
+AC Gilchrist	c GO Jones	b SP Jones	19	13	18	2	0
ML Hayden	lbw	b SP Jones	14	31	24	3	0
*RT Ponting	c GO Jones	b Flintoff	34	69	40	4	0
DR Martyn	c Pietersen	b Harmison	36	78	65	4	0
A Symonds	run out (Collingwood)		74	89	75	6	2
MEK Hussey	c GO Jones	b Harmison	45	76	42	4	0
MJ Clarke	c GO Jones	b Gough	3	8	6	0	0
GB Hogg	c GO Jones	b Gough	2	9	6	0	0
B Lee	not out		21	19	18	3	0
JN Gillespie	c Pietersen	b Gough	1	6	2	0	0
GD McGrath	not out		2	3	5	0	0
Extras 10	(b 1, lb 4, w 4, nb 1)						
Total 261	(9 wickets, 50 overs, 209 mins)						

FoW: 1-34 (Gilchrist), 2-46 (Hayden), 3-95 (Ponting), 4-123 (Martyn), 5-224 (Symonds), 6-234 (Clarke), 7-236 (Hussey), 8-242 (Hogg), 9-254 (Gillespie).

Bowling	O	M	R	W	
Gough	9	0	70	3	(1nb)
SP Jones	10	2	53	2	(1w)
Harmison	10	1	38	2	(1w)
Flintoff	10	0	38	1	
Giles	10	1	44	0	(2w)
Vaughan	1	0	13	0	

England innings			R	M	B	4	6
ME Trescothick	not out		11	25	19	1	0
AJ Strauss	c Gillespie	b McGrath	25	25	18	5	0
*MP Vaughan	not out		0	1	0	0	0
Extras 1	(nb 1)						
Total 37	(1 wicket, 6 overs, 25 mins)						

DNB: A Flintoff, KP Pietersen, PD Collingwood, +GO Jones, AF Giles, D Gough, SJ Harmison, SP Jones.

FoW: 1-37 (Strauss).

Bowling	O	M	R	W	
Lee	3	0	13	0	
McGrath	3	0	24	1	(1nb)

RESULT: No result (rain)
POINTS: England 3, Australia 3
MAN OF THE MATCH: No award

NatWest Series 2005
9th Match Australia v Bangladesh
ST LAWRENCE GROUND, Canterbury, 30 June 2005 (50-over match)

TOSS: Australia **UMPIRES:** Aleem Dar (Pak) and JW Lloyds
TV UMPIRE: MR Benson **MATCH REFEREE:** JJ Crowe (NZ)

Bangladesh innings			R	M	B	4	6
Javed Omar	c Gilchrist	b Gillespie	0	18	10	0	0
Shahriar Nafees	c Gilchrist	b Watson	75	152	116	6	0
Tushar Imran	b Lee		0	2	1	0	0
Mohammad Ashraful	b Lee		7	6	4	0	1
*Habibul Bashar	c Gilchrist	b Watson	30	28	24	5	0
Aftab Ahmed	c Gilchrist	b Kasprowicz	7	14	11	1	0
+Khaled Mashud	not out		71	131	105	4	0
Mohammad Rafique	c Gilchrist	b Watson	15	20	13	1	1
Khaled Mahmud	c Ponting	b Gillespie	22	34	22	1	0
Extras 23	(lb 9, w 8, nb 6)						
Total 250	(8 wickets, 50 overs, 210 mins)						

DNB: Tapash Baisya, Mashrafe Mortaza.

FoW: 1-8 (Javed Omar), 2-9 (Tushar Imran), 3-19 (Mohammad Ashraful), 4-57 (Habibul Bashar), 5-75 (Aftab Ahmed), 6-169 (Shahriar Nafees), 7-193 (Mohammad Rafique), 8-250 (Khaled Mahmud).

Bowling	O	M	R	W	
Lee	10	0	62	2	(1nb, 1w)
Gillespie	9	0	49	2	(1nb, 3w)
Watson	10	0	43	3	(2w)
Kasprowicz	9	0	46	1	(4nb, 1w)
Symonds	10	0	36	0	(1w)
Clarke	2	1	5	0	

Australia innings			R	M	B	4	6
+AC Gilchrist	c K Mahmud	b T Baisya	45	44	36	7	1
ML Hayden	c K Mashud	b M Mortaza	1	9	4	0	0
*RT Ponting	c T Imran	b M Mortaza	66	127	95	5	0
DR Martyn	c K Mashud	b K Mahmud	9	20	16	1	0
MJ Clarke	not out		80	120	104	5	1
A Symonds	not out		42	48	37	4	1
Extras 11	(lb 3, w 5, nb 3)						
Total 254	(4 wickets, 48.1 overs, 187 mins)						

DNB: MEK Hussey, SR Watson, B Lee, JN Gillespie, MS Kasprowicz.

FoW: 1-15 (Hayden), 2-63 (Gilchrist), 3-83 (Martyn), 4-168 (Ponting).

Bowling	O	M	R	W	
Mashrafe Mortaza	9	0	44	2	(4w)
Tapash Baisya	9	0	57	1	(2nb)
Khaled Mahmud	10	0	54	1	(1nb)
Aftab Ahmed	10	0	48	0	
Mohammad Rafique	10	0	44	0	(1w)
Mohammad Ashraful	0.1	0	4	0	

RESULT: Australia won by 6 wickets
POINTS: Australia 5, Bangladesh 1
MAN OF THE MATCH: Shahriar Nafees

FINAL TABLE

	P	W	L	NR	T	Pts
England	6	4	1	1	–	26
Australia	6	3	2	1	–	22
Bangladesh	6	1	5	–	–	6

England play Australia in the final

NatWest Series 2005
Final England v Australia
LORD'S, London, 2 July 2005 (50-over match)

TOSS: England **UMPIRES:** BF Bowden (NZ) and DR Shepherd **TV UMPIRE:** JW Lloyds **MATCH REFEREE:** JJ Crowe (NZ)

Australia innings			R	M	B	4	6
+AC Gilchrist	c Pietersen	b Flintoff	27	43	32	5	0
ML Hayden	c Giles	b Gough	17	29	19	3	0
*RT Ponting	c GO Jones	b Harmison	7	26	18	0	1
DR Martyn	c GO Jones	b Harmison	11	43	24	1	0
A Symonds	c Strauss	b C'wood	29	104	71	2	0
MJ Clarke	lbw	b SP Jones	2	18	19	0	0
MEK Hussey	not out		62	95	81	6	0
GB Hogg	c GO Jones	b Harmison	16	16	22	1	0
B Lee	c GO Jones	b Flintoff	3	6	5	0	0
JN Gillespie	c GO Jones	b Flintoff	0	1	1	0	0
GD McGrath	c C'wood	b Gough	0	11	4	0	0
Extras 22	(b 4, lb 5, w 7, nb 6)						
Total 196	(all out, 48.5 overs, 208 mins)						

FoW: 1-50 (Hayden), **2-54** (Gilchrist), **3-71** (Ponting), **4-90** (Martyn), **5-93** (Clarke), **6-147** (Symonds), **7-169** (Hogg), **8-179** (Lee), **9-179** (Gillespie), **10-196** (McGrath).

Bowling	O	M	R	W	
Gough	6.5	1	36	2	(1nb, 2w)
SP Jones	8	2	45	1	(1w)
Flintoff	8	2	23	3	(1nb, 1w)
Harmison	10	2	27	3	(1nb, 3w)
Collingwood	8	0	26	1	
Giles	8	0	30	0	

England innings			R	M	B	4	6
ME Trescothick	c Ponting	b McGrath	6	15	16	0	0
AJ Strauss	b Lee		2	21	8	0	0
*MP Vaughan	b McGrath		0	12	7	0	0
KP Pietersen	c Gilchrist	b Lee	6	10	10	1	0
A Flintoff	c Hayden	b McGrath	8	14	9	2	0
PD Collingwood	run out (Symonds/Gilchrist)		53	154	116	4	0
+GO Jones	lbw	b Hogg	71	150	100	4	3
AF Giles	not out		18	42	21	1	0
SP Jones	b Hussey		1	2	2	0	0
D Gough	run out (McGrath)		12	26	13	0	0
SJ Harmison	not out		0	1	0	0	0
Extras 19	(b 2, lb 12, w 3, nb 2)						
Total 196	(9 wickets, 50 overs, 232 mins)						

FoW: 1-11 (Trescothick), **2-13** (Strauss), **3-19** (Vaughan), **4-19** (Pietersen), **5-33** (Flintoff), **6-149** (Collingwood), **7-161** (GO Jones), **8-162** (SP Jones), **9-194** (Gough).

Bowling	O	M	R	W	
Lee	10	1	36	2	(1nb, 1w)
McGrath	10	4	25	3	(1nb)
Gillespie	10	0	42	0	(1w)
Symonds	10	2	23	0	
Hogg	6	0	25	1	
Hussey	4	0	31	1	(1w)

RESULT: Match tied
MAN OF THE MATCH: GO Jones
SERIES RESULT: England and Australia shared the NatWest Series 2005
PLAYER OF THE SERIES: A Symonds

NatWest Challenge 2005
1st Match England v Australia
HEADINGLEY, Leeds, 7 July 2005 (50-over match)

TOSS: England **UMPIRES:** MR Benson and RE Koertzen (SA) **TV UMPIRE:** NJ Llong **MATCH REFEREE:** RS Mahanama (SL)

Australia innings			R	M	B	4	6
+AC Gilchrist	c GO Jones	b Harmison	42	68	51	5	2
ML Hayden	c Pietersen	b Flintoff	17	75	47	3	0
*RT Ponting	c Pietersen	b C'wood	14	49	30	2	0
DR Martyn	c GO Jones	b C'wood	43	104	71	4	0
A Symonds	c Trescothick	b C'wood	6	9	10	1	0
MJ Clarke	b Collingwood		2	6	9	0	0
MEK Hussey	not out		46	74	52	4	1
SR Watson	c Strauss	b Harmison	3	13	13	0	0
B Lee	not out		15	19	19	3	0
Extras 31	(b 2, lb 12, w 15, nb 2)						
Total 219	(7 wickets, 50 overs, 218 mins)						

DNB: JN Gillespie, GD McGrath.

FoW: 1-62 (Gilchrist), **2-68** (Hayden), **3-107** (Ponting), **4-116** (Symonds), **5-120** (Clarke), **6-159** (Martyn), **7-168** (Watson).

Bowling	O	M	R	W	
Gough	10	1	50	0	(1nb, 2w)
SP Jones	10	1	28	0	(2w)
Harmison	10	0	39	2	(3w)
Flintoff	10	0	54	1	(1nb, 5w)
Collingwood	10	0	34	4	(2w)

England innings			R	M	B	4	6
ME Trescothick	not out		104	197	134	8	1
AJ Strauss	c Gilchrist	b Hogg	41	110	84	2	0
*MP Vaughan	not out		59	86	65	7	0
Extras 17	(b 1, lb 2, w 3, nb 11)						
Total 221	(1 wicket, 46 overs, 197 mins)						

DNB: KP Pietersen, A Flintoff, PD Collingwood, +GO Jones, AF Giles, VS Solanki, D Gough, SJ Harmison.

FoW: 1-101 (Strauss).

Bowling	O	M	R	W	
Lee	9	0	48	0	(7nb)
McGrath	8	1	26	0	(1w)
Gillespie	10	0	66	0	(1w)
Watson	3	0	16	0	(1w)
Symonds	10	0	32	0	
Hogg	6	0	30	1	

Australia full sub: GB Hogg (ML Hayden, England innings, 22.0 overs).
England full sub: VS Solanki (SP Jones, Australia innings, 31.0 overs).

RESULT: England won by 9 wickets
MAN OF THE MATCH: ME Trescothick

NatWest Challenge 2005
2nd Match England v Australia
LORD'S, London, 10 July 2005 (50-over match)

TOSS: Australia **UMPIRES:** RE Koertzen (SA) and JW Lloyds
TV UMPIRE: MR Benson **MATCH REFEREE:** RS Mahanama (SL)

England innings			R	M	B	4	6
ME Trescothick	c Gilchrist	b Kasprowicz	14	46	36	2	0
AJ Strauss	b Kasprowicz		11	32	25	1	0
*MP Vaughan	lbw	b McGrath	1	5	3	0	0
KP Pietersen	b Lee		15	25	23	2	0
A Flintoff	c Hussey	b Lee	87	140	112	10	2
PD Collingwood	c Gilchrist	b Lee	34	86	56	3	0
+GO Jones	c Katich	b Lee	27	38	33	3	0
AF Giles	c Ponting	b Lee	4	11	6	0	0
D Gough	not out		5	7	5	0	0
SJ Harmison	not out		6	2	3	1	0
Extras	19	(lb 3, w 14, nb 2)					
Total	223	(8 wickets, 50 overs, 207 mins)					

DNB: SP Jones.

FoW: 1-25 (Strauss), **2-28** (Vaughan), **3-28** (Trescothick), **4-45** (Pietersen), **5-148** (Collingwood), **6-193** (Flintoff), **7-210** (GO Jones), **8-214** (Giles).

Bowling	O	M	R	W	
Lee	10	2	41	5	(1nb, 2w)
McGrath	10	2	37	1	(1w)
Kasprowicz	10	2	40	2	(1nb)
Gillespie	7	0	42	0	(2w)
Symonds	7	0	31	0	
Clarke	6	0	29	0	(3w)

Australia innings			R	M	B	4	6
+AC Gilchrist	c GO Jones	b Flintoff	29	23	20	6	0
SM Katich	c Harmison	b Giles	30	87	62	4	0
*RT Ponting	c Pietersen	b Gough	111	157	115	14	1
DR Martyn	not out		39	99	67	2	0
A Symonds	not out		5	4	6	1	0
Extras	10	(lb 2, w 4, nb 4)					
Total	224	(3 wickets, 44.2 overs, 190 mins)					

DNB: MJ Clarke, MEK Hussey, B Lee, JN Gillespie, MS Kasprowicz, GD McGrath.

FoW: 1-36 (Gilchrist), **2-96** (Katich), **3-216** (Ponting).

Bowling	O	M	R	W	
Gough	6.2	0	43	1	(3nb)
SP Jones	5	0	29	0	(2w)
Harmison	10	0	48	0	(1w)
Flintoff	8	0	44	1	(1nb, 1w)
Giles	10	0	38	1	
Collingwood	5	0	20	0	

England full sub: VS Solanki (not used).
Australia full sub: BJ Haddin (not used).

RESULT: Australia won by 7 wickets
MAN OF THE MATCH: B Lee

NatWest Challenge 2005
3rd Match England v Australia
THE OVAL, London, 12 July 2005 (50-over match)

TOSS: Australia **UMPIRES:** RE Koertzen (SA) and DR Shepherd **TV UMPIRE:** JW Lloyds **MATCH REFEREE:** RS Mahanama (SL)

England innings			R	M	B	4	6
ME Trescothick	c Kasprowicz	b Lee	0	13	12	0	0
AJ Strauss	c Gilchrist	b Kasprowicz	36	81	50	5	0
*MP Vaughan	run out (Ponting)		15	38	30	2	0
KP Pietersen	b Gillespie		74	133	84	7	2
A Flintoff	c Gilchrist	b Kasprowicz	5	10	15	0	0
PD Collingwood	c Symonds	b Gillespie	9	17	18	1	0
+GO Jones	c Kasprowicz	b Gillespie	1	11	11	0	0
VS Solanki	not out		53	91	63	5	0
AF Giles	not out		25	26	19	2	0
Extras	10	(lb 1, w 7, nb 2)					
Total	228	(7 wickets, 50 overs, 218 mins)					

DNB: SJ Harmison, D Gough.

FoW: 1-4 (Trescothick), **2-44** (Vaughan), **3-61** (Strauss), **4-74** (Flintoff), **5-87** (Collingwood), **6-93** (GO Jones), **7-186** (Pietersen).

Bowling	O	M	R	W	
Lee	10	0	46	1	(1nb, 3w)
McGrath	10	4	40	0	
Kasprowicz	10	1	46	2	(2w)
Gillespie	10	1	44	3	(1nb)
Symonds	6	1	26	0	
Clarke	4	0	25	0	(2w)

Australia innings			R	M	B	4	6
+AC Gilchrist	not out		121	160	101	17	2
ML Hayden	c GO Jones	b Gough	31	68	47	5	0
*RT Ponting	st GO Jones	b Giles	43	59	44	7	0
DR Martyn	not out		24	27	21	5	0
Extras	10	(lb 2, w 4, nb 4)					
Total	229	(2 wickets, 34.5 overs, 160 mins)					

DNB: A Symonds, MJ Clarke, MEK Hussey, B Lee, JN Gillespie, MS Kasprowicz, GD McGrath.

FoW: 1-91 (Hayden), **2-185** (Ponting).

Bowling	O	M	R	W	
Harmison	9.5	0	81	0	(2nb, 4w)
Gough	4	0	37	1	(2nb)
Flintoff	9	0	34	0	
Giles	10	0	64	1	
Collingwood	2	0	11	0	

England full sub: VS Solanki (SP Jones, England innings, 27.5 overs).
Australia full sub: SM Katich (not used).

RESULT: Australia won by 8 wickets
MAN OF THE MATCH: AC Gilchrist
SERIES RESULT: Australia won the NatWest Challenge 2005
PLAYER OF THE SERIES: RT Ponting

Australian Tour Matches

9 June PCA Masters XI v Australians, Arundel
(20-over match)
PCA Masters XI 167-6 (DL Maddy 70*, MJ Clarke 3-36)
Australians 170-2 (ML Hayden 79, AC Gilchrist 53)
Australians won by 8 wickets

11 June Leicestershire v Australians, Leicester (50-over match)
Australians 321-4 (ML Hayden 107, A Symonds 92*)
Leicestershire 226-8 (OD Gibson 50, GB Hogg 3-56)
Australians won by 95 runs

15 June Somerset v Australians
COUNTY GROUND, Taunton (50-over match)

TOSS: Australians **UMPIRES:** G Sharp and JF Steele

Australians innings			R	M	B	4	6
ML Hayden	retired out		76	64	53	12	0
SM Katich	c Hildreth	b S Francis	12	37	24	1	0
*RT Ponting	retired out		80	81	86	4	3
DR Martyn	st Gazzard	b Smith	44	50	49	3	0
MJ Clarke	not out		63	56	45	7	1
MEK Hussey	b Jayasuriya		51	44	39	4	1
+BJ Haddin	not out		5	5	4	0	0
Extras 11	(lb 2, w 9)						
Total 342	(5 wickets, 50 overs)						

DNB: SR Watson, B Lee, MS Kasprowicz, GD McGrath.
FoW: 1-60 (Katich), **2-101** (Hayden), **3-211** (Martyn), **4-221** (Ponting), **5-320** (Hussey).

Bowling	O	M	R	W	
Andrew	5.2	0	52	0	
SRG Francis	8	0	56	1	(1w)
M Parsons	8	0	57	0	
Jayasuriya	8	0	47	1	(3w)
Smith	7	0	61	1	(3w)
KA Parsons	7.4	0	43	0	
Blackwell	6	0	24	0	

Somerset innings			R	M	B	4	6
*GC Smith	st Haddin	b Clarke	108	94	74	17	1
ST Jayasuriya	c Hussey	b McGrath	101	115	79	9	3
JD Francis	b McGrath		23	42	40	0	0
ID Blackwell	b Watson		25	46	31	0	1
KA Parsons	lbw	b Hussey	1	6	4	0	0
MJ Wood	c Clarke	b Hussey	17	27	21	1	0
JC Hildreth	not out		38	32	24	6	0
+CM Gazzard	not out		21	19	12	2	0
Extras 11	(lb 5, w 2, nb 4)						
Total 345	(6 wickets, 46.5 overs)						

DNB: GM Andrew, SRG Francis, M Parsons.
FoW: 1-197 (Smith), **2-231** (Jayasuriya), **3-254** (JD Francis), **4-258** (KA Parsons), **5-277** (Blackwell), **6-291** (Wood).

Bowling	O	M	R	W	
Lee	4	0	26	0	
McGrath	10	0	49	2	(1nb, 1w)
Kasprowicz	8	0	89	0	(3nb)
Watson	8.5	0	72	1	(1w)
Clarke	10	0	63	1	
Hussey	6	0	41	2	

RESULT: Somerset won by 4 wickets

15–17 July Leicestershire v Australians, Leicester (3-day match)
Leicestershire 217 (CJL Rogers 56, B Lee 4-53) and 363-5 (CJL Rogers 209, SCG MacGill 4-122)
Australians 582-7 dec (DR Martyn 154*, RT Ponting 119, JL Langer 115, JK Maunders 3-89)
Match drawn

30 July–1 August Worcestershire v Australians, Worcester (3-day match)
Australians 406-9 dec (BJ Haddin 94, ML Hayden 79, MN Malik 3-78) and 161-2 (RT Ponting 59*, MJ Clarke 59)
Worcestershire 187 (SC Moore 69, MS Kasprowicz 5-67)
Match drawn

18 August Scotland v Australians, Edinburgh
(50-over match)
Match abandoned without a ball bowled (rain)

20–21 August Northamptonshire v Australians, Northampton (2-day match)
Australians 374-6 dec (ML Hayden 136, MJ Clarke 121) and 226-2 (JL Langer 86*, SM Katich 63)
Northamptonshire 169 (BJ Phillips 37*)
Match drawn

3–4 September Essex v Australians, Chelmsford (2-day match)
Essex 502-4 dec (AN Cook 214, RS Bopara 135)
Australians 561-6 (BJ Hodge 166, ML Hayden 150)
Match drawn

NatWest Series 2005 Averages

Australia
Batting and Fielding

Name	Mat	I	NO	Runs	HS	Ave	SR	100	50	Ct	St
MEK Hussey	7	5	2	227	84	75.66	95.78	-	2	2	-
A Symonds	5	4	1	218	74	72.66	82.57	-	2	2	-
MJ Clarke	5	5	1	184	80*	46.00	64.78	-	2	-	-
DR Martyn	7	6	1	201	77	40.20	67.00	-	2	2	-
SR Watson	4	2	1	36	25	36.00	83.72	-	-	-	-
ML Hayden	7	7	1	205	66*	34.16	81.67	-	1	3	-
AC Gilchrist	7	7	1	201	66*	33.50	95.26	-	1	10	1
B Lee	5	2	1	24	21*	24.00	104.34	-	-	-	-
RT Ponting	7	6	0	135	66	22.50	64.28	-	1	3	-
GB Hogg	6	3	1	28	16	14.00	68.29	-	-	1	-
JN Gillespie	7	3	0	15	14	5.00	71.42	-	-	2	-
GD McGrath	6	3	2	2	2*	2.00	20.00	-	-	-	-
MS Kasprowicz	3	1	0	1	1	1.00	33.33	-	-	1	-
SM Katich	1	1	1	36	36*	-	156.52	-	-	1	-

Bowling

Name	Mat	O	M	R	W	Ave	Best	4w	5w	SR	Econ
A Symonds	5	34.2	3	114	6	19.00	5-18	-	1	34.3	3.32
GD McGrath	6	48	8	176	8	22.00	3-25	-	-	36.0	3.66
GB Hogg	6	40	2	167	10	16.70	3-29	-	-	24.0	4.17
B Lee	5	39	4	174	8	21.75	2-27	-	-	29.2	4.46
SR Watson	4	31.3	0	150	4	37.50	3-43	-	-	47.2	4.76
JN Gillespie	7	50.2	2	251	5	50.20	2-41	-	-	60.4	4.98
MJ Clarke	5	8	1	43	0	-	-	-	-	-	5.37
MS Kasprowicz	3	28	0	154	3	51.33	1-40	-	-	56.0	5.50
MEK Hussey	7	9	0	55	1	55.00	1-31	-	-	54.0	6.11

England
Batting and Fielding

Name	Mat	I	NO	Runs	HS	Ave	SR	100	50	Ct	St
AJ Strauss	7	7	1	378	152	63.00	101.88	1	2	2	-
PD Collingwood	7	5	2	187	112*	62.33	77.91	1	1	4	-
D Gough	6	2	1	58	46*	58.00	96.66	-	-	-	-
ME Trescothick	7	7	2	261	100*	52.20	100.00	1	1	2	-
KP Pietersen	7	4	1	139	91*	46.33	107.75	-	1	5	-
GO Jones	7	5	2	98	71	32.66	70.00	-	1	20	-
A Flintoff	7	5	0	110	44	22.00	77.46	-	-	1	-
AF Giles	5	2	1	22	18*	22.00	91.66	-	-	2	-
MP Vaughan	5	4	1	57	57	19.00	53.27	-	1	-	-
VS Solanki	4	3	0	55	34	18.33	50.92	-	-	-	-
CT Tremlett	3	1	0	8	8	8.00	44.44	-	-	-	-
SP Jones	3	1	0	1	1	1.00	50.00	-	-	-	-
SJ Harmison	6	2	2	11	11*	-	64.70	-	-	1	-
J Lewis	3	1	1	7	7*	-	46.66	-	-	-	-

Bowling

Name	Mat	O	M	R	W	Ave	Best	4w	5w	SR	Econ
PD Collingwood	7	37	1	142	7	20.28	6-31	-	1	31.7	3.83
SJ Harmison	6	57	6	236	15	15.73	5-33	1	1	22.8	4.14
AF Giles	5	47	2	198	1	198.00	1-28	-	-	282.0	4.21
A Flintoff	7	60	6	260	12	21.66	4-29	1	-	30.0	4.33
CT Tremlett	3	24.2	1	111	5	22.20	4-32	1	-	29.2	4.56
J Lewis	3	25	1	124	4	31.00	3-32	-	-	37.5	4.96
SP Jones	3	27	4	142	4	35.50	2-53	-	-	40.5	5.25
D Gough	6	53.1	1	286	8	35.75	3-70	-	-	39.8	5.37
MP Vaughan	5	7	0	46	0	-	-	-	-	-	6.57
VS Solanki	4	2	0	14	0	-	-	-	-	-	7.00

NatWest Challenge 2005 Averages

Australia
Batting and Fielding

Name	Mat	I	NO	Runs	HS	Ave	SR	100	50	Ct	St
DR Martyn	3	3	2	106	43	106.00	66.66	-	-	-	-
AC Gilchrist	3	3	1	192	121*	96.00	111.62	1	-	5	-
RT Ponting	3	3	0	168	111	56.00	88.88	1	-	1	-
SM Katich	2	1	0	30	30	30.00	48.38	-	-	1	-
ML Hayden	2	2	0	48	31	24.00	51.06	-	-	-	-
A Symonds	3	2	1	11	6	11.00	68.75	-	-	1	-
SR Watson	1	1	0	3	3	3.00	23.07	-	-	-	-
MJ Clarke	3	1	0	2	2	2.00	22.22	-	-	-	-
MEK Hussey	3	1	1	46	46*	-	88.46	-	-	1	-
B Lee	3	1	1	15	15*	-	78.94	-	-	-	-
JN Gillespie	3	0	-	-	-	-	-	-	-	-	-
GD McGrath	3	0	-	-	-	-	-	-	-	-	-
MS Kasprowicz	2	0	-	-	-	-	-	-	-	2	-
BJ Haddin	1	0	-	-	-	-	-	-	-	-	-
GB Hogg	1	0	-	-	-	-	-	-	-	-	-

Bowling

Name	Mat	O	M	R	W	Ave	Best	4w	5w	SR	Econ
GD McGrath	3	28	7	103	1	103.00	1-37	-	-	168.0	3.67
A Symonds	3	23	1	89	0	-	-	-	-	-	3.86
MS Kasprowicz	2	20	3	86	4	21.50	2-40	-	-	30.0	4.30
B Lee	3	29	2	135	6	22.50	5-41	-	1	29.0	4.65
GB Hogg	1	6	0	30	1	30.00	1-30	-	-	36.0	5.00
SR Watson	1	3	0	16	0	-	-	-	-	-	5.33
MJ Clarke	3	10	0	54	0	-	-	-	-	-	5.40
JN Gillespie	3	27	1	152	3	50.66	3-44	-	-	54.0	5.62

England
Batting and Fielding

Name	Mat	I	NO	Runs	HS	Ave	SR	100	50	Ct	St
ME Trescothick	3	3	1	118	104*	59.00	64.83	1	-	1	-
A Flintoff	3	2	0	92	87	46.00	72.44	-	1	-	-
KP Pietersen	3	2	0	89	74	44.50	83.17	-	1	3	-
MP Vaughan	3	3	1	75	59*	37.50	76.53	-	1	-	-
AJ Strauss	3	3	0	88	41	29.33	55.34	-	-	1	-
AF Giles	3	2	1	29	25*	29.00	116.00	-	-	-	-
PD Collingwood	3	2	0	43	34	21.50	58.10	-	-	1	-
GO Jones	3	2	0	28	27	14.00	63.63	-	-	4	1
VS Solanki	2	1	1	53	53*	-	84.12	-	1	-	-
SJ Harmison	3	1	1	6	6*	-	200.00	-	-	1	-
D Gough	3	1	1	5	5*	-	100.00	-	-	-	-
SP Jones	3	0	-	-	-	-	-	-	-	-	-

Bowling

Name	Mat	O	M	R	W	Ave	Best	4w	5w	SR	Econ
SP Jones	3	15	1	57	0	-	-	-	-	-	3.80
PD Collingwood	3	17	0	65	4	16.25	4-34	1	-	25.5	3.82
A Flintoff	3	27	0	132	2	66.00	1-44	-	-	81.0	4.88
AF Giles	3	20	0	102	2	51.00	1-38	-	-	60.0	5.10
SJ Harmison	3	29.5	0	168	2	84.00	2-39	-	-	89.5	5.63
D Gough	3	20.2	1	130	2	65.00	1-37	-	-	61.0	6.39

Australia in England
2005 Test Series Averages

Australia Batting and Fielding

Name	Mat	I	NO	Runs	HS	Ave	SR	100	50	Ct	St
JL Langer	5	10	1	394	105	43.77	58.63	1	2	2	-
RT Ponting	5	9	0	359	156	39.88	59.63	1	1	4	-
MJ Clarke	5	9	0	335	91	37.22	54.38	-	2	2	-
GD McGrath	3	5	4	36	20*	36.00	63.15	-	-	1	-
ML Hayden	5	10	1	318	138	35.33	46.97	1	-	10	-
SK Warne	5	9	0	249	90	27.66	70.53	-	1	5	-
SM Katich	5	9	0	248	67	27.55	46.79	-	2	4	-
B Lee	5	9	3	158	47	26.33	65.02	-	-	2	-
AC Gilchrist	5	9	1	181	49*	22.62	71.82	-	-	18	1
DR Martyn	5	9	0	178	65	19.77	53.13	-	1	4	-
MS Kasprowicz	2	4	0	44	20	11.00	67.69	-	-	3	-
SW Tait	2	3	2	8	4	8.00	29.62	-	-	-	-
JN Gillespie	3	6	0	47	26	7.83	21.55	-	-	1	-

Australia Bowling

Name	Mat	O	M	R	W	Ave	Best	5w	10w	SR	Econ
RT Ponting	5	6	2	9	1	9.00	1-9	-	-	36.0	1.50
SK Warne	5	252.5	37	797	40	19.92	6-46	3	2	37.9	3.15
GD McGrath	3	134	22	440	19	23.15	5-53	2	-	42.3	3.28
B Lee	5	191.1	25	822	20	41.10	4-82	-	-	57.3	4.29
SW Tait	2	48	5	210	5	42.00	3-97	-	-	57.6	4.37
SM Katich	5	12	1	50	1	50.00	1-36	-	-	72.0	4.16
MS Kasprowicz	2	52	6	250	4	62.50	3-80	-	-	78.0	4.80
JN Gillespie	3	67	6	300	3	100.00	2-91	-	-	134.0	4.47
MJ Clarke	5	2	0	6	0	-	-	-	-	-	3.00

England Batting and Fielding

Name	Mat	I	NO	Runs	HS	Ave	SR	100	50	Ct	St
KP Pietersen	5	10	1	473	158	52.55	71.45	1	3	-	-
ME Trescothick	5	10	0	431	90	43.10	60.27	-	3	3	-
A Flintoff	5	10	0	402	102	40.20	74.16	1	3	3	-
AJ Strauss	5	10	0	393	129	39.30	57.79	2	-	6	-
SP Jones	4	6	4	66	20*	33.00	67.34	-	-	1	-
MP Vaughan	5	10	0	326	166	32.60	60.82	1	1	2	-
GO Jones	5	10	1	229	85	25.44	57.97	-	1	15	1
AF Giles	5	10	2	155	59	19.37	50.65	-	1	5	-
IR Bell	5	10	0	171	65	17.10	45.35	-	2	8	-
SJ Harmison	5	8	2	60	20*	10.00	84.50	-	-	1	-
PD Collingwood	1	2	0	17	10	8.50	22.07	-	-	1	-
MJ Hoggard	5	9	2	45	16	6.42	19.65	-	-	-	-

England Bowling

Name	Mat	O	M	R	W	Ave	Best	5w	10w	SR	Econ
SP Jones	4	102	17	378	18	21.00	6-53	2	-	34.0	3.70
A Flintoff	5	194	32	655	24	27.29	5-78	1	-	48.5	3.37
MJ Hoggard	5	122.1	15	473	16	29.56	4-97	-	-	45.8	3.87
SJ Harmison	5	161.1	22	549	17	32.29	5-43	1	-	56.8	3.40
AF Giles	5	160	18	578	10	57.80	3-78	-	-	96.0	3.61
PD Collingwood	1	4	0	17	0	-	-	-	-	-	4.25
IR Bell	5	7	2	20	0	-	-	-	-	-	2.85
MP Vaughan	5	5	0	21	0	-	-	-	-	-	4.20

Australia in England 2005
Australian First-Class Tour Averages

Batting and Fielding

Name	Mat	I	NO	Runs	HS	Ave	SR	100	50	Ct	St
BJ Haddin	1	1	0	94	94	94.00	97.91	-	1	2	-
JL Langer	7	13	2	574	115	52.18	59.11	2	3	3	-
RT Ponting	7	12	1	557	156	50.63	61.20	2	2	5	-
ML Hayden	7	12	1	472	138	42.90	56.05	1	2	14	-
DR Martyn	6	10	1	332	154*	36.88	61.14	1	1	4	-
GD McGrath	3	5	4	36	20*	36.00	63.15	-	-	1	-
MJ Clarke	7	12	0	412	91	34.33	58.11	-	3	3	-
BJ Hodge	1	2	0	59	38	29.50	45.38	-	-	1	-
SK Warne	5	9	0	249	90	27.66	70.53	-	1	5	-
JN Gillespie	5	8	2	149	53*	24.83	40.59	-	1	1	-
SM Katich	7	11	0	266	67	24.18	46.34	-	2	5	-
B Lee	6	10	3	164	47	23.42	64.31	-	-	2	-
AC Gilchrist	6	10	1	207	49*	23.00	72.12	-	-	20	1
SW Tait	3	4	2	30	22	15.00	65.21	-	-	-	-
MS Kasprowicz	4	5	0	52	20	10.40	69.33	-	-	5	-
SCG MacGill	2	0	-	-	-	-	-	-	-	1	-

Bowling

Name	Mat	O	M	R	W	Ave	Best	5w	10w	SR	Econ
RT Ponting	7	6	2	9	1	9.00	1-9	-	-	36.0	1.50
SK Warne	5	252.5	37	797	40	19.92	6-46	3	2	37.9	3.15
GD McGrath	3	134	22	440	19	23.15	5-53	2	-	42.3	3.28
SCG MacGill	2	44	6	207	7	29.57	4-122	-	-	37.7	4.70
SW Tait	3	61	9	261	7	37.28	3-97	-	-	52.2	4.27
B Lee	6	218.1	30	953	25	38.12	4-53	-	-	52.3	4.36
MS Kasprowicz	4	99	15	417	10	41.70	5-67	1	-	59.4	4.21
SM Katich	7	12	1	50	1	50.00	1-36	-	-	72.0	4.16
JN Gillespie	5	110	16	445	7	63.57	2-40	-	-	94.2	4.04
MJ Clarke	7	7	0	42	0	-	-	-	-	-	6.00